D0056308

HILL COUNTRY HARVEST

OTHER BOOKS BY HAL BORLAND

THE OUTDOORS

An American Year
This Hill, This Valley
The Enduring Pattern
Beyond Your Doorstep
Sundial of the Seasons
Countryman: A Summary of Belief
Our Natural World (Editor)

PEOPLE AND PLACES

High, Wide and Lonesome
The Dog Who Came to Stay

FICTION

The Seventh Winter
The Amulet
When the Legends Die
King of Squaw Mountain

FOLKLORE

Rocky Mountain Tipi Tales
The Youngest Shepherd

POETRY

America Is Americans

HILL COUNTRY HARVEST

HAL BORLAND

J. B. LIPPINCOTT COMPANY
PHILADELPHIA AND NEW YORK

Third Printing

PRINTED IN THE UNITED STATES OF AMERICA

Library of Congress Catalog Card Number 67-15498

A portion of this book has appeared
in *Audubon* magazine.

For Barbara

If you would number all my thoughts of you,
Count diamond drops of spiderweb-caught dew;
If you would know the times I sing your praises,
Count asters when you've counted all the daisies;
If you should ask the times I think your words,
Count birds.

FOREWORD

Before someone else beats me to it, maybe I should say that this is a book of personal essays. I don't think of it that way, but maybe I'm like the man who was surprised to learn that he had been speaking prose all his life. I think of it as a running account of life, salted with opinions and flavored with convictions, here in a somewhat remote corner of New England. Maybe it's even a chronicle, though I doubt that; chronicles are long, serious, scholarly accounts of important events. This book started the wrong way to be such a chronicle.

Almost ten years ago an editor from Pittsfield, Mass., forty miles or so up the Housatonic valley from where I live, asked me to write a weekly column for his daily newspaper. "What about?" I asked. "Nature," he said, "the outdoors, life in general. Whatever seems important or interesting to you." The idea itself seemed uninteresting and unimportant at the time. I was helping Barbara, my wife, plant a vegetable garden, and I was having trouble with a book I was writing. I said, "I'll think about it." And I promptly forgot it.

A few weeks later the editor asked, "What did you decide?" By then the garden was planted and the book as well in hand as it ever would be. I was feeling rather amiable, so I said, "I might give it a try." The editor said, "Fine! Let's start next week."

That's how it started. It has continued ever since, partly

out of habit, partly because I have enjoyed writing it, partly because there were things to say that interested me, at least. And there is the added factor that a writer is, by trade, a talkative fellow on paper and appreciates an audience.

Anyway, some months ago I looked back over my files and found that I had written close to half a million words in those columns. My publisher saw some of the files and said, "We've got a book." I said, "Half a million words make quite a long book." He smiled. "It won't be that long when you get through with it," he said, and I knew what he meant. He meant that I was going to have to carve a book out of all that material. So I carved and revised and whittled and shaped, and the result is this personal book about human hopes and dreams and laughter and indignation and disappointment and triumph.

It is, of course, also about nature and the outdoors, and it deals with the neighbors, both wild and tame. It also deals, from time to time, with tradition. The tradition of such values as truth, decency, faith, love, beauty and honesty, verities that reach far back in human history. No matter how much we change our environment, those verities persist. Some of them go out of current fashion from time to time, but we always come back to them simply because we need to know who we were and where we came from to have any understanding of who we now are and where we are going. They are the cultural memories, the foundations of our civilization and the dreams we have. Dreams, after all, have little substance without memories. And, since it reflects life as I know it, there are trifles here too, nonsense and tomfoolery and japery. Life would be intolerably dull and depressing without them.

So here it is, a book that was ten years in the writing, bit by bit and week by week, and a good many months in the choosing, cutting and revision. I hope it now reflects some of the cherished things I have felt and seen along the way—the cool of a May morning, the heat of a July afternoon, the bite of a January night; the hoot of a great horned owl, the jeering of a jay, the ecstasies of a brown thrasher; the marvelous grace of a deer, a shrew's deadly pursuit, the pranking of a fox; the laconic neighbor-talk, the fireside opinion of close friends, and the laughter of my beloved companion in the moonlight. If it does that, I am content.

H.B.

Salisbury, Conn.

1967

I

Every winter when I see what snow and ice can do to life in the cities I think how improvidently we have organized urban existence. In terms of cold logic, every city north of Virginia should be abandoned from Thanksgiving till the first of April; and I have seen Richmond all tied up in knots by a 6-inch snowfall. Out here in the country we just push the snow aside and go on with our daily life, even in the villages. But the cities have to fight it. New York spends I don't know how many million dollars every winter just getting itself free of snow, dumping it into the rivers, and every major city spends enough fighting snow to feed most of its hungry the whole year round. Even with all that outlay, the cities are in a mess after every snowstorm.

Twice in the past two weeks I had to go to one of Connecticut's major cities. The first time was just after a 6-inch snowfall. My back road had been plowed out and my driveway cleared, and the highways were plowed and sanded. I made the trip in good time. Then I came to the city. Plows, snowloaders and trucks were still at work, traffic was snarled, policemen were frantic, pedestrians were miserable. It took me forty minutes to go 2 city miles, and when I got within sight of where I wanted to go the side streets were still clogged, the going treacherous. But I picked up my passenger, made my slow way back through the city to the highway, and came from there home safely and with dispatch.

My second trip was a week later and after a 2-inch snowfall. Again the country roads and highways were in good shape, but the city was worse off than before. The original snow had become rutted ice on the side streets, where it probably will remain most of the winter. The new snow made the going doubly treacherous. Streets that had been cleared of the earlier snow now were deep in icy slush, slick as glass. I was glad to get away without at least a smashed fender. Out, into the country again, and safely home.

My urban friends sometimes say, "You aren't going to spend this winter up there in the country, are you?" And when I say yes, of course, they look at me as though I were crazy. "It's bad enough in the city," they say. "It must be simply awful up there." And when I say that it's simply grand up here, they know I am crazy.

What they are doing, of course, is thinking of their own urban troubles and multiplying them four-fold in imagination. What they should do is divide them by four instead of multiplying. I think one reason is that we in the country have learned to live with the weather instead of fighting it. We expect to wear boots and warm clothes when we go outdoors in cold winter weather. Before the deep cold strikes in, we prepare our cars for it with snow tires, antifreeze and a reliable battery. We know how to drive in and on snow and ice, something too few urban drivers ever learn. We revise our schedules, taking some of the haste out of them. We still know how to use a snow shovel. We depend on the local road crews to open the roads as soon as possible, but beyond that we know that things are pretty much up to us.

So we snug our houses early, and make sure there is a

full pantry, the freezer is amply stocked, the water supply lines are safe from freezing. Since electric lines can go down in a severe storm—ours hasn't been "out" more than an hour at a time since we've lived here—we lay in a supply of firewood and candles and oil lamps for any emergency. Then we settle back and take the weather as it comes, knowing that no storm lasts more than a day or two.

There are few privations, even in winter, and few real dangers here in the country. A couple of years ago a man who lives a few miles from me was stricken with an appendicitis attack in the midst of a howling snowstorm. Their driveway was drifted deep. They couldn't get out. Fortunately, the phone still worked. His wife called for help. Two township snowplows opened the driveway. A doctor was brought in by the state police. The stricken man was taken to the hospital in the trooper's car and was operated on within a matter of hours. That's the way things are taken care of. I read the other day of a critically sick man being trapped for three hours in an ambulance in New York City with only an intern to ease him. I prefer our country way. It seems safer, somehow.

Cities are nice places to visit, particularly in the spring and fall. Summer there can be rather uncomfortable. But deliver me from life in the city in the winter! I have had a worse time in the big city in a winter storm than I ever had in a sod house on the lonesome plains in a week-long blizzard. If they would only take advice, those city folk who have summer places in the country would quit the city every fall and move to the country for the winter. After the first shock they would find that life in the country in the winter is a lot easier than it is in the city. Besides, the snow out here is clean. It actually is. The snow all over the place right now is so white it dazzles the eye. Beautiful snow!

THE SUBWAY BUILDERS have been at work in my backyard again. I don't mean moles, though one was there again last fall; I mean the red squirrels, who wait for winter and snow to do their tunneling and are no menace whatever to the grass.

I was first aware of the red squirrels' hidden runways winter before last. We have several bird feeders hung in the big apple tree just back of the house, and the tree sparrows insist on kicking out at least as much millet and other grain as they eat. This, of course, is a boon to the ground-feeding birds, such as the juncos. It also is a lure for the squirrels, who have to eat too. But the birds and squirrels never seem to eat all the grain on the snow, and each new snow covers it so that after a time there is a kind of icy layer cake with a scattering of seeds on each layer. The squirrels seem to know this and they, particularly the gray squirrels, dig down to reach the hidden food, uncovering it as miners in open pits uncover the layers of pay ore.

But two winters ago I noticed that the red squirrels were also salvaging that hidden grain, and when I went out to fill the feeders the red squirrels simply vanished. I soon found that they were diving into holes in the snow, like woodchucks into their dens. But when I watched to see where they went I was astonished to see them emerge from the snow again near other apple trees, some of them 50 or 60 feet away. Curious, I did a bit of excavating myself and found runways radiating in all directions from—or perhaps to—the apple tree with the feeders. And each of these runways led to another tree. The runways themselves were about 2 inches in diameter, ample for the little red squirrels. But the thing that was most surprising was the fact that each of them was ruler-straight, as though surveyed and laid out by an engineer with a transit. And they were just beneath the surface crust on the snow, 2 inches or so down in the soft snow. None of them had a heap of snow at its mouth; each exit was a clean hole in the surface crust that went down a few inches, then turned sharply to the tunnel itself.

Apparently the squirrels found a weak spot in the icy crust, or a hole already there—some of the tunnels had their entrances in footprints I had made—and simply took a sight on an objective before they went to work. And apparently they simply pushed the soft snow aside, packing the walls of the tunnels. There was no evidence of pawing or actual digging; it was as though a small piston had been thrust through the snow, a miniature battering ram, and had compressed the snow on each side. And, as I have said, each runway was arrow-straight toward its objective.

I can only guess at the reason for these tunnels. First, of course, they insure safety from attack in the open. If a squirrel is hidden under the snow in his comings and goings he isn't going to be a victim of fox or owl. Second, such runways provide access to the source of food—in this case the grain from the bird feeders—in any weather. I have seen the red squirrels busily eating under the feeders when the snow was coming down in blinding sheets, and when they were alarmed they dived into the hole and had no need to flounder through several inches of soft surface snow to get to safety.

I wonder if they dig such tunnels back in the woodland, to reach stores of acorns or other wild food. I have never seen such runways anywhere but here in my dooryard. Field mice and voles do have such runways, a vast maze of them. When the spring melt comes I can see them in the pasture and even in the woods, networks then marked by icy trails so hardpacked by use that they are slower to melt than the surrounding snow.

Anyway, the red squirrels in my dooryard make their own network of subways every winter, and they are using them right now. They waited till the snow was deep enough to give them at least 6 inches in which to work, and until it had a firm crust to keep the runways from caving in. The central station, so to speak, is under the bird feeders. From there the subways lead to three other apple trees all the way across the yard, to the pasture fence, and to the woodshed, where at least one family of red squirrels dens among the firewood each winter. There is also a separate subway between the big spruce close beside the house and the pear tree 50 feet away at the edge of the vegetable garden. How many other runways there may be, I have no idea. But I am amazed at the instinctive skill they represent. None of them seems to deviate an inch from the most direct route toward its objective.

LAST NIGHT, one of those crisp, clear nights bright with starlight on snow, I ran across an old description of New England's winters. It was written by one William Wood about 330 years ago and it was called "New England's Prospect." I can find no record of William Wood's identity except that he was promoting colonization here and that his pamphlet was written for English readers. It was one of the first pieces of promotional advertising for this country.

"It is for certaine the best ground and the sweetest Climate in all these parts," Mr. Wood wrote, "being high land, and sharpe Ayre . . . not often troubled with Mists, or unwholesome Fogges, or cold weather from the Sea . . . And whereas in England most of the cold windes come from the Sea . . . in this Countrey it is not so, but otherwise; for in the extremity of winter, the North-east and South windes comming from the Sea produceth warme weather; only the North-west winde comming over the land, is the cause of extreme cold weather, being alwaies accompanied with deepe Snowes and bitter Frost, so that in two or three Dayes the Rivers are passable for horse and man.

"No extremes last long," he goes on, "so this cold winde blowes seldome above three dayes alltogether, after which the weather is more tolerable, the Ayre being nothing so sharpe, but peradventure in foure or five dayes after this cold messenger will blow a fresh, commanding every man to his house, forbidding any to out-face him without prejudice to their noses; but it may be objected that it is too cold a Countrey for our English men, who have been accustomed to a warmer Climate, to which it may be answered, there is Wood good store, and better cheape to build warme houses, and make good fires, which makes the Winter lesse tedious."

Then Mr. Wood says, "Moreover, the extremity of this cold weather lasteth but for two Monthes to ten weekes, beginning in December, and breaking up by the tenth of February."

It is always satisfying to come across such information, particularly when it is this specific. I now look forward to February 10. But not without a degree of doubt and distrust. As I recall, Mr. Wood's prophecy has been wrong every year since I have lived in New England. This, of course, could be the year he is right.

Then Mr. Wood adds, "It is observed by the Indians that every tenth year there is little or no Winter." And that is just a step too far. I have been here ten years, and longer, and winter has never yet skipped an engagement here. But he was trying to lure settlers. And he goes on to say, with a strange frankness at the beginning, that "the piercing cold of this Countrey produceth not so many noysome effects as the raw Winters in England. In publick assemblies it is strange to heare a man sneeze or cough as ordinarily they doe in England; yet not to smother anything lest you judge me too partiall in reciting good of the Countrey, and not bad; true it is that some venturing forth nakedly in extremity of cold, being more foole hardy than wise, have for a time lost the use of their feet, others the use of their fingers; but time and Surgery afterwards have recovered them. Some have had their over-growne beards so frozen together, that they could not get their strong-water bottles into their mouthes." Then he goes on to tell of an Englishman and an Indian, out hunting, who were overtaken by a storm and frozen to death. The Indian was found "reared back against a tree with his Aquavitae bottle against his head." There is no mention of the Englishman's bottle.

He also tells about fishermen being frozen to death in their boats, in this gentle winter climate, and of a servant lost in the woods four days and "a certaine Maide" lost six or seven days. Both, he insists, survived, refreshed and nourished by water from a spring miraculously unfrozen, though he makes no mention of whether they ever recovered the use of their feet and hands, "Surgery" or not.

All in all, he speaks well of this New England climate. He even makes a pitch for the womenfolk. "In New England," he says, "both the men and women keep their naturall complexions, in so much that Sea men wonder when they arrive in these parts to see their Countrey-men so fresh and ruddy: If the Sunne doth tanne any, yet the

Winters cold restores them to their former complexion."

After I had read Mr. Wood's tract through to the end, I went back and checked in my own journal for last year. On the night of Feb. 10, when Mr. Wood says winter ends, just like that, it was 6 above zero on my front porch. It was an even zero on Feb. 13 and again on Feb. 17.

One thing in Mr. Wood's account, though, might well be taken to heart. Don't grow a beard. If you do, it may freeze and you can't get the strong-water bottle to your mouth. I shall remember that.

THEY CAME DOWN across the pasture from the mountainside just as though they knew where they were going, but as they came through the dooryard they looked both weary and bewildered. They stopped at the roadside for brief counsel, then the older of them led the way and they went down the road. They had bright new Christmas guns on their shoulders, sopping Christmas mittens on their hands and they trudged as though their boots were full of snow.

Ten minutes and they came back up the road, obviously as lost as two puppies. Barbara went out on the porch and hailed them and they came, so cold and bewildered and tearful they couldn't talk. She told them to come on in and get warm, and they struggled with their boots. I went down and helped and they came into the living room, where I lit a fire for quick warmth and began to rub their frosty hands and feet. Barbara brought hot soup from the kitchen. Their teeth were chattering so much they couldn't talk, but they managed to drink the soup. And the older one, who was about eight years old, managed to say, "My grandfather's house," before he choked on the tears again.

I wrung out the younger boy's socks and hung them to

dry, and I emptied the snow and ice water from his boots. I asked his name and his brother said, "He's David and I'm Timothy, and my grandfather—" Then he ran out of breath and words. They sat on the rug, warming their hands and feet and the tears began to subside.

I asked if they'd shot a deer, and six-year-old David managed a smile. Timothy said they hadn't even seen a rabbit, but they saw tracks. He said they saw other tracks too, big tracks. "Like this," and he shaped his red hands in a circle. "A cat?" I asked, and he nodded. "A bobcat?" He nodded quickly and his eyes grew big. It could have been, for a big bobcat has been prowling the lower mountainside. "Did you get a shot at him?" I asked, and David smiled at me and shook his head. Their guns were rifles, the flint-lock kind that shoot caps and make a fine, loud noise. But not if your fingers are too cold and stiff to load them and pull the triggers. And those small fingers were still stiff with cold.

Finally Timothy asked what time it was. Barbara said it was a quarter till twelve. "We have to catch the train at two o'clock!" Timothy said. "We have to go home!" And I asked, "Where do you live?" Timothy said, "Bridgeport," and I had a hunch.

"Do you have an Aunt Christine?" I asked. "And an Aunt Mary?"

"Yes!" they exclaimed, and for the first time they brightened.

"Well, I guess you aren't too far lost," I said. "Your grandfather's probably out looking for you right now." And Barbara said, "I'll call and tell them," and she went to the phone.

It's terrifying to be lost, whether you're eight or fifty-eight, and the winter woods can turn you around in five minutes, especially if you've followed rabbit tracks among the trees and through the brush. The hollows you may have known so well on a summer visit are all strange country when covered with snow. Grown men forget to go downhill and follow the road in the valley, when they are lost, and they even forget to follow their own tracks back to where they started. Small boys with brand-new Christmas guns that shoot caps forget too.

But we didn't talk about being lost, while they sat there in front of the fire and toasted their toes. We talked about being found, which is altogether different. Being found is being with friends and knowing your family will come and get you. Being found is a fire and a cup of hot soup and knowing that Grandmother won't scold because your pants are soaked and your boots are full of ice water. Being found is being able to smile again, even if you can't really laugh until tomorrow.

Then Grandfather came and the world was almost back in place. Grandfather said they wanted to go hunting and they'd been on the mountain before, in summer. But when they didn't come back he went to look for them. They wandered all over the place, following rabbit tracks. Then they started down toward the road, and he thought they'd gone home. But they weren't there when he got back and he was about to go look for them again when Barbara phoned.

David and Timothy got into their coats and boots and picked up their guns. Their ammunition was wet, so they couldn't have shot that bobcat even if they'd seen him. But it didn't matter now. They got into Grandfather's car and waved goodbye, two hunters who had a big adventure and came back safely. Back to Grandfather's house, just half a mile up the road.

I WISH THEY would leave the moon alone. It has done very well without any human help, and without letting man in on most of its secrets, for a long, long time. We did learn long ago that it isn't really made of green cheese, and somewhat later we found that it has a lot of craters and no oceans. Now I think it is time we told the space agencies to keep hands off and leave that moon to the people who enjoy it the way it is. There are a great many such people, including me.

Did you ever see such a series of full moons as we have had these past four months? I can't remember a time when we had four full moons in a row with brilliant, clear nights at the time of fullness. First came the Harvest Moon, in October, with a whole series of nights when it seemed to fill the sky with radiance. Then came the Hunter's Moon in November, almost as brilliant and prolonged. December's full moon, the Beaver Moon, was equally brilliant though somewhat less prolonged. And now, this past week, we had the January full moon, which the Indians called the Wolf Moon, with just enough snow on the ground to make a full week of nights so bright that only the biggest stars were visible.

We all have special moonlight memories. One of mine is of an autumn moon that seemed twice as big as the sun when it rose, and it was a special coppery yellow such as I have seldom seen. I saw it many years ago, but the memory holds on, not because of any special incident but because of the moon itself. In fact, I watched that moon all alone, and I sat on a hilltop for several hours in the moonlight. Strange memory, but both poignant and beautiful. Maybe it was that night that made me feel I had a special ownership of the moon.

Long afterward there was another night, when Barbara

and I were returning home from a trip to the West Coast, and we had planned to stop for the night in Ithaca, N.Y. But when we got there, the hotel was jammed with a convention and there was a mixup about our reservation, so we gave up and got back in the car and drove on. It happened to be a night when the moon was a day past the full, and we drove in the darkness for an hour, wondering whether to try to push on home, tired as we were, or to look for a roof and a bed in the next town. Then that moon rose, directly ahead of us, a marvelously beautiful moon, and we kept on driving. The whole night was filled with magic, and we thanked the convention that had kept us from stopping in Ithaca. Eventually we stopped, around ten o'clock that night, at a roadside inn somewhere near Cherry Valley, I forget just where. But I will never forget that moon.

About ten years ago we experienced a special moon on the river. A friend was visiting us, a noted Shakespeare scholar who had been lecturing in England and was on his way back to his post at the University of Colorado. He came up from New York to see us, and late in the afternoon we took him out in the boat to watch the sunset. The sunset didn't amount to much, but when we started back upstream the full moon rose. Our friend George sat and watched it for maybe five minutes, then whispered, "I never saw such a moon!" It was a rather special moon, but it was doubly special in the way it cast its glittering beams on the river. We slowed the boat and seemed to ride in the moonlight itself. And George began quoting Shakespeare, not only the moon speech from "Romeo and Juliet," but lines and whole passages from half a dozen plays. He wasn't reciting to us, really. He was talking to that moon, and in words of incredible beauty. George is gone now, but every time we see the moonlight on the river we remember him and hear his voice, which was music itself.

There are perhaps a dozen other special moon memories, including thin crescents as well as full-blown golden or silver spheres. Midsummer moons as well as brittle, frosty winter moons, spring moons twinkling the newest of young leaves, autumn moons making the crisp leaves an incredible wealth of gold and jewels. Daytime and suntime are the times for work, for the everyday chores of this world. But nighttime and moonlight are for dreams and poetry and the whole incredible magic of life.

And that is why I say I wish they would leave that moon alone. We need the magic, and the dreams and the poetry. We need that moon just the way it is. I don't care what they find, if they ever get to the moon, they won't find the moonlight. We already have that, and whatever they find can't be one half so precious.

WHEN WE FIRST came here I said we would let the woods on the mountainside grow as they would, see what happened. I didn't want a woodlot, trimmed and tended, and I didn't want any logging done up there, either for lumber or pulpwood. It was what is listed on the tax books as "sprout land," a mixed stand of trees that had been cut over a number of times, first by the original settlers to open fields for cultivation, then by loggers, then by charcoal burners, then by loggers again and, finally, by the farmer who owned the place to get building lumber. The lumber in this house and most of the outbuildings was cut and sawed there, I have been told. Anyway, fourteen years ago it was a rather brushy stand of maple, oak, ash, birch, white pine and hemlock, with red cedars in almost every opening, especially on the lower slopes.

The first few years I had to say no to a whole series of people who had ideas about that woodland. A sawyer wanted to take out the white pine and oak. A pulpwood man wanted to cut the birch and poplar and market it on shares. A forester wanted to come in and trim and clean out the "weed trees" and "give the really good ones a chance." It took some time to convince all these people that all I wanted was to leave that mountainside alone, let the pests have their way, let the trees grow, crowd each other perhaps, die and rot. I just wanted to watch those trees for a few years, ten or twenty years, say, and see what happened to them and to the mountainside if they were left alone.

This fall and winter I have been taking a kind of inventory, making an appraisal of what has happened. And since we have had a series of drouth years it has been particularly interesting to see how well the trees have done. Not only the trees but the soil and the whole ecology. I have no big, important conclusions to draw, but certain facts do stand out.

The trees have grown steadily, of course. Some of the hemlocks have doubled in height. The white pines have spread amazingly. There was a knoll with only half a dozen medium-sized pines and at least 5 acres of open grass when we came here. Today the original pines are 40 feet tall and the open grass is almost gone; young pines have taken virtually all of it, pines ranging from 2 feet to 15 feet tall. I have never cut or planted a tree on that knoll, but they are almost as evenly spaced as though I had planted them by chart, with plenty of room to grow another thirty years. And one of the lower slopes which also was open grass, with only a clump of big sumac at the far edge and a few big pines at its foot, now is more than half covered with young pines, the oldest of them showing eleven annual whorls of branches.

Those big pines at the foot of that slope all seem healthy except one. It died about five years ago. I saw that it was in trouble and when two big branches lost their needles I was tempted to cut and burn it to check whatever was attacking it. But I kept to my resolution, hoped the other pines would survive. They did, and now that dead pine has been well worked over by the woodpeckers, who must have gotten every grub and insect.

Two beautiful clumps of white birches grew old and brittle and developed an inner rot. A winter storm took down several of their big boles, and now they look sad and forlorn. But other white birches not far away have grown to take their places, apparently in good health. The gray birch grows like a weed, is borne down by snow and ice, falls, quickly rots, and is replaced by vigorous new shoots from the roots. The clumps of big sumac, some of it 20 feet high, have largely died out, shaded by the growing pines and the oaks and shagbark hickories. Ash saplings have sprung up and shoot toward the sun, slim as fishpoles. Old chestnut stumps still send up shoots that live a few years and blight away.

When we came here there were several old logging roads up there that gullied deeper year by year. Now, filled with the woodland litter, they have stopped gullying and are full of absorbent leaf mold. The whole woodland is a spongy bed of decaying leaves and woodland litter, new soil building year by year. And, even in these past few drouth years, the old seep springs continued to ooze. Two of them flow better than they did ten years ago, creating small brooks that dry up only in July and August. And the big spring, which for years supplied the house and barnyard, hasn't gone dry in three years, even in August. When we came here, long before the drouth, it went dry every summer. I think I was right, to let those woods alone.

TWO GRAY SQUIRRELS were out under the bird feeders on the big apple tree back of the house the other morning, making a breakfast of the seed that the juncos usually eat. I was surprised to see that the small birds, chickadees, sparrows and juncos, weren't afraid of the squirrels, though they did keep a wary eye open. And the squirrels made no hostile gestures, not even at the jays that came from time to time to glare indignantly and hop around, just out of reach of the squirrels. Maybe the cold weather had enforced a truce among them. Jays and squirrels usually seem to think they should call each other names and have any feed-ground to themselves.

These two squirrels raise a question in my mind to which I have no ready answer. One is a typical gray squirrel with its salt-and-pepper winter coat, somewhat ruddy over the shoulders and almost white on the under parts. Its ears are smooth.

The other, which is a trace larger, has quite a patch of ruddy color on its back, a reddish patch at the base of each foreleg, and it has long, reddish-tan hairs on its ears. They aren't really tufts like the ear tufts on the Abert squirrels of the Southwest, along the Grand Canyon of the Colorado, but they are noticeable.

Red squirrels often have ear tufts, especially in the winter. But this is no red squirrel. Red squirrels are small, not much over a foot long, tail and body, and I have never seen one that wasn't some shade of red, certainly not salt-and-pepper. This one I speak of is big, even for a gray squirrel, and most of its pelt is typical gray-squirrel color. Maybe the ear tufts are not as rare on grays as I thought they were.

Or maybe I keep seeing odd squirrels. Last fall I saw one in the edge of the pasture that was also a baffler. It was the size of a small gray, but its back was the color of a red. The really strange thing, though, was a white tip to its tail. I didn't have my field glasses at hand, and before I could get them this squirrel headed for a tumbled-down stone wall 50 yards away. There it sat on its haunches for perhaps a minute, watching me, and I saw its light belly, its reddish-brown back and, again, that tail with a white tip. I never saw it again. And I have yet to find any reference to a squirrel with a white-tipped tail. I wondered if it might have been a flying squirrel, which is about that color. And I wondered if I had imagined that white tail-tip, seeing the white underside of a typical flying squirrel tail. But I know I didn't imagine it. That squirrel had a white tip to its tail.

A couple of years ago I saw a white squirrel, all white except its tail, which was beautiful silver. It was, of course, an albino. Albinism is rare, but occasionally occurs among the grays. Usually, though, the tail is white too in the albino. Melanos also occur among the grays, more frequently than albinos, but I have never seen one. The melano is the opposite of the albino, an excess of pigment instead of a lack of it. Melanos are black.

I saw the albino around for several weeks, and I suspect that some young hunter shot it. It would have made an eye-catching target. I have heard that other animals and birds don't like albinos and usually kill them, but I suspect that this is mostly human imagining. The other gray squirrels treated the albino I saw just as they treated each other, no worse and no better.

Most animals are color-blind, of course, and see everything in shades of black and white, but even to eyes that could not distinguish color a white squirrel would be different from a gray one. I doubt that such differences are as important as we think they are, except that they increase the natural hazards. An owl, a fox, any natural enemy of a squirrel, could see an albino more easily than a gray one.

The two grays that have been feeding under the bird feeders have also been at work in a nearby apple tree that still has quite a few withered apples on it. They take those withered apples, nip away the dried fruit flesh and get the seeds. Squirrels are fond of apple seeds. And they have been watching the suet I have out for chickadees and the small woodpeckers, no doubt trying to figure a way to reach it. Last fall I bought a cocoanut, cut it in half and hung the open half-shells on wires for the birds. When they had cleaned out the cocoanut meat I decided those shells would be good containers for suet, so I melted enough suet to act as an adhesive, packed them with raw suet and poured the melted tallow over it. It made an excellent suet pack, and the birds love it.

But gray squirrels also like suet. I have even known them to steal bacon rind. But those suet shells are hung on long wires, and they haven't yet found a way to reach them. If it can be done, they will do it. A gray squirrel is a very bright fellow—whether he has tufts on his ears or not.

I AM FIRMLY of the opinion that temperature, like virtue, is relative. When I listen to the weather reports morning after morning I know that I have to discount the temperatures cited at the weather stations. Why? Because their thermometers are sheltered, and mine isn't. Theirs is an official temperature, for comparative purposes in the record books. Mine is a practical temperature, taken right out in the open where I have to go to do the outside chores that morning.

Official temperatures are essential, and they are useful because they are taken at various stations under uniform conditions. But when someone begins to talk about temperatures now as compared with those of fifty or a hundred years ago I begin to rally reservations. I doubt that the records are actually comparable. Maybe those of fifty years ago are, but those of a hundred years ago should be taken for what they are—the same kind of practical temperatures that I get on the thermometer on my front porch.

At one time or another I have poked around in the old records, most of them in diaries kept by folk who lived close to the weather. Now and then a weather entry says, "temp at thermometer on clothes line post, -30 at 6 A.M." Or "temp're at water trough, -25 at 6:15." Occasionally some mention is made of the wind blowing at the time the thermometer was read, but not always. And I know that if a 20-mile wind was whipping that mercury, it was shrinking 10 degrees or so below the level it would have showed under shelter.

There are other factors besides the wind. Some years ago Dr. Charles F. Brooks, one-time Weather Bureau meteorologist, checked temperatures at Milton, Mass. Three feet above the snow-covered ground the temperature was -19 degrees. At the surface of the snow it was -27 degrees, a difference of 8 degrees on the same spot but 3 feet lower. Then he thrust his thermometer 7 inches into the snow and it showed 24 degrees *above* zero, 51 degrees difference between the snow's surface and 7 inches below. That only proved the insulating capacity of snow, something every farmer knows. To me, the important variation was that 8 degrees' difference between the snow surface and 3 feet above it. Temperature varies with where you hang your thermometer, high or low.

It also varies from hilltop to valley. Dr. Brooks, in other observations made at Worcester, Mass., found 10 degrees' difference between a hilltop and its base, 250 feet below. Working downhill, he found as much as 8 degrees' difference between two places only 30 feet apart in terms of elevation. That was because cold air flows downhill and collects in the valleys. My house here in the valley probably is 10 degrees colder, on any calm winter day, than it is even halfway up Tom's Mountain, perhaps 20 degrees colder though I doubt that there's that much difference. The presence of the Housatonic in this valley is another factor in temperature variation, easing the extremes.

But this proves to me that the old weather records, especially those taken by volunteers and noted in the journals, are all relative. To compare them with modern records one would have to know exactly where the thermometers were placed, and half a dozen other factors would have to be taken into account.

My front porch thermometer is about 8 feet above the ground, unsheltered from the wind, and far enough from the house itself to be little influenced by inside temperatures. Its situation probably is equivalent to that of most of the thermometers read by amateur rural observers a century ago. Since I have lived here the coldest it has registered was -32 degrees. That was on January 19, 1957. I have no record of the official temperature that day, but it probably was in the minus-20s for this area, perhaps as low as -25.

I was outdoors a good deal on that cold January day in 1957, doing outside chores, and it did not seem brutally cold to me. In my journal I noted that there was not much wind and the humidity was low. I know I have been much more uncomfortable here in temperatures above zero. And that brings up another factor, humidity. A humid zero can be punishing. A dry -30 can be comfortable. As a boy, in the thin, dry air of mile-high Colorado, I knew -40 a number of times. I once rode a horse 30 miles in -35 weather and didn't suffer, though I found later that my nose had been frostbitten. But when I first came East I thought I was going to freeze to death on a street in mid-Manhattan on a December day when the official temperature was 10 above zero. There was a wind, and the humidity on that river-bounded island was in the 60s. It was brutal weather.

So it's all relative. Three weeks ago it was bitter cold at zero, with a cutting wind. Two days later it got up to 30 and felt like spring. I was comfortable out of doors in my shirtsleeves. A wool shirt, I admit; but after that punishing zero a calm 30 above was actually mild.

WHEN I TOOK PAT, the dog, outside to feed him one evening there was a scurry and Pat chased some small animal away from the dooryard. I held my breath, hoping it wasn't a skunk. It wasn't. It was an opossum. I got a light and cornered the silvery gray beast beside the woodshed and watched it for a few minutes. It was the prettiest possum I ever saw, in prime pelage, silvery body and white head, very pink nose, and eyes that glowed like rubies in the light. It wasn't particularly afraid of me, and apparently Pat knew this particular animal and had some kind of truce with it. All Pat had done was chase it away from his food pan and, apparently, tell it to tend to its own business. Pat finished his meal, came to me, looked at the possum and as much as said, "It's just that old moron. Why are you interested in him?"

But I was interested, and I followed the possum around for half an hour while he poked in the compost heap, tasted a shriveled windfall apple, looked in a grass clump for some insect life that wasn't there, and finally wandered down a cowpath across the pasture. There was snow on the ground, and he paused from time to time to hold up a cold foot in distaste. And he snuffled as though he had a cold. He obviously didn't care for the weather. He wandered off, quite aimless, and I came back in the house, thinking that nature had shortchanged the possums.

I remembered some statistics I had on relative brain capacity of animals, and I looked them up. Vernon Bailey, a government biologist, once measured the brain boxes of several animal species by filling the cavities completely with beans, then counting the beans. The results, which provide a comparison if not absolute measurements, were: Opossum, 21; porcupine, 70; raccoon, 150; red fox, 198; coyote, 325; gray wolf, 438. In other words, the raccoon has seven times as much brain as the possum, the red fox nine times as much. Even the porcupine, which is a pretty stupid animal, has three times the brain capacity of the possum.

I doubt that these figures will surprise anyone who has ever spent much time watching a possum. Not only is the possum short on brains, but his nervous system apparently is subject to short-circuits. Some who have investigated the matter say that when a possum "plays possum" in the presence of an enemy, it isn't an act at all; that the animal faints and goes into a coma, a nervous wreck. But this I cannot vouch for.

Why the possum ever extended its range from the South into the Berkshires and even into southern Canada is a mystery to me. Winters up here certainly are difficult for such an animal. Last year I met one on the road when the snow was a foot deep and the temperature was flirting with zero. The road hadn't yet been plowed and the possum was in a wheel track and didn't seem to know how to get out. I stopped and watched. The beast fumbled, hesitated, sat back and almost wrung its cold forepaws. It looked at me like a youngster lost in a storm, tears in its eyes and its nose red and running. At last it climbed out of the rut and wallowed off up the hillside, pausing often to lift a cold paw and look bewildered. I watched until it blundered into a clump of cedars and took shelter. The creature just shouldn't have been out alone, that's all there was to it. It needed a nurse or a guardian.

But here they are, those incompetent possums, up here in the inhospitable North. And they survive and multiply. They are marsupials, kin of the kangaroo, the only marsupials in North America. They have several primitive characteristics, including a gestation period of only twelve days. The young, which are little more than embryos, are so small at birth that a whole litter of fifteen can be put into a tablespoon. They squirm into the mother's abdominal pouch, begin to feed and stay there until they are two months old. When they are three months old they begin to forage for themselves, eating almost anything, vegetable or animal, living or dead. And they, in turn, are eaten by bobcats, foxes, owls and hawks. They have a disagreeable musky odor, their only protection except their faint, or their ability to play dead, whichever it is.

The possum specially interests me because of its feet. For years I was told by those who should know that man became a superior creature because of his opposed thumb, a thumb which enabled him to hold tools and use a pen or pencil to make a record of his ideas, if any. That opposed thumb seemed to be a critical matter.

But an opossum also has an opposed thumb. It is particularly evident on the hind feet, though the forefeet are almost as clearly divided into fingers and thumb. But did the possum ever learn to hold a hammer or to use a pen? He never even learned to use those unusual feet very adeptly for most simple animal tasks. He can't even climb very well without the help of his tail. And up here in the North the possum sometimes loses part of his tail to frostbite, which complicates his whole existence. Actually, the raccoon, with conventional paws, is one of the most dextrous of all wild animals, and the possum is one of the most inept.

So when someone begins to pontificate on the amazing things man has done because he has an opposed thumb, I ask, "What about the possum? The possum also has an opposed thumb." And the talk shifts to the matter of brains, where it really belongs.

TODAY I should like to poke around in my memories of the Model T Ford because late yesterday my lowslung modern car got caught in a snowdrift that shouldn't have trapped a kiddy-car. I had to shovel snow for half an hour and carry two bucketfuls of sand to get it out, and I wished I had the first car I ever owned, a Model T.

It was secondhand to start with and had been piled up in a ditch, which wrecked the body. I didn't want the body anyway, so I bought the wreck, stripped it to the running gears, put on a pair of bucket seats, a big gas tank and a new hood. I drove it close to a hundred thousand miles. Then I sold it to a rural school teacher who drove it for five years. She sold it to a rural mail carrier who made it into a "mud buggy" and used it several months a year on the unpaved back roads of eastern Colorado until the late 1930s. I don't know what happened to it after that. I'm sure it didn't die. Not that car! Maybe it is in somebody's old car museum by now, properly restored. It should be.

The Model T stood well off the ground. That one of mine originally wore different size tires front and rear, 30x3s in front, as I remember, and 30x3½s in the rear. Clincher tires. Remember those? They came before remountable rims. I changed to 30x3s all around to simplify the problem of spares. The car had 15 inches of clearance. It could waddle through a foot of snow without a whimper or, if need be, a foot of mud. It had a magneto, no battery, and no lights when the engine stopped. It had no selfstarter; you cranked it, and if you weren't careful you got a broken wrist when it kicked.

There were two small levers on the wheel, one to advance the spark, the other to feed the gas. It had three pedals. You stepped on one to start it in low, let the pedal up and it jerked into high. One pedal was for reverse. And the third was the brake. When the bands on the brake pedal wore down you used the reverse pedal for a brake. Nobody had yet thought of such a thing as a windshield wiper. When it rained, you stuck your head out around the windshield and looked, or you opened the two-piece windshield and got soaked looking.

The motor was a marvel of simplicity. Every thousand miles you pulled off the head and scraped off the carbon, put back the head and went your way. Once I blew a head gasket 40 miles from town and cut a new one out of the only material at hand, a Uneeda Biscuit cracker box. It worked. I drove a couple hundred miles with that cardboard gasket. A friend of mine once burned out two rod bearings on a lonely road and replaced them, on the spot, with pieces of bacon rind. He drove a thousand miles with those makeshift bearings.

In the winter, on a road with deep snow, you bucked your way, plowing ahead as far as you could go, backing up, taking another shot at it. I once drove 30 miles through snow 14 inches deep that way. It took three hours, but I got through. The radiator boiled dry a dozen times, and I packed it full of snow each time, which melted and satisfied the beast. Some people used kerosene for anti-freeze, but the smell stayed with the car the year around. The womenfolk didn't like it, so if it was a family car you drained the radiator every night.

I forget just what was the horsepower of the Model T motor, but it seemed to have more "pull," more effective power at the wheels at least, than the big cars of today. And we didn't have snow tires, either. Chains, yes. If you were caught without chains you wrapped rope round and round the tires—it had wooden "artillery" wheels, with spokes, not steel disc wheels, so you could wrap the tires that way.

The gas tank on the Model T was under the cushion on the front seat. To fill it, driver and passenger had to get out so the man at the gas pump could lift up the cushion. In a pinch, if you had half a tank of gasoline left you could fill up with kerosene and the motor would run on that mixture. It smoked like a woodburning locomotive, but it ran. There wasn't any door on the left side in front. The driver either got in first or climbed over the side. It had a folding top—the closed cars came later—and isinglass side-curtains that buttoned on. It was probably the coldest vehicle ever built, colder even than a buggy because it went faster and had more cracks for the air to get in.

In the winter, you filled the radiator with boiling water, covered the hood with a blanket, let it set half an hour, then cranked it. If you were lucky, it started in about five minutes. That was its only winter drawback. Once the motor was started, you could go anywhere in it. All you needed was patience and a degree of fortitude. I paid $37.50 for the one I owned, and I would give $50 to get it back. Might even go to $52.50, but no higher.

I RECENTLY RAN onto a botanical puzzle that was a little hard to unravel but seems to come out at a point that could make quite a few faces red. Since I am only a spectator, not really a participant, all I can do is report the matter the way it came to me.

It concerns the common field flower generally known as Joe Pye weed and listed in all the botany books I know as *Eupatorium purpureum*. It grows all over New England and in many other places, a tall, rather rank plant with large pointed leaves growing opposite and with a dense cluster of dark magenta or reddish purple soft-bristly florets that appear in late summer. It was named for an obscure Indian herb doctor, Joe Pye, who seems to have brewed a fever medicine from it.

For years I have wondered just who was this old Joe Pye, about whom little was known. From time to time I asked various friends who were interested in botany or old-time herb medicine, and none of them could come up with any identification for him. Among those I asked was John Bakeless, of Seymour, Conn. Mr. Bakeless is an author and historian with curiosity and wide-ranging interests in natural history. He couldn't turn up anything new on Joe Pye. But because he, too, once considered writing a book about the old herb doctors—writers get such notions, nurse them a while, put them aside, come back to them again and again—we kept in touch.

Then Morgan Bulkeley turned up brand new material about Joe Pye with tavern records of his accounts here in the Berkshires. I sent a copy of this material to Mr. Bakeless. He sent it along to Dr. Edgar T. Wherry, distinguished botanist at the University of Pennsylvania and author of one of the best wild flower books to be had.

I am not quite sure of the sequence from there, but somewhere along the way it came out that Joe Pye weed isn't really *Eupatorium purpureum* at all. Somebody, I don't know who, went to the Linnaean Herbarium, in London, and took a close look at the type specimen of *Eupatorium purpureum,* and it isn't Joe Pye weed. Not the Joe Pye weed we know, anyway. Further research in the Herbarium seems to have shown that Joe Pye weed actually is *Eupatorium fistulosum,* closely related but actually a cousin, so to speak, not even a brother.

The Linnaean Herbarium, with its vast collection of type specimens, is generally taken as the final authority in such matters. Yet even Gray's Botany, right through the seventh edition at least, identifies Joe Pye weed as *purpureum,* and so does Dr. Wherry's botany text. Somebody made a slip-up, and apparently quite a while back, and the error has been perpetuated right down the line. It's the same old story, I suppose. The scientists, just like the historians, tend to go to their predecessors for facts when they don't actually rewrite them.

Mr. Bakeless tells me that when Dr. Wherry visited him last fall they went for a walk and on a back road they found a woodland species of *Eupatorium* that baffled them both. Dr. Wherry agreed that it was a *Eupatorium* but he couldn't completely identify it. It was the only plant they saw that he couldn't name. Maybe, Mr. Bakeless speculates, it was the Joe Pye weed that is over in London as the type specimen in the Herbarium. Though it looked a good deal like the openfield Joe Pye weed we all know, it wasn't the same.

So there it is. I know little about Joe Pye except that he was an Indian herb doctor and he bought several quarts of rum at a tavern in Stockbridge, Mass., in the late 1770s. But I do know that the professional botanists are fallible, even the revered Asa Gray. Either that or the Linnaean Herbarium got the labels mixed, and that is almost like suspecting that Moses mixed up the tablets when he handed down the Mosaic Laws.

But to a layman like me the whole matter is quite reassuring. If the men who write the botany books can get themselves into such an embarrassing situation, I shall no longer hem and haw when asked to identify all the wild asters along my roadside. I shall just do the best I can, and if some eager beaver who has had one year of college botany challenges me I shall calmly ask, "On what authority?" He will undoubtedly cite Gray. I shall cock an eyebrow and say, "Gray was wrong about Joe Pye weed. Are you sure he isn't wrong about this aster?" And that, my friends, will be that.

IT SOMETIMES SEEMS that I go out and fill the bird feeders three times a day, and even then they are empty by sundown. Somebody said the other day that if the birds would just slow down a bit, maybe take a few tranquilizers, they wouldn't burn up so much energy and need so much to eat. But maybe grain is cheaper, considering the markups on tranquilizers. Anyway, the birds need a lot of food because they run a temperature, sometimes as high as 114 degrees, and everybody knows you should feed a fever. Or is it the other way round? I forget whether you starve a cold or a fever. It's one or the other.

Right now I'm sure you starve them both, at least as far as I'm concerned. I haven't a cold and I'm not running a fever, but there are moments when I look at that bird feed and am downright envious. I've been whittling off a few pounds, and if you must know, that's why I think the birds around this place are gluttons. I wonder if they ever stopped to count up the calories.

Let's see, now. There are 100 calories in ¾ cup of rice. Cracked wheat has 100 calories in half a cup. There are 100 calories in every slice of white bread. One biscuit is 100 calories. One apple dumpling is 300 calories! And just one piece of raisin pie packs 400 calories. Time was when I liked raisin pie above all other things.

But there are other things to eat. Oh, yeah? Yams, 250 each. French fries, 25 calories per *piece.* Baked beans, 300 c. per small helping. Roast pork, 170 per thin slice.

But why go on? If one can't eat bean soup, or beef stew, or spaghetti even without meat balls, or a couple of pats of sausage, without facing the threat of 300, 400, even 500 calories a mouthful . . .

I don't know how the birds get away with it. A chickadee, for instance, can and often does eat one-seventh of its own weight in twenty-four hours. But does a chickadee get—well, call it overweight? Not so you could notice it! Moles are even worse. They often eat their own weight in twenty-four hours. They begin to starve if they don't get at least half their own weight in food every day. Think of it! If an ordinary-sized man, like me, ate that much—No, don't think of it. Forget it. I'm sorry I brought it up at all.

It wasn't on doctor's orders. The last time I saw the doctor he said, "You're looking well. Eating well, I see, too." And I said, "I always put on a little extra in winter. You know Barbara's cooking. And I don't get quite as much exercise, in the winter." He smiled, and checked my blood pressure, and said, "O.K., boy. I don't know how you do it, but it's still down there around a hundred and forty."

No, it wasn't the doctor. And Barbara didn't egg me into it, either. She just said, "I hope you can still get into those good brown slacks of yours. If you can't, you'd better see Tony and get a pair you *can* get into." And she said, "I think we'll have a clear soup for dinner. And how about turnip instead of mashed potatoes?" Which was all right with me. But a fellow has to have something to eat, too. He can't fill up and do any work on clear soup and turnip. For a while I thought Barbara was doing it, though. Then I found that when she went out to the kitchen before we went to bed, "to see that all the food is put away," she was having herself a baked bean sandwich or two and a glass of milk. I don't know how she does it. She can still get into her clothes. Maybe she has some chickadee blood.

Blue jays don't put on the pounds either, even though they spend their days out at the corn crib. Boy, are they working on that corn! Let's see. Cornbread packs 130 calories into "one small square." Imagine that! You wouldn't think it, would you? Cornbread, rich and golden and hot enough to melt the butter right into it, plenty of butter . . . Well, forget the cornbread, too.

And juncos are sleek and slim. They are ground feeders and don't just gobble at the feeder, as chickadees do. But when I put a handful of grain on the ground, I don't see the juncos holding back. I doubt if they even know how to spell "diet."

Well, time to fill those feeders again. I really think I walk off a few ounces a day that way. That fellow who said you have to walk five miles to work off one slice of bread must have been crazy . . . Ho, hum. Wonder what bird seed tastes like. Maybe with plenty of cream and sugar . . . Well, forget that, too. Come, birdie, come birdie! I hope you choke, you gluttons!

A YOUNG FRIEND asked, the other day, "I wonder what they did with the snow fifty years ago? They didn't plow it off the roads and streets. What *did* they do?"

I said, "Here in New England they used to roll it, pack it down, with big wooden rollers. Where I grew up they just tromped it down, wore it down with bobsleds, and sleighs." And in saying that I was remembering winters of years ago.

Cold weather came early, in the small town where I was born. Or so I remember. Cold, but little snow before Christmas. There was a pond not far from town and by Thanksgiving Day it was iced over. From Thanksgiving till Christmas we skated there, on the clear white ice. Everybody used the clamp skates, the kind that had jaws to grip the soles of your everyday shoes and bite into the heels. Girls' skates had no heel clamps; they had straps that came up over the insteps to hold the heels in place.

The boys played shinny, with a home-made wooden puck and clubs cut from the osage orange trees that lined the roadsides. We skated there after school and on Saturdays, with a big bonfire to warm us when hands and feet were numb with cold. And when we took off the skates and tried to walk home our feet were so cold and our ankles so numb it was like walking on stubs, legs amputated somewhere between knee and ankle.

Then it snowed, usually Christmas week, and there was no more skating. Out came the sleds. You went out to the edge of town and waited for a farmer coming in to do his Saturday trading, and if you were lucky and he was willing you threaded your sled rope through a runner-strut on his pung or cutter, flopped on your sled, the rope-end in your hand, and had a free ride. Then you waited for another farmer, his trading done, to start for home, and you caught a tow from him back to the edge of town.

There was an unwritten law that there must be no knot in the end of your rope. One Saturday my rope began to fray and I knotted it, and when I tried to cast loose the knot jammed on the cutter. The farmer, bundled to the ears, didn't hear my shouting and I was hauled two miles from town in the deepening dusk and the bitter cold before he turned and saw me, like a fish at the end of a line. He stopped and let me loose, and I started back to town. I was seven, or eight at most, and the snow was up to my knees. Fortunately, another farmer, a friend of my father, came along before I had gone half a mile, and turned around and took me home, tucked in beneath his old buffalo robe. That was my last session of "hooking rides" that winter. I got my orders, which ended with, "You might have frozen to death."

When one was older, in his teens, he could go bobsledding on one of the hills in town or nearby. Bobsleds were built at the local blacksmith shop. They consisted of two sleds perhaps 3 feet long, with a long plank between them, the rear sled bolted in place, the front sled on a pivot for steering. A good bob would hold eight or ten riders and required a skillful helmsman. Most of the bobsledders used the steep hill on the town's main street. With a full load and a skillful pilot, one of those big bobs would run half a mile, all the way across the Burlington tracks at the far edge of town.

The older crowd, the highschool boys and girls, now and then took a big bob out on the winding country roads for more exciting runs. One moonlit night ten of them came down Jackson's Hill, where the road curled like a snake before it crossed Nemaha Creek on an iron bridge.

The pilot took the first three curves successfully, but on the sharp curve just above the bridge the runners chattered and lost their grip on the rutted ice. Going more than 20 miles an hour, the sled slewed broadside into the bridge abutment. The screams were heard in town, half a mile away. Two boys and a girl were dead when help arrived to count and care for the casualties.

That was the end of bobsledding, not only on country roads but on Main Street Hill.

We moved away, and it was a good many years before I was there again in winter. I drove in on hardtop roads that had snowplow heaps 4 feet deep on each side. The town's streets were all plowed out. Youngsters were coasting, but not on the streets, which were salted and sanded; they were coasting on a pasture hillside at the edge of town, safely away from traffic. I drove out Main Street, looking for the big hill. But it wasn't there. I didn't even have to shift gears. It never had been there, I found when I asked a boyhood friend. And the pond down across the tracks, where we used to skate? "Oh, that little puddle," he said. "Just a mud hole. It always was." And I knew that hills are twice as steep, ponds three times as big and deep, when you are eight years old.

A COUPLE OF WEEKS AGO a friend in Canaan, N. Y., the place to which inattentive mail clerks send mail addressed to Canaan, Conn., and vice versa, phoned and asked what are sun dogs and could she see them about now. I told her sun dogs were leftover rainbows that were sawed up for fence posts and set out, one on each side of the sun, in cold winter dawns or sunsets.

She said, "Well, I guess we've got them," making it sound like measles.

"How many?" I asked.

"One pair a day. I see them every morning while I am taking my vitamins. Haven't you got them?"

"Not yet. But we've been exposed."

"What causes them?"

"Look," I said, "this is your call. It could run to five bucks if I went into all the symptoms. They'll show up down here, and I'll write a piece about them and save you a bit of cash."

"O.K.," she said. "But don't forget. How long will it take them to get there?"

"Depends on the weather. Were they big dogs?"

"Big as elephants!"

"A week or ten days," I said, "if they don't get lost."

"I'll leave directions in a milk bottle," she said.

She must have made the directions plain, because yesterday afternoon I saw the sun dogs down here, so I'd better write that piece for Helene.

Sun dogs are vertical shafts of color like segments of rainbow that appear near the horizon soon after sunrise or just before sunset on cold winter days. If the sky is clear you can sometimes see a faint circumzenithal arch, as the meteorologists term it, high overhead. That is the top of the rainbow curve of which the sun dogs are the lower ends. But usually you see only the sun dogs, the vertical bars, down near the horizon.

Sun dogs are caused by clouds of tiny ice crystals in the air, but they are unlike rainbows because rainbows are opposite the position of the sun in the sky. Sun dogs are always alongside the sun—you face the sun to see them. If you are mathematical-minded, the sun dogs usually are between 20 and 25 degrees from the sun.

It is sometimes said that the appearance of sun dogs is a warning of an approaching storm, but I have seen them in the past in the midst of a long, cold, stormless period. The ones I saw last Wednesday could possibly have foretold the weekend weather, but I doubt it. This winter we have had here in the valley few sun dogs but no lack of stormy weather.

The ones I saw were visible from 4 P.M. till about 4:45. They were sunset dogs. The western sky was striped with cold, gray clouds that parted from time to time enough to let the sun shine brilliantly. Off to the left was a gap in the clouds, and there I saw one sun dog, as brilliant as any I ever saw. The sky to the right was dark with twin clouds that thinned only once while I was watching, but when they did I had perhaps a minute's look at the other sun dog. It was equally brilliant, but only a fragment of it was visible. The sky overhead was almost clear, but I saw no sign of the circumzenithal arch. Just those two dogs, those astonishingly bright bands of color, red predominating but with yellow and deep purplish blue also visible.

It wasn't a particularly cold evening, around 30 above zero at the time by my thermometer. The day before had been much colder, 20 below zero at daybreak and not above 20 all day; and the day after, Thursday, it was exactly zero at sunrise and again around 20 at the day's warmest. I haven't yet seen sun dogs at sunrise this winter, though there have been a number of what I consider ideal days for their appearance.

There are also moon dogs, a similar phenomenon that occurs at the rise or set of a moon near the full on a cold winter dusk or dawn. They are not as brilliant as sun dogs, but easily recognizable and even more spectacular, I think, perhaps because they seem so strange. I have seen them only a few times in my life and those times rate with the two rare occasions when I saw rainbows at night, also caused by a moon near the full. Once in a great while a light pillar will be seen near sunrise or sunset, a vertical bar of red or white light directly across the sun, and sometimes it has a crossbar, making a heavenly cross. This, too, is caused by ice crystals in the air.

"THE CLIMATE" Henry said, "is changing." Henry has firm opinions about everything. I sometimes think he stops in just to try them out on me, though he says he stops for a drink of my spring water. Once in a while I offer him something stronger, and he never refuses.

"Of course the climate's changing," I agreed. "There was a time when this valley had half a mile of ice in it. Woolly mammoths were grazing on the ice sheet, and there was a herd of polar bears up there on top of what is now Tom's Mountain."

Henry snorted. "How do you know? Were you here? Did you see those polar bears?"

"Do I look that old?"

"With your cap off you do."

"You were talking about the climate," I reminded him.

"Yes. Well, back in eighteen eighty-eight—"

"Oh, please! Not that again. Anyway, the Blizzard of Eighty-eight was in March."

"All right. There was another big blizzard in eighteen ninety-nine. In February, the eleventh to the 14th. They had fourty-four inches of snow at Atlantic City and almost that much in Philadelphia."

"How about New England?"

"I don't recall how much we got here, but plenty. In eighteen sixty-seven we got five feet of snow in one storm. Five feet, measured and verified, in Dorchester, Mass. That was a January storm, January seventeenth." He shook his head. "We used to get snow that really was snow, back in the old days."

"You don't have to go that far back," I reminded him.

"In nineteen thirty-four in February as I recall, we had more than two feet of snow right here in Connecticut. And up in Maine they had—or said they had—eight feet in that storm. It seemed to get deeper the farther north you went. Up on Gaspé a whole freight train was buried and they said it was fifteen feet deep on the level."

"Seen anything like that the past few years?" he asked.

"No," I admitted.

"Well, the climate's changing. We don't have old-fashioned winters any more."

"We don't have old-fashioned summers, either. Or much of old-fashioned anything. Times are changing too; or hadn't you noticed?"

"The climate's getting warmer," he said.

"Thomas Jefferson said it, quite a while back. I doubt that he originated the comment, but Jefferson said, 'We don't have old-fashioned winters any more.' "

"He did? When?"

"Oh, around eighteen-ten, or thereabout. What would you say is responsible for the change?"

"People, the way we live. All these overheated houses. They give off heat into the atmosphere."

"I wish my house would give off enough heat to melt the ice at the eaves from time to time."

"And cities," he went on. "You'd be surprised how much heat even a medium-sized city gives off. Heat and fumes. And motors. How many motors have you got in your house?"

"I'd have to count up. A dozen or more."

"See what I mean? Every one giving off heat. And cars. How many million are on the roads, burning up gas? And all those roads!"

"What have roads got to do with it?"

"In the good old days," he said patiently, "we rolled the

snow on the roads, left it right there to reflect the sun. Now what do we do? Scrape it off, salt it off, clean them right down to the cement and blacktop to *catch* the sun's heat. How many miles of roads and throughways have we got?"

"And parking lots," I suggested.

"Right! And electric lights. Every light bulb gives off heat. How many light bulbs have you got in your house?"

"Enough to light a factory. You should see my electric bill." I paused to light my pipe.

"That, too," he said.

"What?"

"You smokers. Ever figure out how much heat your pipe gives off? And all those cigars and cigarettes!"

"I hear that folks are cutting down or trying to."

"High time! And aeroplanes. You know how much heat an aeroplane makes? Just from the motors, and not counting the friction on the air. Tremendous. Then there are—"

How about a drink?" I suggested. "Even you are beginning to warm up."

"Don't mind if I do. Getting that time of day. Make it an old-fashioned, please."

TOMORROW IS GROUNDHOG DAY, but I will lay heavy odds that there won't be a groundhog awake anywhere in New England. Even in an early spring the groundhog, which most of us call a woodchuck, doesn't come out of hibernation till March; the earliest I've ever seen one out in this area was March 16. And when a woodchuck does wake up he doesn't go looking for shadows. He looks for a mate and for something to eat, usually in that order.

The Groundhog Day legend is so tangled in half-truths and errors that it is almost ludicrous. The basic idea is very old, reaching back at least to the pre-Christian Romans who seem to have taken a still earlier ceremony and built upon it a mid-February ritual of purification. The exact date, by the modern calendar, is not altogether clear; it may have been closer to mid-March and the vernal equinox. That would explain, at least in part, the idea of an animal seeing its shadow and forecasting the season. The identity of such an animal is obscure, but various animals were of symbolic importance in many of those early rituals.

As with a number of pagan rituals, this one eventually was incorporated into a church ceremony, the Candle Mass, and the date was established as February 2. The animal legend persisted and was transferred in western Europe to the badger and the hedgehog. It was even elaborated to the point that the emerging animal must see, or fail to see, its shadow at 11 A.M. And when the early colonists came to America they brought with them this legend, one among many in their miscellany of weather lore and animal tales.

But the early colonists were not too careful in their naming of native animals. They called the large, ruddy-breasted American thrush a robin simply because someone thought it looked like the warbler-size English robin. And someone mistook a woodchuck for a badger. Before you could say *Marmota monax,* the animal aspect of the Candlemas Day legend was pinned on that unsuspecting sleepyhead and he was called a groundhog, as some called the English badger.

Further complicating the whole matter was the name "woodchuck." It came into currency as a corruption of still another corruption, "wejack," which apparently came from the Cree "otchek" and the Chippewa "otchig," which actually were the Indian names for another animal entirely, the fisher. Just to follow this through, the fisher is a valuable fur-bearer closely related to the marten and is no kin whatever to the animal we know as the woodchuck.

So there we are. Candlemas Day started as a pagan religious festival. Some unidentified animal became involved with its significance. Centuries later that animal was identified in western Europe as either the badger or the hedgehog, varying locally. The legend was brought to New England and pinned on an animal mistakenly identified as a badger and named, also in error, for a fisher. So we arrive at Groundhog Day and the woodchuck.

As far as the woodchuck itself goes, it is one of the most persistent of all animal hibernators. Actually, it is endowed with the ability to revert, seasonally, to prehistoric status. It virtually becomes a cold-blooded animal, its bodily processes depressed to the minimum necessary to keep a thin flame of life flickering. In late fall, provisioned with a thick layer of fat, it crawls into its den, seals the entrance and goes to sleep. Its breathing slows almost to a stop. Its pulse becomes slow and faint. Body temperature drops as low as 40 degrees, usually about the same as the surrounding earth. In this condition it sleeps as long as five months, living on the fat stored beneath its skin.

Finally something happens, nobody knows exactly what. The woodchuck rouses from its coma, perhaps wakened by rising daily temperature, perhaps by sun angle or daylight length, though how the signal reaches him underground is a mystery. Anyway, the 'chuck wakens, digs out of the den, and emerges into the springtime full of rampant hormones. Male woodchucks fight bloody battles for mates. Then they settle down to work on the burgeoning green of this world.

The appetite of a woodchuck amazes me. One year we

were unwilling hosts to a 'chuck who ate only two things in the garden, choice young cucumbers and, at the opposite end of the garden, the shoots of young dill. I never found out where he got the vinegar. Another year we had one who ate nothing but beet greens. From time to time we have had one who loved sweet corn; I accused the 'coons of this depredation till I caught this 'chuck at it in broad daylight. And one year we had Ferdinand Woodchuck, who ate nothing but zinnia buds.

In later years, however, I lost touch with the garden variety of woodchuck. Pat came to live with us, and although Pat's training was as a rabbit dog, he thought his real mission in life was to rid New England of woodchucks. One June he averaged one a day for two weeks and laid them out, one by one, on the lawn for me to find. Nobody can fail to find a dead woodchuck after a few hours in the broiling sun.

But even Pat knew that there wouldn't be any woodchucks out as early as February 2.

THIS HAS BEEN a difficult winter for wild life, I am sure, but I doubt that the hazards we know are as serious to life in the wild as we sometimes think. Man has a persistent tendency to interpret conditions anthropomorphologically. That big word simply means that we attribute to non-human creatures the thoughts and feelings of the human species. Wild birds and animals live and have experiences on another plane from ours.

The normally migratory birds that are wintering over in this area no doubt are having trouble. Theirs is a somewhat marginal existence every winter here and a good many of them are dependent on the charity of those of us who maintain bird feeders and supply them with grain and suet. I have a theory, however, that some robins are developing a particularly hardy strain, and perhaps some of the other normal migrants are, too. When such a strain is developing, weaklings always perish. It's a part of the natural selection process.

But the birds that normally live here the year around probably are doing about as well as usual. They are equipped to stand our winters. They are well feathered, they live on a diet obtainable in the woods and fields all winter, and they know how to conserve energy in prolonged cold spells. Take the partridges, the ruffed grouse. They eat a great many buds, which are never completely covered by the snow, and they add to this an assortment of wild berries. They are well clothed, even to their feet. I have never looked into this very deeply, but it is my belief that a partridge's feet are seldom feathered in a mild winter. I know I have seen them with feet as naked as those of a chickadee in late December, if there was little snow.

Owls, of course, have no special winter problems. They thrive, in fact, when cold and snow force mice and rabbits into the open. The snowy owls, incidentally, come south every few years regardless of the weather. Their coming and going in our area seems to coincide with the supply of lemmings up north, and the lemmings have a four-year population cycle. Apparently there are few lemmings up there this winter.

Crows and jays are omnivorous and truculent enough to drive other birds away from any food they find. Both will invade barnyards for waste grain, and crows eat small animals killed on the highways. They make out in any winter. The small woodpeckers, hairies and downies, will not starve as long as there are trees in the woodland, and no winter ever buries the trees. They are ready customers at the suet cage, but they can get along without such handouts. And the same goes for the nuthatches.

Life is somewhat more difficult for the smaller birds. That is one reason there are so many juncos, sparrows and chickadees at the feeding stations. But for every one of them that lives on handouts there are thousands that work for their living all winter long. I know that the grain that I put out couldn't wholly sustain the flocks that come and go here. Some of them are habitual beggars, but a good many of them live in an old pasture just down the road, and live rather well. I can always flush a big flock of juncos there, feeding on weed seed, and I often see several mixed flocks of sparrows and chickadees there. And every time I go up into the woods I find flocks at work in the underbrush and the cedar thickets. Redpolls do very well for themselves, too, and so do goldfinches, and pine siskins, all feeding on weed seeds. And by no means all the weed seedheads are covered with snow.

Evening grosbeaks take care of themselves, both at the feeders and in the open. And cardinals are downright independent. The cardinals that come around my place seem to visit the feeding stations only for dessert.

Thus far we have had no ice storms, which cause real trouble for the birds, not only by icing their feathers but by sealing in their food. Most winter kills of birds occur during and soon after an ice storm. But it has now been fairly well proved that most bird casualties, especially in the winter, are a result of predators—hawks, owls, etc.—rather than weather. And such death is normal. Few small birds, and that includes most of the songsters, live as much as five years. And that means birds that survive the nest. The casualties at nesting time probably are greater than any normal winter toll. Two days of cold rain when eggs are hatching probably kill more chicks than two days of zero cold and snow kill off adults.

It isn't an easy life. But birds all live a hazardous life. Nature takes pretty good care of them, as long as they abide by fundamental rules. Feeding stations help some of them out in hard times, but there were birds here long before there were feeding stations. And millions of birds today never go near a feeder.

FROM TIME TO TIME we all get a letter of sympathy from someone who went to Florida or Southern California or maybe Arizona for the winter. I do. And they always make me want to laugh. The person who wrote the letter was so obviously saying, in a backhand way, that he or she was homesick for New England weather. The heart wasn't in the invidious comparisons, really not in them.

Sure, most of us yelp about the cold, and when we get it we holler about the snow. But what we are doing is bragging, in our own way. I've known some weather braggarts, in my time, but none can compare with those here in the Berkshires. Oh, maybe those in Alaska can, but they really have something to brag about. I know that Midwesterners who are so inversely proud of their blizzards and their simmering summers are pikers, compared to a real New Englander. And the folks up in Minnesota just sort of glum up, as though their vocal cords were frozen. The most eloquent tales of Minnesota weather I ever heard were years ago, when they talked about how a streetcar smelled when all those bearskin coats began to warm up. Now there aren't many bearskin coats left, and few streetcars, so that one is passé and nothing has taken its place as a braggable winter topic.

But we have weather, and we know how to talk about

it. We go around comparing thermometers, and cheating a few degrees just to make things properly rugged. We measure snow, when we have a normal winter, and we fudge a few inches there, too. Last winter at this time I was telling everyone we had 3 feet of snow in the back pasture and the drifts and piles along my driveway were 8 feet high. I have referred to those measurements a number of times since and shall continue to do so in years to come. But the other day, just to be sure I wasn't making light of the matter, I looked back in my journal for last year. I hesitate to quote the figures I set down at the time, but I must have misread the yardstick. I did say that I could see over the piles along the driveway, but I failed to mention that all I could see was the peak of the houseroof. I now remember that quite clearly. I wonder why I didn't mention it then. You just can't trust such journals, I guess.

When it comes to temperatures, last Sunday morning a friend phoned me, just to gab and ask about a bird he saw. Finally he asked, "Cold at your house?" I knew the gambit. I said, "Oh, a bit chilly. How cold was it at your house?" He said, "Well, uh—what did your thermometer show?" I said, "Fourteen below," lying by a couple of degrees, just to be safe. It probably dropped two degrees after I looked. But he had trapped me. "Mine," he said, "was a couple of degrees below yours." And he couldn't keep the note of triumph out of his voice.

Then I went to the village for the Sunday paper, and someone asked, "How are things over in your valley?" And I said, "Chilly." He asked, "How much snow have you got?" I said, "We always get more than you do. Six or eight inches, I'd say." And he said, "Ten inches in my backyard." But I noticed that he wasn't wearing galoshes, and his low shoes weren't even wet. To tell the truth, we had only about four inches of snow. But that's the way it goes. In a few places it drifted deeper than that, and I wore my high boots just to prove it.

I won't give an inch, though, on some things. The other evening we were out under a brilliant moon, and the beauty of it was breathtaking. We just stood and looked at the way the shadows lay, ink-black. Then we went up the road a bit and the moonlight shifted, or the angle of the bank was different, and the light burst into a dazzle of color on the snow. The whole surface was covered with snow crystals, and every one of them was a tiny prism. They shone red and blue and green and orange, almost fiery. It was as though the snow was completely covered with twinkling sequins.

As we walked, with the temperature down to—well, down there a way, near zero—the snow sang underfoot. That whine of cold snow underfoot is winter music, like nothing else in the world. Then the river began to boom, the way it does when the cold bites and the ice freezes even deeper and has to open expansion cracks. It boomed and echoed, and boomed again, and a breeze on the river ice scurried the light snow in curls and swirls, like smoke. It never rose more than a few inches above the ice, but it made gorgeous fluid patterns in the moonlight.

We walked until our noses began to tweak and our cheeks were tingling, threatening to become numb, and our breath was twinkling in the moonlight. A barred owl began asking, "Who cooks for you-all?" up on the mountain, and we laughed at him and came home. To a house that was snug and warm and full of winter comfort.

I never get letters from down South about anything that can match that. All they talk about is sunshine and 65-degree days. Who wants a 65-degree day at this time of the year? Besides, I've been there. I know that they aren't lying in the sun—they're lying in their teeth, just as we so often do. The only difference is that their teeth aren't chattering.

FROM TIME TO TIME I wish that those who lived here before I came had sat down with pencil and paper and planned this farm's buildings a little more sensibly. Not the buildings themselves, but their placement. Besides the house, there are six structures: the woodshed, the corn crib, a small brooder house, a big chicken house, the big barn and the old milk house. I am told that there once were also a small ice house and a large tobacco barn. If they were still standing this place would look like a village, one laid out by a cross-eyed man who had just emptied a jug of hard cider.

The woodshed stands just back of the house, but separate from it; it is still used as a woodshed, as well as for storage of garden tools and many other odds and ends. The milk house, because it is close beside the road I suppose, was made into a garage some years ago. The corn crib is still a corn crib and filled with corn every fall. Pat, the dog, took over the little brooder house for his own quarters. I re-roofed the big chicken house, moved my power tools and bench in there, and found ample room left for a ping pong table. The big barn is used for storage of hay, straw, lumber and farm machinery.

I suppose my complaint really is directed at the hardihood of those who put the buildings where they are. If they had come from 50 or 100 miles north of here, habit, custom and common sense would have persuaded them to group the outbuildings closer to the house. Probably they would have run them all together, with a covered runway from house to woodshed, an open wagon shed joined to the woodshed, and the barn walled right up to the wagon shed. Those who originated such an arrangement didn't care to face a sleet storm or shovel unnecessary snow any more than I do. And even in summer they didn't really want to get soaked to the skin when they went to the barn to do the chores.

Incidentally, the architects who created breezeways between house and garage for suburban dwellings probably took a leaf from those farmers whose layouts I admire and envy. Maybe some of them even grew up on such farms and, though they fled from the land, remembered some of the wisdom of their forebears.

Farm architecture and design have strange echoes. The old barns, of which mine is an example, hark back to the shipyards, as did most of the really old New England houses. Both my barn and my garage, which once was the milk house, are framed horizontally and the sheathing is put on vertically. The framing in both structures consists of hand-hewn timbers which were mortised and tenoned. Those in the barn obviously came from some earlier building, for the timbers have mortises in odd places and for no present purpose.

That type of construction carried over to the big chicken house, which is of much later date. Its framing is of sawed lumber, but it too is basically horizontal and the sheathing is vertical. But by the time the brooder house was built, the fashion had changed. It has vertical studding, the common type of modern construction, and its sheathing is horizontal. The builders were far from the sea and the shipyards, both in time and tradition.

For a time I wondered if some of the outbuildings couldn't be moved closer to the house. Then I considered building a covered runway to the woodshed; but it didn't seem practical and it certainly wouldn't have improved the architectural effect. Instead, I put a wing on the house, at the back, in keeping with its rather stark farmhouse lines, and I moved the back door a few feet closer to the woodshed. That gave the illusion of greater ease in fetching wood in January. But that still left 50 yards of rain or snow to navigate when I put the dog to bed, and another 20 yards to the shop when I wanted to make a minor repair to something for the house.

I suppose everyone who lives in the country puts up with things like this and occasionally dreams of the ideal house and the perfect arrangement. I remember one charming old lady who bought an old country house because she loved it, and spent the rest of her life complaining about its inconveniences. The kitchen floor pitched almost 3 inches, and she had quite a time leveling her refrigerator and getting her electric stove set so that the pans would stay aboard. But every time someone suggested that she have that floor leveled she exclaimed in horror, "And ruin it!"

We have no such problems, since the house belongs to this century. It has a dry cellar, stout walls, a good roof, and level floors. I just wish those who built the woodshed and garage hadn't been such hardy souls. I'm not.

IT'S A QUARTER AFTER FIVE on a Sunday morning and here I am at my desk with a second cup of coffee. The late moon, which entered its last quarter last night, is a rather ragged fragment but casts enough light to throw long shadows of the maples across the road toward the house. I saw them and stood looking for five minutes before I turned on the lights. A worn, late moon and a cold night, 12 above zero five minutes ago and it will drop another few degrees before sunup.

The world is so asleep and deserted at this hour that one can either feel like the last man or think how wonderful it is that so many people are at rest. There's a lot of room and quiet, at this time of day. That's one reason I get up early. But just to be sure, I turned on the radio and listened to a news broadcast with my first cup of coffee. It was the same news I heard last night, which is in a way comforting. Nothing crucial happened, just the normal doing of mankind, if there is a norm, which I doubt.

Another reason I get up early is because there is less of a sense of pressure before the rest of the world is up and stirring. You can feel the slow rhythms of time and the stars and you can see the day begin. The days are just as long as they were 10 million years ago. If they seem short it is because man has tried to pack them so full of hurry.

I don't know where we are hurrying, but haste has become habitual. I wonder what most people do with the time they save by hurrying. I doubt that haste makes life any richer. It usually just makes life more complicated, and complexity isn't really richness, is it?

We have become so impatient. We want instant-everything—instant coffee, instant cake, even instant thinking with electronic computers. We try to teach our children instant reading with such things as flash cards, and achieve what? Approximate reading, with no knowledge of words as such and little knowledge of spelling. We want instant solutions of everything from how to deal with China to how to cure a cold. And such "solutions" are drummed at us hour after hour by those who either forget or want us to forget that the world wasn't created yesterday and probably won't be de-created tomorrow. Probably.

I read where one man says that if we don't use an instant insecticide, we will lose our woodlands. The trees, he says, will die if they are defoliated twice, or is it three times, or only once? No matter. I look around me and I see woodlands that have been defoliated several times and still are woodlands. I read where another man says that gypsy moths and linden loopers will do irreparable damage this year. I wonder how he knows. Gypsy moths have been here, right here in New England, since 1869, almost a hundred years, and they have seventy-five insect parasites. The sprays that kill the moths kill the parasites, too, so what is gained beyond a brief and local respite? Linden loopers have been here, as far as we know, forever, and so have linden trees. The loopers, too, have their parasites.

Is there instant control? Put it this way: If one female gypsy moth survives she will lay 1,000 eggs from which 1,000 larvae will hatch and feed and become moths which will lay 1,000 eggs apiece, and the cycle will start all over again. Man has utterly destroyed several species of birds and animals, but up to now he has never eliminated one species of insect.

It is getting lighter now, dawn. I look out and see the trees, the persistent trees, with their unhurried buds awaiting April and May. I am not a patient man, but such patience as I have was taught me by the trees and grass. Grass, the insistent and ubiquitous greenery of this world, so gentle a plant that I crush it under foot when I walk the pasture, so persistent that some species takes over every waste spot of ground. Trees which, if I turn my back for a season, will reclaim the land I think I own, even driving out the grass. I can destroy the trees, for a time, but not forever. I and my own species are the real devastators of the woodland, but even we will be outlived by the trees.

It is a cold dawn. I just looked at the front porch thermometer, which shows 10 degrees above zero. But some of the birds are already up, probably roused by hunger. Two jays are at the feeders. Seeing them I think of bird diets and scientists who carefully counted insects in bird stomachs. In one flicker, for instance, they found 5,000 ants; in one nighthawk 500 mosquitoes; in one yellow-billed cuckoo 250 tent caterpillars. I think of the brown thrashers that will be here in my yard in a few more weeks. A thrasher eats insects all day long, 6,000 or more a day.

It is almost sunrise, another day begun. Time for breakfast.

WALKING ALONG THE STREET in the village today, turtled in my coat against the raw wind, I heard a strange sound, one I hadn't heard in a long time. I looked around; there was a boy about fourteen, whistling his way happily down the sidewalk. I stopped and stared and listened. Several others stared too. The boy was oblivious. He whistled his way around the corner and was gone. And another man turned to me and said, "Now there's a happy kid!"

Obviously, the boy was happy. I don't know why, and it doesn't matter. All I know is that he was whistling, and I hadn't heard anyone, man or boy, whistling out loud in a long, long time. I wondered why, and I still wonder. Whistling seems to be a lost art. Boys once learned to whistle before they began to lose their milk teeth, and sometimes girls learned too, especially if they had older brothers. I'm not really an authority on the subject, because I never did learn to put two fingers in my mouth and deliver a blast that could be heard a mile away if the wind was right. That used to embarrass me, that failing of mine. But I could whistle between my teeth, and I could carry a tune pretty well, well enough to be one of the gang, anyway. I can still whistle-in a dog. Sometimes.

But what I am talking about is whistling just for pleasure, as a kind of self-expression. They used to say that no song could be really popular unless it had a tune that you could whistle. Then times changed and they said no musical comedy would succeed without a couple of tunes you could hum. Now they don't seem to need whistleable tunes or hummable tunes. All they need is a stable of disc jockeys. I can count on the fingers of one hand the musical shows of the past five years that made me want to whistle a tune. And I don't hear anyone else whistling, or even humming, their tunes either.

But I suspect it's something besides the songs themselves. Maybe it's the radio, after all, and the TV. They get blamed for all sorts of things, as well as the crimes they should be blamed for. Maybe we have got so used to hearing someone else make the music that we don't bother to make it ourselves any more. Or maybe we have grown too sophisticated, have outgrown our respect for the amateur. Whistling was, despite a few professionals, strictly an amateur performance, after all. Anybody could do it, and lots of people did.

A while back a friend, looking through the files of *The Connecticut Western News,* a local weekly newspaper, found a piece titled, "Virtue in Whistling," and copied it off and sent it to me. I remembered it when I heard that boy whistling in the street, and here it is:

"An old farmer once said that he would not have a hired man on his place who did not habitually whistle. He always hired whistlers. Said he never knew a whistling laborer to find fault with his food, his bed, or complain of any little extra work he was asked to perform. Such a man was generally kind to children and to animals in his care. He would whistle a chilled lamb into warmth and life, and would bring in his hat full of eggs from the barn without breaking one of them. He found such a man most careful about closing gates, putting up bars, and seeing that the nuts on his plow were tight before he took it into the field. He never knew a whistling hired man to beat or kick a cow, or drive her on the run into the stable. He had noticed that the sheep he led into the yard and shed gathered around him as he whistled, without fear. He never employed a whistler who was not thoughtful and economical."

The date of that piece was April 11, 1878.

The whistler is in our language. We whistle in the dark. We whistle up our courage. We whistle down the wind. If a demand seems unjustified, we let the other fellow go whistle.

But do we whistle? No! It is unseemly, or something bad, to whistle. Oh, there are wolf-whistles here and there, but not in the better circles, I understand. Too primitive, or too brazen—does anybody ever use *that* word any more? —or too juvenilely delinquent. Why, we even buy the whistles we use to call our dogs, whistles that nobody but a dog can hear! Incidentally, I once tried such a whistle on my dog Pat, and he looked at me as though he thought I had gone off my rocker. I have no idea what it sounded like, but Pat obviously thought it didn't sound like me. I gave the darned thing to a friend in the city who used it to torture his wife, who had freak ears and could hear some of its super-sonic tones. She finally left him. So much for mechanical whistles.

I see that I haven't got very far with this; but someone should speak up for honest whistling before everyone forgets what small boys and uninhibited men used to do with their spare breath. They used to whistle tunes, right out in public, and I still miss them.

IT WON'T BE LONG NOW before we will be watching that age-old phenomenon, the spring migration of the birds.

Even in a severe season, I usually see a flock of migrant robins here in the valley by mid-March. The male red-wing blackbirds usually appear about the time of the robin, and around that time I nearly always hear the geese high overhead, chattering with a sound like the distant barking of small dogs.

All the migrant birds, of course, wait for hospitable weather. They know, as well as the meteorologists, it seems, when spring temperatures set in. The robins and the geese and, as far as I can learn, the red-wings too, follow rather closely the northward advance of the isotherm of 35 degrees. Watch the weather map, and when that isotherm begins to approach the Berkshires you can be fairly sure you will soon be seeing migrant robins. Apparently it takes a 35-degree temperature to bring out their natural food. No robin in its right sense will migrate into a starvation area. Those that spend the winter here are something else again. They aren't many, and they have their own food sources, which wouldn't support big migrant flocks.

The spring migration is always slower than that in the fall. Apparently when the birds sense cold weather coming they want to get out in a hurry. But they follow spring north in March and April, seldom outrunning it. They could easily outrun it, of course. The American robin can fly as much as 32 miles an hour, and migrating geese have been timed at 45 miles an hour. But the robins seldom fly as much as a hundred miles a day in the spring migration. In the fall they may cover more than three hundred miles a day.

Among the smaller birds, most of the seed-eaters, such as the sparrows, prefer to migrate by day and rest at night. The insect-eaters, such as the robins, usually make their migrant flights at night and rest and eat in the daytime.

This may be in part because insects are more active and easier to find in the daylight. Swallows and other birds that catch and eat insects in flight are an exception to this general rule. But once at their destination, even the insect-eaters sleep at night, reverting to their normal habits.

Observers watching migrations by radar or by telescope focused on the moon have found that the heaviest night migrations occur between 10 P.M. and 1 A.M., with the busiest hour between 11 P.M. and midnight. There seem to be few flights after 4 A.M., for some reason, perhaps because of the approach of dawn.

Early guessers at the cause and conditions of migration greatly overestimated the altitudes at which the birds travel. Some even said they all fly at 20,000 feet or more, where they are invisible from the ground. Now we know such an idea is wholly wrong. Most small birds on migration fly less than 250 feet above the ground, though they have been seen as high as 5,000 to 10,000 feet. Geese have been seen flying at 9,000 feet and often migrate a mile high. Golden crowned sparrows have been seen migrating at 10,000 feet in California and cranes have been known to migrate at 15,000 feet in France. Altitude apparently varies with the weather.

In the fall migration, the young birds are sometimes the first to go south, followed by the females, then the males. In the spring, however, the two sexes usually migrate together most of the way. Then the males push on ahead. We see this most vividly among the red-wings, with the males here and *ka-reeing* loudly a week or two, sometimes even longer, before the less conspicuous females arrive.

Aretas Saunders, of Canaan, Conn., whose studies of bird songs are classic, charted the spring arrival dates of fifty species of Connecticut migrants over a period of about forty years. His study showed conclusively that the arrivals varied with the weather. Early spring brought them early, late spring delayed them. The variation for some species was as much as four weeks.

Why birds migrate at all is still an unanswered question. We know the answer involves weather and food, environment and psychology. But we still don't know why out of one nestful of robins, for instance, one may stay north for the winter and the rest will go south. In his *The Migrations of Birds,* Jean Dorst rallies close to four hundred pages of data and opinion, but his conclusion is substantially that birds migrate for reasons of their own that man hasn't been able to pin down.

HOW EAGERLY we look for signs of spring, now that February is in its final week! A week ago it was so mild out that Barbara went to the vegetable garden and looked for the first green tips in the chive bed, and I went to the most favored part of the flower beds to look for a crocus tip. Of course we didn't find either chives or a crocus. There were still huge patches of snow in the pastures, the woods on the mountain showed no sign of life, and the river just across the road was still iced in. And by Friday night it was down to zero again. Still February, not March or April.

But there were reports, last week, of sugar maple sap running here and there. By the weekend it wasn't running, and unless all the forecasts are wrong it won't be running again this week. But there was a note of triumph, just the same, in the news that it did run, even briefly. It will run again; that we know.

There were the robins, too. People keep seeing winter robins and announcing triumphantly, "The robins are back! I saw two in my front yard this morning!" Of course they saw robins, but not migrant robins freshly in from the South. We have had robins in our yard every decent day all winter. A few hardy robins stay here all winter, every winter, feeding on cedar berries and sumac berries and such like; and when a mild day comes and they can find a patch of open grass, they look for the insect food they hunger for as people hunger for fresh greens. People also hunger for the sight of robins, which is why they are so triumphant in announcing that they saw one. I heard a report of bluebirds the other day, too, five or six of them. But a few bluebirds spend the winter here too. Winter before last a friend of mine saw a flock of a dozen or more, in mid-January, down in the Cornwalls.

One woman I know has her own way of hurrying spring. Some people cut forsythia twigs and force them in the house, but this woman picks a mild day, usually in February, and goes with a trowel and a flat-bottom basket and brings in a half-frozen chunk of soddy soil from the foot of a ledge where early wild flowers bloom in April. She digs it carefully, with as much root tangle as she can get, and when she gets home she puts it in a flat pan and sets it in a south window. Within two weeks she has a fine little green garden there, with violets and cinquefoil and anemones poking eagerly up and beginning to bud. Sometimes she has violets in bloom before the vernal equinox. One year she had a whole hatch of tiny grasshoppers, too, jumping around the room like outsize fleas. She had inadvertently brought in a clutch of grasshopper eggs with her pat of sod.

And that reminds me of another friend who, in March, brought in a handful of apple twigs to force some blooms. The apple blossoms opened, in due time, but the same day a pod of eggs hatched and she had young praying mantises all over the place, unexpected hitch-hikers on one of the apple twigs. You never know what you will get as a bonus, when you try to bring April or May into the house in February or March, but you can be sure it will be some phase of spring.

We don't have to bring spring into this house. During that warm spell spring came down from the attic, as it always does, in the form of wasps. I have tried for years to be rid of those wasps, which are plain, everyday mud-daubers. But they had a foothold here when we came and apparently they will be here long after we are gone. Every fall I go through the attic, on a cool day when the wasps are properly lethargic, and announce that this time I have got them all. Then comes that first warm spell, and the wasps appear. How they get down to the bathroom, the bedroom and the studies, I do not know, but they do. Last week I killed six in the bathroom within an hour, two in Barbara's study and three in the bedroom, all the same day. Then I went to the attic and killed almost a dozen of them. The next day I had it all to do over again. By the weekend they had subsided; but they will be back.

The first reliable signs of spring, the ones I can count on, are the flush on the red osier stems and the quickening amber color of the willows, especially of the big weeper. When I see those signs I know I can find fattening willow buds down at the little bog a mile and a half from here. It won't be long after that before willow-pussies will be in sight, and when they come I begin to look and listen for redwing blackbirds. But there is still no flush on the red osiers. It's still February, and I keep looking only because I, too, am hungry for spring.

IT WAS THE CHICKADEES that impressed them most. I was proud of the little beggars and the way they responded; but it wasn't my doing. It was the weather.

These three people had come up from the city, an editor, a girl with the title of researcher, and a photographer. It could all have been done by telephone, but that isn't the way they do things. So they drove up here, on a chilly, rainy day with a forecast of snow and possibly sleet. And we talked in front of the fire, mostly about the country and rural living and how and why one writes about the outdoors.

The editor was city-born. "I don't even know a robin when I see one." He spent some time "in the country, sort of," over in Providence, and was glad to get back to New York where everything was citified and familiar. He wasn't a fanatic about it. The country was nice but rather sparsely populated, and country hours were incomprehensible to him. He tried to understand, and seemed to, at least up to a point.

The researcher turned out to have a country background. Her father wrote a fish and game column for some years, one of the best such columns I ever read. And when Barbara spoke of foxes barking, this girl smiled and knew what she meant. She even knew that "birds" mean partridges, and she asked the right questions about the fishing. One didn't have to explain too much for her.

The photographer had the tools of his trade slung around his neck and didn't care much about the talk. He saw the world through a lens. The only times he really sparked was when two other photographers, both masters of their trade, were mentioned. And when he spotted an original Stieglitz in my study. That meant something important to him. He would have given one of his cameras for it.

We talked, and we seemed to have things pretty well wrapped up. Then we wandered out to the sun porch and looked at the mountainside. The rain was turning to sleety snow. The big old apple tree just beyond the house was a busy place as the birds gathered at the feeders for a last meal before the storm iced things in. I had filled the feeders earlier that morning, but the jays had scattered most of the grain and the sleet was beginning to cover it.

One of the chickadees saw us at the windows and came and perched on the sill, begging as they often do. The editor exclaimed, "What's that bird? Is it a tame one?"

I tried to explain about chickadees. "Sometimes they practically poke into my pocket for sunflower seeds," I said.

"Suppose they would now?" he asked.

"I doubt it. Another ten minutes of this sleet and they'll hightail it for the pines, get under cover before they are all iced up themselves."

"Would you mind trying?"

So I got into a coat and the editor and the photographer went with me out to the feeders. The jays fled, the two female cardinals headed for the woods and the juncos rose in a windswept flurry. Even the sparrows had left. It looked hopeless.

Then I heard a chickadee in the big apple tree. I held out a handful of sunflower seeds and called, "Come and get it!" The chick, a wary little glutton I knew rather well, flew around the big feeder twice, then swooped to my hand, grabbed a seed and was gone, too fast for the photographer.

There wasn't another bird in sight. I was about to give up when I heard another chick. He came out of nowhere, perched almost within arm's length, a little fellow who always seemed to get crowded out at the feeder. But this was his chance. I would swear he looked at the photographer, squared his shoulders, put on an almost jaunty look, and came gently to my hand. He perched on my thumb, posed, took his time about choosing a seed. He posed again, put back the seed, took another, posed still again. He put that seed back, chose two at once, and flew away.

As we went out to their car the editor said, "That was worth the whole trip, that one little bird." I wanted to tell him that chickadees are a dime a dozen and that a hungry chick will come to anybody's hand for a sunflower seed. But it seemed a shame to spoil it. They were going back to the city, back where people feed pigeons, back where starlings outnumber chickadees a thousand to one.

II

The ice went out of the river as quietly as mist, with no fuss whatever. Now it flows free and calm—and polluted. It is a bilious green even at sunny midday, when it should have a tinge of blue even if it were roiled and muddy with early runoff. But it flows, and a few mornings ago I saw the first black ducks on it. They looked rather bewildered at the quality of the water, flavored with paper-mill sludge and Massachusetts sewage; but I suppose any open water is welcome on a migratory flight. The ducks used to nest by the dozen along the river, but the past few years their numbers have steadily decreased. I haven't yet seen a merganser, though they, too, used to spend several weeks on the river each spring. Maybe they gave up on it, too.

And the Canada geese are back. The biggest flock I have seen was on a spring pond on old Route 7 just above Ashley Falls. Very few geese have been on the river the past few years. They have shifted to the ponds, both those that are perennial waters and the shallow ones that gather from the melt in the hollows and dry up by May. I suspect that this flock is the same one that has been on the Ashley Falls pond the past three years. Last year there were a couple of snow geese in the flock, but they seem to be missing this year. Maybe they joined a flock of their own kind. Mixed flocks of geese are not rare, however.

I haven't yet seen a red-wing blackbird, but the other

morning I saw a flock of at least a hundred grackles. They were at the little bog down the road a mile and a half from my house, and at first I thought they were red-wings. But when I stopped to look and listen there was no doubt of their identity. You can't mistake the sound of a flock of grackles, which often is like a vast chorus of creaky gate hinges. And there wasn't a red epaulet among them. They had the iridescent grackle sheen on their black feathers. No mistaking them. The red-wings may be along any day now. Males first, of course. The females don't arrive for at least a week after the males; and the females look like big sparrows, streaky brown and white, not at all like the males.

Cardinals have been around all winter, as usual. A couple of females have come into our yard from time to time, to feed under the bird feeders and add a bit of brilliance. I heard the males whistling but didn't see one until Saturday morning, when he came down from the woods and foraged for half an hour under the feeders. And when he had gone back to the woods, he whistled quite imperiously and at length. It's getting that time of year.

A week or so ago a friend in Philadelphia wrote to say that he had seen a gray squirrel carrying off a robin's egg. Could that happen, he asked, at this time of year? I said no, it was most unlikely, even in Philadelphia. I suggested that it might be a starling's egg, which is somewhat the same color as that of a robin. Starlings sometimes nest very early, though not as early as owls. Apparently it was a starling egg; my friend says there were starlings around and acting as romantic as starlings ever do.

The robins here are all year-rounders, thus far. We have half a dozen that have been in the yard every time there was a bare patch of grass, and they all looked fat and prosperous. Winter robins go on a cereal diet, eating seeds they wouldn't give a second look in the summer. I suppose they pick up a bit of insect fare now and then, but not much. I can always tell the migrants from the year-rounders because the minute they arrive they scatter over the pastures and forage for hatching insects. They never head for the woodland to eat seeds and dried berries.

The chickadees are getting independent. A few weeks ago they swarmed around me, demanding food, every time I went outdoors. Three or four really brash ones perched on my shoulder and begged, and one oddball thought the beak of my cap was a good place to sit and make himself heard. But now I have to beg *them* to come and get the sunflower seeds, and even then they take their time about it. Chickadees are foul-weather friends, and the weather has faired up.

The jays are singing. I mean really singing. They have a quiet musical spring song that many people know but don't identify. It has a kind of bell-tone quality, not at all raucous. They sing it only briefly, a few weeks, then quit, possibly because by then there will be real songsters around. By April the jays will be jeering, as usual. But it isn't April yet, and any singing is welcome.

IT IS HARD TO SAY why they came, whether they were restless or hungry or what, but a big doe and a gay red fox visited us this week. Best of all, they came in broad daylight and on snow-clad mornings when the visibility was perfect.

The doe appeared just after 7 A.M. A couple of inches of soft, wet snow had fallen during the night. I first saw her beside Millstone Brook just beyond the vegetable garden, not 50 yards from the house. She had come down from the mountain and across the home pasture, with no sign of fear. She didn't pause under the two old apple trees, where the windfalls had pretty well rotted anyway, but went to the roadside fence, leaped it gracefully, and came up the road. I thought she was going right past the house, but instead she turned, just below the house, and went down to the river where she walked in and began swimming toward the far bank.

But for some reason she didn't go ashore there. Ten yards from the far bank she turned and swam upstream as though enjoying the swim. She swam close to 200 yards upstream, then turned and came back across the river. I went out to see what she would do next, but instead of coming ashore she turned still again and swam on upstream, now close beside the near bank. I hurried up the road and had almost reached the railroad bridge when the town snowplow came thundering along. The driver didn't see the doe, which was close beside the bank; he went roaring on up the road. But the doe heard the clatter, turned and swam directly across the river, lunged up the far bank just above the bridge, shook herself, climbed the embankment, flirted her tail almost defiantly, and stood there a long minute before going on down the far side and into the woods.

She had been in the water fully ten minutes, had crossed the river three times and had swum at least a quarter of a mile. She didn't even appear to be puffing when she got out. I don't know whether she saw me, but if she did she paid no attention. But that snowplow was a clattering, menacing monster.

The fox appeared Sunday morning, at almost exactly the same time, seven o'clock. Barbara saw it first. It was in the same place where I first saw the doe, beside the brook just beyond the garden. It had come down Millstone Brook, investigating the grass clumps with their tufts of Saturday's snow. I thought at first that it was hunting mice, but if so it was very casual about it. It turned and went down the pasture a little way, then went through the fence and came up the road, like a dog. I wondered if it, too, was going for a swim. But it turned back into the pasture and through the garden fence into the garden itself. There it nosed at a pile of matted maple leaves I left there last fall to mulch, investigated the old Brussels sprout stalks, nosed at the asparagus bed.

Then it came up the garden path to within 40 feet of the house. It glanced at the house once, then ignored it, poked at another pile of moldering leaves, and went through the garden fence again and back into the pasture.

It ranged the pasture almost ten minutes, back and forth, sniffing now and then, nosing the air from time to time, catching nothing, not even trying. It went to the far fence, followed the fencerow to the old stone wall, came along the stone wall down to the barn. There it stood for a long moment, as though considering whether to come back to the house and investigate the compost pile. Instead, it went around the barn once, spent another five minutes in the small upper pasture beyond the barn, and at last went up the railroad embankment and disappeared. I suspect that it was a neighbor of mine, a resident in a den up that way that I know was used several times by vixens and their litters in the past few years.

Why the doe and the fox came, I don't know. Neither seemed to be hungry. The fox was ready to take any available snack, of course, but it wasn't actually hunting mice. It never hurried, beyond the normally nervous gait of a fox in the open, and it showed no fear of the house or anything else. If I had gone outdoors it would certainly have streaked away, but I stayed indoors, watching it through various windows. Its coat glistened, its brush was full and graceful. I could have counted its whiskers while it was in the garden; I plainly saw the shine of its dark eyes through the binoculars.

Both came on snowy mornings, which provided sharp contrasts. And we had grandstand seats, which doesn't happen too often.

THE VERNAL EQUINOX doesn't occur till the end of this week, but I saw and felt and smelled winter preparing to call it quits yesterday, around four o'clock in the afternoon. That doesn't mean no more snow or ice or sleet. All it means is change, which is slow and often interrupted. In fact, yesterday, today and tomorrow are the anniversary dates of the Blizzard of '88, which dumped 30 inches of snow on this area and is cited every time anyone talks about spring in March.

But I am not talking about spring. I am talking about that time of change between winter and spring, which may last two weeks or six weeks. The best word I can find for it is interregnum, a period between reigns, between administrations, if you will. By the almanac, winter will be in power until the equinox; after that spring will be in office. But it always takes a while to get a new program launched and that is the period between reigns, the interregnum. The earth, where spring really has its roots, not in the stars, takes its own time about making the adjustment.

Here is what I mean about yesterday.

The sun came up at 6:09 according to the almanac, and was visible here by 6:15. It was a clear sun, and the night temperature had been in the upper 20s. By 9:30 it was into the 30s and there were trickles of melt at the roadside. In the side yard, where the drifts were least, there was a patch of open grass for the first time since mid-December. As the morning passed that open patch widened, inch by inch. A pair of cardinals that have been around here most of the winter explored it, and so did half a dozen purple finches that came here for the first time earlier in the week. Tree sparrows and a couple of song sparrows were there, too, acting as though open grass were something very special.

Noon, and the melt continued. All around the big spruce in the yard were small holes in the snow. Each one had a spruce needle in it, and every one of those tiny dull green needles collected extra warmth from the sun, enough to melt the snow under it. Holes began to appear around the fence posts at the garden, heat again collected by the dark posts.

Just before three o'clock I was outdoors, filling the bird feeders before the late afternoon time when all the birds come for the late meal that will tide them over the night. Chickadees swarmed, as always, begging their special ration of sunflower seed. They got it, and one of them sat in a lilac and sang a five-note song over and over, a song I hadn't heard since last April. Then a tree sparrow in the big apple tree sang, not much of a song but the best a tree sparrow can do; it, too, was a new sound.

When I tried to cross the drifts to the pussy willow bushes I sank almost to my waist at every other step. The various crusts in those drifts were beginning to rot. The pussy willow buds were fattening but showed not even a crack. Then I found one that showed a tiny fleck of green beneath it, brand new green. Only one bud, though. I wallowed on through the snow to the big weeping willow, whose fountain of wythes had a warm, honey-colored glow. That glow often comes before the riverbank red-osier dogwood stems look alive. But the weeping willow buds were still tight and tiny.

A touch of a breeze came down the valley. It had a new

feel, not warm, but not edged. A March feel, not the feel of February. I came back to the house and out onto that bare patch of lawn, which had almost doubled in size during the day. It had an oozy feeling underfoot but with the firmness of frost just beneath. Curious, but not hopeful, I looked for signs of new life. That is the warmest spot anywhere around, sheltered from the wind and in full sun. Crocuses bloom there first. I looked for crocuses, and I found one tiny thrust of twin tips in the brown grass. The first crocus, the rash one. It meant little, and yet it did mean that change is coming.

A little later I drove down the road on an errand and saw tiny red beads along the twigs of the swamp maple at the bend. Flower buds, no longer winter-brown. They can wait till April to open but, like that crocus, they mean change is coming. I didn't get home till 5:30, but it was full daylight till well after 6. Not spring yet, but spring definitely in the making.

THIS IS THE TIME of year when I have the feeling that anything can happen. It could snow 2 feet tomorrow, or it could turn so warm next week that the birches would skip their catkins and burst right into full leaf. I know that won't happen, of course. I know what time it is by the clock of the stars and the calendar of the seasons. But it's partly the way the sun shines now, and it's partly the way my own senses react. There's a stirring in my own vitals, and there's a bit of chlorophyll in my blood, clamoring for a chance to go to work. And that's not wholly a figure of speech. The hemoglobin in my own blood, in any human being's blood, is chemically akin to chlorophyll, the difference being an atom or two of iron, the chemists tell me.

I suspect that the plants and the birds and even the animals have something of the same reaction. It would be amazing if they didn't, for we are all a part of that mysterious stream we call life. The old earth slowly heaves over and we here in the Northern Hemisphere find ourselves under the direct rays of the sun again. The sun begins to penetrate instead of glancing off, like a ricocheting bullet, as it did all winter. And all things are possible, including such minor matters as crocuses in bloom and maple sap running, and such major matters as the end of winter and the beginning of spring.

And, to the surprise of all of us, there is a pristine something in the air and even in the earth. A sense of newness.

Look at the sunrise, just as an example. Yes, I know it comes at 5:52 today, and two months ago you could stay abed till 7 and still see it. But a January sunrise occurs away off there toward the South Pole, and usually it has a case of the sulks. Sunrise now comes in the east, where it belongs, and sometimes it arrives with the power and the glory of creation. It's the start of a brand new day. A day that has practically twelve hours of daylight. Isn't that something new? So new that even the astronomers and the atomic physicists can't match it; all they can do is look at the charts and tell you that it has so many hours, minutes and seconds. Probably microseconds, too, if you ask them. But they can't stretch or shrink it one iota.

Or look at the sunset. That's available to anyone, and it is a brand new one every day. I've watched sunsets for a lifetime and I've never seen two alike. Nobody has. But the newest ones of all seem to come right now. I don't know why, and I'm not going to ask. Some things you take on faith. The kind of faith that convinces me that there are no two leaves exactly alike, and never will be.

And there's a moon. A moon in its first quarter, which is there in the sky at sundown and doesn't set until after midnight. How long is it since you looked at a waxing moon in mid-March? Well, take a look, if it's clear to-night, and see something brand new and yet as old as—well, who knows how old the moon is? It's new to anyone who looks, because it's never twice the same, from where we stand. Why? Because we keep changing, we funny, blinking, upright animals who can count the stars but still don't know why they are what and where they are.

But most of all, look at this earth around you, which despite all prodding and probing and guessing and figuring still defies our curiosity. We live here, along with all the other amazing plants and animals, and yet someone finds out something new about it every day. New to him, at least. And what is newer than a new idea or a new glimmer of understanding?

That's what I was trying to say. Tomorrow brings the vernal equinox. The bells won't ring and there won't be any Roman candles, but tomorrow, according to the stars, will be the first day of spring. I doubt very much that my apple trees will care very much which stars have lined up for that event, but I am sure that something down at their roots is already responding to the angle of the sun. And to the temperature of the air and the depth of the frost, which a grave-digger tells me is about four feet. That may be a grim way to find out, but spring reminds me that life and death are facts to be faced, and that is just as important as any equinox. Anyone can chart the seasons, but it takes a seed to perpetuate life, some kind of seed. Give a seed a place to grow and anything can happen.

I know that, down in my viscera as well as in my brain. It is instinctive as well as intellectual. I am not sure that it is intellectual at all, on second thought. But I do know that it comes to the surface now, when I see the first crocus shoots. I know that a crocus can happen, and if crocuses can happen again, then anything can happen. Tomorrow I may see a bee. Or a woodchuck. This morning when I watched the sunrise I know that I saw a brand new day, a world that had the look of Genesis about it.

SO IT'S SPRING, by the almanac. The vernal equinox occurred yesterday morning at 9:43, and the daylight was already a bit longer than the darkness, one of those things that prove that the mathematics of celestial mechanics are imprecise at best. Maybe not imprecise, in their own terms, but certainly unrealistic. In any case, anyone who lives within hailing distance of the land knows that spring doesn't originate up there among the stars. Spring is a matter of mundane matters such as a thaw and an ice-break-up and mud in the fields and the maples coming to blossom and the redwings ka-reeing in the bogland and the peepers yelping their hearts out.

Almost a month ago I met a woman who lives 20 miles south of here and she said triumphantly, "I have daffodils up!" She said it with one of those challenging smiles, daring me to say, "No!" I fooled her. I said, "All right, so you've got daffodils up. I'll bet I can tell you where they are." She said, "Where?" And I said, "Out in your side yard, over the septic tank." And she said yes.

I didn't have to guess. The same thing happens here. We had the first green tips of crocuses up, too, out there over the septic tank that gets the warm bath water and the hot water from the kitchen sink. It's a natural hotbed. The first year we lived here I wondered why the snow always melted over that area so early. Then, the last week in February, the crocuses came up there, and the daffodils soon after them. Considering the weather, I wondered if we had some special Arctic breed of bulbs. But there wasn't another one up elsewhere. Only in that circle about

6 feet wide. And then it came to me. That septic tank. The man I bought the place from had waved his hand in that general direction and said, "The septic tank's over there."

So we always have a few early crocuses out there, and half a dozen daffodils that come to bloom two or three weeks ahead of normal time. Which proves that spring is a matter of only a few degrees of temperature. I suppose if I were properly curious about such things I would go out with a thermometer and see just how much warmer the soil is there than in the surrounding area. I never have.

But I see somewhat the same thing happening naturally. Several brooks flow down off the mountain and across my pasture-land, and their water is not much warmer than the surrounding air, probably not more than 2 or 3 degrees. But along the banks of those brooks the grass always grows green and fresh several weeks ahead of the grass 20 feet away. Violets come up and bud and even blossom at least two weeks early when they have their roots in the brookside mud. There are a few gray birches, little ones, along one of the brooks, with their roots in the edge of the water, and they come to catkin earlier than the birches elsewhere.

And along the river I already see that warm red glow in the red osier dogwood brush, that livening color which means spring is not far off. Those bushes are warmed by the river, maybe only a couple of degrees, but enough to wake them early.

The equinox hasn't anything to do with these matters. In a sense, the equinoxes and the solstices, which mark off our seasons on the calendar, are not much more than convenient coincidences. They don't correspond to the seasons, really. By the calendar and almanac, for instance, spring ends and summer begins with the summer solstice, about the twenty-first of June. That means that all through summer, by the calendar, the days are getting shorter. Logically, fall would begin with the summer solstice. But the logic of the seasons doesn't tally with the logic of the almanac.

If I were in charge of the almanac and the calendar I would go back to the old-time order and start the year with the vernal equinox. That would make sense. It made sense to the old-timers, anyway, who thought the year should begin with the time when daylight exceeded darkness. That happened to be the natural new year, too, for the green world began to wake up and get going about then. Not precisely, but near enough if one were going to tie the year to the stars. But they were farmers and herdsmen, and the fellows with the telescopes and the mathematical formulas thought they knew a better way to order things. So we got the new year where it is now, without any relationship even to the stars, which was really something for a mathematician to achieve in the name of logical order.

I'm not in charge of any calendar or almanac, and officially this is the second day of spring, the eighty-first day of the year. But the trees are stubborn about these matters, and so are the buds and the bulbs. They have their own calendar, just as the birds do. They won't be hurried. The almanackers can have their equinox. I don't expect to see spring, real, mild, green spring, till the first of May. Not up in these hills. I hope it comes sooner, but I don't expect it.

FOR WHAT IT IS WORTH, the migrant robins now are back in the valley. Today I heard them scolding when I went outdoors at 7 in the morning and an hour later I saw a dozen of them out in the home pasture. This afternoon I saw the whole flock, as eager and interested as homecomers from a winter vacation. Which, in a sense, they are of course. I think of any bird's home as the place where it nests and rears its young. Their trip south each winter is little more than my occasional trips down to the city. There's a time difference, and they travel farther, but that's about all.

And I have seen the red-wings that I heard two weeks ago. Half a dozen of them came up the valley the other morning, as though announcing that they were here, and sat in the trees and chattered for half an hour or so. Then a few grackles appeared and there was a lot of noise. Grackles in full cry always make me think of the sound of rusty hinges, unless there is one of those huge flocks of them. A whole flock of grackles is absolutely beautiful to see, but a chorus of their voices is not in any sense a symphony.

The mergansers are here, too. At least two pairs of them. They have been up and down the river, swimming, flying, floating and diving, making a great show. Sometimes I think they dive and swim breathtaking distances under water just to show the black ducks what astonishing birds they are. The ducks are up to their usual tricks. A few nights ago one old loudmouth among them began quacking at 3:15 A.M. He has quacked at 3:15 every morning since, and if he doesn't mend his ways I'm going to post notices. It wouldn't be so bad if he just woke up and quacked a few times, but he is a loud-mouth and long-winded. Maybe he's a politician conducting a filibuster. Anyway, I wish he would stop thinking he can keep owl hours and get away with it.

The mourning doves have been calling, even at mid-day, for the past ten days or so. The doves have been around all winter, some of them anyway, but they haven't been calling till recently. I suppose they are getting hot blood too.

The other day, down at the little swamp, I got one

quick flash of what I was tempted to say was a redheaded woodpecker. I still can't think of any other bird it might have been. I didn't see the red head, but all the other markings seemed to be right. It was there for only that one quick look, then was gone, and its flight followed the typical woodpecker pattern. I've heard that a couple of redheaded woodpeckers were around, so maybe this was one of them.

I've kept watching for bluebirds, but without success. They should be here about now. But I didn't see a bluebird last year, and I heard of very few in this whole area. Strange, sad things seem to have happened to the bluebirds, and it's a shame because they are lovely to look at and beautiful to hear, as well as being exemplary citizens. I sometimes think, the way we spread poison around, that we don't deserve to have bluebirds.

It won't be long now before the first flocks of flickers are back. And soon after that we will have orioles and grosbeaks and brown thrashers and all those wonderful vocalists. I already hear some morning song, just about sunrise, but most of it comes from the robins. They aren't really in good voice yet, though. A few phrases and a lot of chattering, the scold-notes, but not really scolding. And I was sure the other morning that I heard song sparrows.

The other birds, the feeder patrons, are going about their business but with a somewhat more jaunty, carefree air. And they are doing their best to sing. Any time in March it is a heartening sound when a chickadee begins to sing, even the old, familiar song. He puts a touch of April into it, and that makes all the difference. He makes me think that the spring peepers will be out before too long, and that is a very pleasant thought.

As for other, related matters, the buds on the big popples are fat and now make a brand new pattern against the sky. I opened one of those buds and found the catkin all ready to grow. The male catkin, it was, and when I peeled away the layers to reach it I found a yellow trace of pollen on my fingers, the fine, golden dust of silvan life. The shadbush is also swelling its buds, but more deliberately. In the dooryard, the twin buds on the lilacs are fat and faintly green; and the crocuses are up, but still very cautious about even unfurling a leaf. I guess spring has signed its lease and will move in eventually. But there's a lot of redecorating to be done first.

THE RED-WINGS ARE BACK in my pasture and I have been quietly celebrating their return. To some people the red-wings are only swamp blackbirds, rather noisy at times, early arrivals in the spring but otherwise undistinguished. But to me they are old friends and welcome here. I knew the red-wings when I was a boy in a land of little rain, and they meant water and cattails and cottonwood trees and shade in a place where shade was rare.

Each time we went from the hot, dry plains to the town on the South Platte River where we bought our groceries once a month I saw and heard the red-wings as soon as we came to the irrigated land a few miles from the river. They lived in the reeds along the irrigation ditches and they gathered in the towering cottonwoods and filled the air with their cries. And now and then a great flock of red-wings and yellowheads took to the air, gleaming black speckled with red and gold, magnificent.

Later I knew the red-wings along the Rio Grande in New Mexico, and again they were symbols of water and shade and lush patches of green, and I knew them along the Green River in the desert of eastern Utah. Then I knew them along the lower Mississippi, near Shreveport, where they were detested because they ate rice in the fields. And in the Carolinas, where they were regarded as a pest.

And now I know them here, and still they make me think of cool water and cool shade, even in this land of plentiful water and shade. For they nest and flock in every bogland and along all the streams, and from late March till autumn I hear them, their calls sometimes like the contralto of the wood thrush, sometimes like the arrogant challenge of the jay, sometimes like the sweet nothings of the oriole. Nobody need agree in this matter, which is quite personal; but even my Barbara, to whom red-wings are just red-wings, says that one of the red-wing phrases is, "I love you, I really love you." And she thinks their glistening jet and their startling scarlet epaulets are lovely. Especially now.

I have no idea why those few which nested beside the small brook in the pasture chose this site. They came two years ago, and I had thought they were nesting beside the river, so close at hand. Then one day when I walked beside the brook I found a nest in the tall grass with five pale greenish-blue eggs marked with fine sepia lines and I knew whose eggs they were. The brown-striped female, so unlike her mate in color, screamed at me from a nearby mullein stalk, and Mr. Red-wing came swooping in and called me every name in the book. I retreated, and in due time the eggs hatched and the fledglings learned to fly and sing.

The brook dries to a trickle, often to no flow at all, by mid-July, and I had thought the red-wings would not return another year, particularly with the Housatonic so handy and with patches of swampy land both up and down the valley. But they came back last year and nested again beside the brook. And here they are once more, apparently annual residents now although the cows are in that pasture all summer long and there isn't a cattail the whole length of the brook. There are a good many grass-hoppers, though, and the red-wing diet includes them in quantity. Maybe that's why they stay.

They come early, always, as early as the migrant robins. Some of them winter over. A few were seen from time to time all winter in the little swamp just down the road beside the old Weatogue Cemetery, and now and then they were seen in Canaan. I heard them in my pasture three days before I heard the mourning doves this year, the dove on the mountainside calling in late afternoon to the dove across the river.

And always the red-wings are here and making music, to me at least, well before the peepers come out of hibernation and salute the afternoon and evening. We went up the road to a little bog the other evening to listen for the peepers, though we knew there wasn't a ghost of a chance they would yet be out, and there were the red-wings, a whole flock of them, making so much noise you would have sworn it was late April. We sat and listened for twenty minutes, and quite forgot the peepers, which, incidently, weren't out.

We listened. To that typical call, which some transcribe as "O-ka-lee," "O-ka-lee." And to that throaty phrase: "I love you, I really love you." And to that wonderful liquid note, so like the fall of a pebble into a pool of water, a kind of sweet "Cliunk," and to the twittering undertones, the embroidery of the red-wing songs, the lace on the fabric, which I can't begin to describe or transcribe. Listen to a dozen red-wings all making music and you hear a medley, with all kinds of variations. Or maybe you don't. Maybe I'm just hearing the play-back of my own memories.

Anyway, the red-wings are here in my pasture for the

third year in a row, here beside the brook. And I welcome them with a kind of grateful wonder. They sing to me of a time when I had to drive 30 miles to see and hear a red-wing beside flowing water. And here they are, nesting practically in my back yard 2,000 miles from those high, wide and lonesome plains I knew as a boy.

THE VERY WORD "April" has a warm, green sound to it, and the word "March" somehow sounds raw and muddy. Part of this is a result of association, I am sure; but so are the connotations of a great many words. To continue with the months, July sounds hot to me, and August sounds humid and sweaty. Since all four of these month names go back to Roman gods or emperors, the sensations they prompt in me are obviously not valid. When I think of Julius Caesar, I certainly don't have the same reaction I have when I think of July. And when I think of Mars, I don't get a raw and muddy reaction, though Mars was a god of growing things as well as of war. And, to cap this list, October's very name makes me think of colorful woodlands, balmy days and falling leaves, which is ridiculous if I remember that originally it simply meant the eighth month in the Roman calendar. The word "eight" has no such connotations, nor does the Latin equivalent.

Words are peculiar that way, full of overtones and memories and semantic subtleties. It's an old game to pick the most beautiful, or the most unpleasant, words in the language. Playing it, some people have chosen "cellar door" as the most beautiful combination of sounds, with liquid consonants and soft vowels. To me, however, it has no such beauty. Perhaps I have worked too long with the meaning of words rather than with their sheer sound. Even so, I think "oriole" is a beautiful word, a most pleasing combination of sounds. "Robin" hasn't the same sensation at all. And, though I love the infinitely varied songs of the brown thrasher and think it is a beautiful bird, the words of its name do not make any kind of music to me.

"Brook" is a beautiful word. Yet "book" lacks something, probably that rolling "r," which give "brook" its sensation of music. "Rill" has some of that same music. "River" lacks it. Maybe it is the liquid "l's" which have a pleasanter sound than the "v" and "r" in river. "Creek" is a harsh word, probably because of those long "e's," possibly because its homonym, "creak," signifies an unpleasant sound. Again we are dealing with semantics.

"Home" has a pleasant sound, though "hum," so close to it, is rather nondescript. Maybe it is that long "o" combined with the soothing "m" sound. And "smoke" has a sound that pleases, perhaps also because of that long "o." On the other hand, "fire" is not reassuring, and it isn't only because of the literal meaning; it may be that combination of the long "i" and the rather growling "r" sound.

Years ago I took a course in the origins of the English language. At the time I hated it, though now I go back often to the textbook and get pleasant satisfaction from it. I know now that I disliked the course because the teacher was a rasping-voiced man who never did get at the music of words. I didn't know it then. I simply disliked him and all his works. Now I know that he was also a pedantic fellow who had not even a hint of poetry in him. Poetry is basically song, or should be, and the words of poetry should sing, not only in their meaning but in their very sound.

Later, after I left college, I found that I was following the path that course should have set me on. Words became very important, not merely as meanings but as sounds. I had discovered that how a thing was said was often as important as what was said. The substance was essential, but the form could alter the meaning in subtle ways, even make it more easily understood. And that, of course, is the purpose of words—to make meanings understood.

We all grow up with words in our mouths, so automatic that we use them with only casual care. That is why we use such expressions as "see what I mean?" and "in other words," and "what I am trying to say." We fumble with words, settle for the approximate, then try again. We have countless generalities, and yet we invent such words as "gadget" and "whoozit" and "dingus" and use them to death simply because we are too lazy or slipshod to pick the word we really mean. And those three words, by the way, strike me as among the ugliest words we use, both in sound and meaning, or lack of meaning.

"Storm" is an ugly word to me, though when taken apart it hasn't an ugly sound in it. "Cloud" is a beautiful word; yet when you take away the initial consonant it becomes an unpleasant "loud." "Spring" is not a beautiful word, nor is "rain." "Water" is sweet to the ear, unless it is given that pinched, upper-Midwest pronunciation. But "April" sounds right. Thank goodness, it starts tomorrow.

RUSS SAID the woodcocks were putting on their courtship flights every evening soon after sunset, so we drove up to his place, the house on the knoll above the alders and the slow brook and its small boggy area. The sun had set before we got there but the lengthening twilight made headlights unnecessary. With sunset a breeze had sprung up, twitching the treetops. It was a cool evening.

Two others had come to watch and listen, and after introductions the five of us stood on the porch and waited, watching the alders below us. Nothing happened. "Sometimes," Russ said, "you can hear them from up here. Maybe the wind will stop them tonight."

So we walked slowly down the driveway. The big black dog came along, but he didn't trust fortune—he brought a big bone, just in case we decided to make a night of it. Halfway down the slope we stopped to watch and listen. Five minutes and there was a faint peep. "Robin," Russ announced. The peep was repeated, then became a full-length song, the robin's evening song. It was in a pine 50 yards away.

"Last night the woodcocks were in flight by this time," Russ said. "No wind last night, though, and a full moon besides."

There was a loud "Whooonk!" behind us, and we looked up and around just as a flight of Canada geese went over, so low we could hear the slight whistling of their wings. They were in a rough V and they talked among themselves as they arrowed north. I counted fifteen of them. "Must have come from Mill Pond," Russ said. "Sometimes they go over so low I can hear the hiss-hiss of the air through their wings."

Still no woodcocks. The dog was gnawing at his bone. We went on down the lane, paused at the brook, hoping for some woodcock action. No luck. We crossed the highway, went a little way up the slope beyond to a small brush-grown meadow that was a little pond until someone bulldozed it full and then let the brush take over. Another brook flowed along its edge, burbling softly. Russ pointed to a shallow curve in the brook. "That's where I saw my first water shrew. I was looking for a water snake I saw there the day before and this little animal suddenly took off from the far bank and walked right across, on the surface of the water. I couldn't believe my eyes."

A beautiful oak loomed against the western sky, still faintly pink with sunset. A bur oak, sometimes called mossy-cup because the acorn cup is very rough and almost covers the acorn. There were several of them in the woods nearby, Russ said. But there weren't any woodcock. Not a twitter, not a peent, not a hissing wing.

The wind had a slight edge by now. In the east was a cloud bank through which the moon made a streaking glow, just above the horizon. Another ten days or two weeks and the peepers probably will be making the night echo in that damp valley. But not even an owl hooted this night, and the few robins seemed to have sung their evening songs and tucked in till dawn.

We went back across the highway and started up the slope toward the house. The dog drank noisily at the brook, found his bone again, carried it a little way, then left it for some future time of need. He was going back where he knew the food came from.

Halfway up the slope we heard a peep, or thought we did, and stopped and listened. It may have been a sleepy robin. If it was a woodcock, he was merely announcing that there would be no performance tonight. We turtled into our collars, tucked chilly hands into our pockets, and went on. Off to the west, Venus was brilliant and other stars had begun to appear overhead. Twilight had faded but there was enough sky glow for us still to see the ground underfoot.

The lights from the house began to blind us to the night. Only the treetops were visible, silhouetted. The alders were a shadowy mass of darkness. And somewhere down among those alders the woodcocks were quietly waiting for another evening when the air would be calm, when whatever stirs a woodcock to twitter and make that fantastic courting flight would stir them again.

We went back to the house, warmed ourselves, talked a bit and called it an evening. Russ apologized for the woodcocks, and we promised to come back another time. He was there on the porch, bareheaded, listening to the night, as we drove away.

Mr. Chip was out and chirping this morning. He wasn't the first chipmunk I heard; several others had been calling for almost two weeks, in the stone wall beyond the barn and from the stone footing for the garage. Mr. Chip may have slept late. If he did, he wakened full of sound and energy, for he sat on the front step for fifteen minutes, chirping, and his notes were like the musical drip from a leaky faucet into a deep pan of water, liquid and loud. I could have heard him a hundred yards away.

Mr. Chip lives under the cement slab at the foot of the wooden steps to the front porch. He—or at least a chipmunk that looks exactly like him—has lived there the past three years. I think it has been Mr. Chip, for he is clever enough and has a sufficiently secure home to have survived that long.

We are friends, Mr. Chip and I, but not so friendly that he comes at my call and eats from my hand. Occasionally he will allow me to sit on the top step and watch him, 5 feet away, but only if I sit very quietly. Now and then I put out a few peanuts for him, but beyond that we draw the line. He is not a pet. We agreed on that arrangement two years ago. I feel that once you make a pet of any wild animal you not only take away its independence but you rob it of the wariness it needs for its own safety. He seemed to agree.

I am not even sure that Mr. Chip is not Mrs. Chip. There may be baby chipmunks in that den under the cement slab right now. But it pleases me to call the chipmunk, whatever its sex, Mr. Chip. I have never seen young chipmunks playing there, however, so I suspect that the name is right. Baby chipmunks, in any case, will not be leaving the nest till late May or early June. And when they do come out they will be almost full grown. That is why we almost never see what we would call baby chipmunks. By the time they appear they have the same kind of coat, the same markings, as the adults, and they are already eating adult fare. The only difference, and it is not easy to see, is slightly less fullness to the tail.

Mr. Chip lives what we would call an easy life, I suppose. He sleeps most of the winter, rousing only from time to time to satisfy his hunger from well-stocked storerooms in his den. In very cold weather he goes into semi-hibernation, by no means as deep as that of the woodchuck. He may appear on the first warm days of spring, but when it turns cold again he goes back to sleep. He doesn't do much chirping until he is awake for the summer. Mr. Chip obviously had ended his sleeping, except at night; he chirped for fifteen minutes the other morning.

He is seldom short of food. Even this early in the spring he eats well, mostly from his own pantry. He is primarily a vegetarian, living on seeds, and nuts. For a while, now, Mr. Chip will make trips to the back of the house to forage under the bird feeders, where he finds millet and cracked corn and an occasional sunflower seed that the chickadees have overlooked. As soon as the first berries are ripe he will eat them. He loves wild strawberries, and if we grew tame strawberries he would be a nuisance there. I think, but am not certain, that he raids the tomatoes occasionally, when they are ripening. Beyond that, he haunts the vegetable garden chiefly for weed seeds and grasshoppers, with which he varies his diet. I have never seen him at it, but I know his kind will also occasionally climb a tree and eat an egg or even a nestling from a bird's nest. But that is only an occasional crime, and in his lexicon it is no crime at all. Blue jays eat ten times as many eggs and nestlings as all the chipmunks in existence.

When the maple keys are ripe and begin to spiral down, Mr. Chip will really feast. He will also stow maple seeds, their vanes neatly clipped off, by the pint in his underground pantries. When the basswoods come to seed he will harvest those little round nuts and stow them. And when the oaks drop their acorns he will be busier than a bee. Since he carries all his harvest in his cheek pouches, he will nip off the sharp points of the acorns before he carries them away. Find an acorn with its tip bitten off and you can be sure a chipmunk marked it as his own.

Mr. Chip will work most of the summmer, but not too hard. He lives in a world of plenty, and he is a provident little creature. When he is working he will chirp and play, and keep a wary eye for hawks, and foxes, and for barn cats. He has his enemies. But he also has a special pleasure in life. That is why he was out there chirping the other morning. His world was in order and it was good just to be alive.

ONCE the spring peepers begin to yelp there isn't much doubt about what time it is. They are even more sensitive to temperature than crocuses and daffodils. My records show that they don't quit their hibernation until the daytime temperature gets up to 50 degrees and stays there three or four days in a row. It doesn't much matter if it gets down below the frost line at night if the days continue warm. But if the days drop into the low 30s the peepers retreat into the silence if not actually into the mud. One year they came out the last week in March, called loudly for two days, then were frosted out and didn't utter a sound for a full week. Another year I heard them yelping during a 3-inch snowstorm; despite the snow, the temperature didn't drop below 40.

Peepers sometimes are called treetoads, though they actually are frogs. The distinction between frogs and toads, generally speaking, is that frogs have smooth skins and toads are warty. Both toads and frogs lay their eggs in the water and the eggs hatch into tadpoles. When the tadpoles have developed lungs to replace their gills, have grown four legs and lost their tails, they are ready to come ashore. From that point on the toads are primarily dry-land creatures and the frogs are amphibians, spending a good part of their life on land but always near water.

The scientific name of the spring peeper is *Hyla crucifer*; the *Hyla* stands for treefrog and the *crucifer* refers to the cross on its back. It is a very small frog, no more than an inch and a quarter long, and it bears a dark cross mark on its orange-tan or reddish-brown back. It has long toes with little sticky pads on their tips. There are eight varieties of treefrogs in the United States but only two are found in our area, the spring peeper and the gray treefrog, which is almost twice as big as the peeper and varies from light brown to gray-green in color. The peeper yelps or peeps in a high, shrill call. The gray treefrog trills.

Peepers are marsh dwellers, wetland creatures. You almost never find them far from water and their preference is a bogland with a growth of willow brush or alders. I seldom find or hear them here on the banks of the Housatonic except where there is a backwater bog, as at the mouth of the Blackberry. One evening a few years ago, however, one came to our house and spent the evening.

It was a warm April evening, so warm we had a couple of windows open. I was in the living room near an open window, reading a book, when I heard a peeper. It was very close by, so close I thought it must be in the bushes beside the front steps. I got a flashlight and went out to search, but the peeper fell silent and I couldn't find a trace of it. I came back in and resumed my reading, and the peeper sounded off again, so close it seemed to be right in the living room.

I went out three times to look, with no success. Then I glanced at one of the open windows when I heard the peeping start, and there was the peeper, on the window screen. I might not have seen it then—there is a strange ventriloquistic quality to the peeper's call—if it hadn't puffed up like a toy balloon as it called. That slight motion caught my eye. Most frogs inflate an air sac under their jaw when they call, but the peeper inflates its whole body.

The peeper is the first of the toads and frogs to call in the spring. Soon after, the leopard frog starts its rumbling, guttural *gr-r-r-r-ock,* rolling those middle "r's." Next comes the wood frog, followed by the American toad, whose voice is a high, musical trill. After that come the green frog, Fowler's toad, the gray treefrog already mentioned, and finally the bullfrog's deep *gr-r-r-rump.*

Some years ago the *New England Naturalist* assembled a timetable for first frog and toad calls. It was timed for the Boston area and because of the difference in altitude and distance from the ocean the dates would be at least two weeks later for our area. The schedule runs thus: Spring peeper, March 24; leopard frog, March 28; wood frog, March 31; American toad, April 1; pickerel frog, April 3; green frog, April 7; Fowler's toad, April 15; Gray's treefrog, April 28; bullfrog, May 20.

My records show that the earliest I have heard the peepers was March 20. The latest date I have for them is

April 15. Most years I hear them between April 5 and April 12.

Some people think the peeper's calls sound like a chorus of tiny bells. Some say they are too shrill to be musical. On Nantucket the peepers are called pinkletinks, a name that sounds to me much like the sound the peepers make. I wouldn't want to live in the middle of a peeper bog, but from a little distance I think their calls are one of spring's most exhilarating sounds.

EVERY YEAR I think I shall remember, and every year I forget. I see the robins and hear the red-wings and drive down past the bog and listen to the old, old clamor of the peepers newly emerged from hibernation, and I ask myself if they aren't all a little late this year. Then I go to my own records, and I find nearly every time that they were all here about the same time last year and the year before. Seldom do I find more than a week or ten days difference, certainly not more than one year in five.

It happened again this year, and I think I know why. Like everyone else, I am so eager to have spring come that I keep watching and listening and hoping. I want spring by the middle of March, at the latest, and it never comes then, not in these parts. The calendar in my head and heart is a wishful thing, not in keeping with the reality that the birds, the peepers, the buds and the blossoms all recognize.

Just to cite a few examples. I heard the peepers for the first time this year on April 12. That doesn't mean that was the first time anyone heard them around here; it means I didn't hear them till then. But the same qualification applies to last year, when it was April 15 when I first heard them.

I saw the first grackles this year on March 29. They

may have been around a week earlier, but I didn't see them. Last year I saw them on the same date, March 29. Last year I heard the first red-wings on March 26. This year I heard them three days earlier, on March 23. Last year I saw the first migrant robins on March 21. This year, for some reason, probably because I wasn't where they were, I didn't see them till April 8. I am sure they were around earlier, for I had reports of them two weeks before I saw them.

That's the way it goes. I thought the ducks were early on the river this year, and the mergansers late. But they both appeared at almost exactly the same time they did last year and the year before.

Spring's timetable really is keyed to the angle of sunlight and the length of daylight. Local conditions of weather can hasten or delay it somewhat, but not too much. The averages even out, and by the middle of May everything is in line with the longtime schedule. My lilacs began to open leaf, still a bit cautious, in last week's hot spell. I thought they were rushing things. Then I looked it up and found that last year they were opening leaf by April 20. And when I saw a poplar all tasseled out in catkins I checked and found that the very same tree was in catkin just two days later last year.

I had thought that the bird migration might be delayed this year by the snow and cold in the South. Obviously, that didn't much affect the robins' schedule or that of the grackles and the red-wings. And that seems to point to a theory about migration that has always seemed plausible to me. That theory holds that the migrants time their coming and going by the length of daylight and alter the schedule only slightly to meet local weather conditions. I know I thought the big flock of migrant robins that came to my pasture in the midst of a snowstorm one spring must have been quite mad. But they knew what they were doing. The snow ended by nightfall and the next morning it swiftly melted, leaving the pasture open to the robins and apparently full of the food they wanted.

There is a seasonal sense, or whatever you wish to call it, in nature that man apparently has "civilized" himself away from. Or maybe man, as a species, is too young to have acquired it. The hylas, the spring peepers, have been here on earth for a long, long time, 60 million years or more, and if they don't know when to come out of hibernation by now they never will learn. I'm inclined to believe that those who come out too early, over the eons, were killed by the cold and those who came out too late found mating season over with. So only the bright ones, or those who conformed to the demands of the season itself, survived.

Seeds and roots and bulbs have the same "sense," the same response to the seasons. Quite a few scientists have investigated this and have shown the way this response comes about, but so far as I know nobody has found where it came from. It is there, and that's all we really know. Seeds sprout and bulbs send up shoots and buds open into leaves and blossoms, and all at the proper time. They don't have to look at the calendar. I do. I even have to look at my records to see how wrong I was in my memory. But I'm just a man, a creature who has been here only about one million years. Maybe when my kind is as old as the frogs we won't need a calendar, either.

THE RED SQUIRRELS that tunneled under the snow last winter are still here, and just as long as they stay out of my attic they are welcome to remain. All spring they have been as busy as bees and as amusing as monkeys. One pair of them seems to have nested in the apple tree beside the woodshed, which has a number of fine holes for squirrels and woodpeckers. Another pair is in the woodshed, where they or their parents took over the pile of fire logs several years ago. I haven't looked under the maple sugar tub that hangs on the wall there, but two years ago I found half a bushel of nesting material in it and three startled and indignant red squirrels. It may be that there is another nest there now.

It is almost time for the litters to be born, so I suspect that the more active little reds I have seen the past week or so are males. The mothers will have litters of four or five late this month or early in June, and the young will be nursed six weeks or two months, seldom leaving the nest. By the end of the summer they will be on their own. Next spring they will mate and have families of their own, if they survive till then. They have many enemies, hawks, owls, foxes, bobcats, domestic cats, even black snakes.

One red squirrel, who seems to live in the woodshed, has been matching wits with me for weeks over suet and bacon rinds that I put out for the birds. We have a large suet container with a flat board back, half-inch wire mesh for the front and sides, and a wooden lid hinged at the back. It hangs from a long wire on an outstretched limb of a tree just back of the house. I thought when I hung it there that the squirrels couldn't reach it. It hadn't been up a week when this red squirrel went up the trunk of the tree to a point 5 feet above the suet box, leaped out and down about 7 feet, and almost thumbed his nose at me as he sat on the lid of the suet container.

The first day he picked morsels through the mesh, as the birds do. A few days later he got cute, found that he could lift the lid, went in and helped himself to a chunk of suet as big as my hand. I took a cord and tied the lid down and he gnawed off one whole corner of the wooden lid and helped himself as usual. I put a new lid on and covered it with heavy gauge aluminum. But I forgot to tie it down. He lifted it, as though he had been doing it for years, and went on helping himself. So I found a coil spring, fastened the lid down with that. And watched to see what happened.

Mr. Red went as usual, the aerial way, to get his suet. He nosed at the lid. It opened part way. He thrust in one paw. The lid snapped shut. Maybe I should have been ashamed, but instead I laughed. He got his fingers pinched, drew back and called down the wrath of the gods. He tried again, got pinched again. Then he got it open enough to thrust his head inside, almost got trapped, banged his head, backed out and chattered in anger. And had to take his suet bit by bit, through the mesh. He didn't like it one bit.

He has been back every day since, testing that spring. Some days he pinches his paws. I keep watching to see if he gets far enough inside to pinch his tail, but he hasn't yet done that. Maybe I have won this engagement, but I wouldn't bet. By next fall I wouldn't be surprised to see him unlatch the spring.

Meanwhile I admire his persistence almost as much as his beautiful pelt, his big, dark eyes, and his eloquent tail. His eyes look almost as large as those of a flying squirrel, probably the better to see all the enemies he has. His back is a beautiful red, just a shade lighter than cinnamon, and his belly is pristine white. During the winter his ears had bristly little tufts that gave him a perpetually startled look, but he lost them with the spring shedding. He will have them again when his winter coat comes in.

He is one of the most nervous, energetic, perpetually alert of all the small animals in my area. He is not really at home on the ground, never seems to feel safe there.

When he has to cross the yard between trees he travels in great leaps and often in a kind of zig-zag path, a kind of evasive action that would at least puzzle a hawk intent on mayhem. Once in a tree, however, he is completely at home, racing, leaping, chattering, enjoying life. Twice I have seen red squirrels fall from trees, each time because of a miscalculated leap. Both times they spread their legs in the same manner a flying squirrel does and managed to ease their fall. They didn't seem even to have the breath knocked out of them, for they scrambled up at once and fled up the tree again. Wonderful little hellions they are—just as long as they stay out of the attic.

THE LITTLE RAINS of last week may not have amounted to much statistically, and they did little to abate the fire hazard in the woods, but they certainly roused the grass. They were practically green rains, and by the end of the week the meadows and pastures here in the valley had come to life again. Ten days ago they were winter brown, with only a hint of green, but by Saturday morning they were almost solid green. How the grass responded!

The aspens and the willows responded, too. The big weeper beside my garage was a dainty fountain of lacy green by the week's end, and all down the river I could see the aspens in a gauzy green mist, their leaf-points showing. In the dooryard the lilacs threatened to open bud within a day or two; but they are not dependable prophets—they can dawdle along like that for another week or two. They tantalize, and they temporize. But when they finally say "Yes" they really do their stuff. No other buds that I know except those of the hickory family have so much packed into them or open with such magician-like opulence.

The other evening I was browsing in a volume of English poetry and was struck, as I have been before, by the ecstatic praise of April. From both the poetry and prose about it, spring comes earlier over there and comes with more of a rush than it does here. That accounts for the April ecstasies of the English poets.

As a matter of fact, even our early nineteenth century New England poets had their ecstatic moments about April. But, to my mind, that doesn't prove anything about our season. It simply shows that those poets of ours were still seeing their own outdoors through the eyes of English poets whom they persistently aped. Too many of them sat indoors and wrote "library poems" instead of going out and seeing what their own April was really like.

It wasn't until Thoreau went out into the woods on the margin of Concord and set down his day-to-day observations that we began to get at the season as it really is. Thoreau was just cantankerous enough to get satisfaction out of noting that the ice didn't go out of Walden Pond until April in four years out of seven, not until April 18 in 1852. Such facts made absolute absurdity of "library poems" praising April's wealth of spring flowers. Those flowers grew mostly in the imitative poets' imagination.

We have flowers in April, of course. But no great wealth of them in the woods or meadows. Bloodroot will bloom, no doubt, and anemones. And hepatica is already in bloom here and there. Within this week I am quite sure I shall find an occasional violet in bloom, but only in a sheltered place such as beside a stone wall that accumulates the sun's heat. Of the early tame bulb flowers, we had daffodils in bloom here last week and tulips are in bud. Squills and chinodoxa have been making their expected display, and a few of the big hyacinths have come out, as they usually do by now. But they don't really count, welcome as they are.

One thing I did note, though, was the way the birds began to sing by last weekend. I hesitate to think they were waiting for the showers and the green grass, but they hadn't been making more than token sounds before the pastures burgeoned. Then, on Saturday morning just before sunup, quite a chorus of robin song saluted the day. Listening to it, I knew that the few robin songs I had heard a week ago were mere tune-ups. I suppose it takes even a songbird a little while to get back into form. But from now on the dawn chorus will be increasing day by day, with the orioles and the tanagers and the grosbeaks of the red weskits soon adding their own arias. And by the first week in May we should have brown thrashers back and in business, singing like mad and repeating their choice phrases just to be sure they are properly appreciated.

It's all a part of the green pattern, in a way. The elements of spring are here, but they don't come together until the grass turns green and the first leaves deckle the twigs of the willows. April is the setting, but the signal comes from the earth, not the calendar. It takes just so much sun and just so much rain to get things going, and neither one can do it alone. The longer I live and the more I read, the more certain I become that the real poems about spring aren't written on paper. They are written in the back pasture and the near meadow, and they are issued in a new, revised edition every April.

THERE ARE, I suppose, two ways of looking at it. So I shall be charitable. This squirrel was being helpful rather than critical. The lawn here at the side and the back is a little mangy in spots and I haven't had time to reseed as I suppose I should. This fellow—he is a male; the females are busy taking care of the small children just now—had been looking over the place for some time, and he knew what had to be done, so he did it. And I should thank him, even if the lawn turns out to a corn patch.

It happened just the other morning. I glanced out the window and saw this gray squirrel on the side lawn with an ear of corn in his mouth. He had come from the corn crib, where he has a private entrance, and I expected him to climb the big Norway spruce, as usual, and sit on a favorite branch and eat his fill of corn germ, spitting out the bulk of the kernels. But he didn't. He laid the ear on the ground, carefully chose one kernel from the middle of the ear, held it in his teeth, found a bare spot in the lawn, and dug a hole with his forepaws. He tucked the kernel in the hole, patted it carefully with his nose, then covered it with a dozen deft strokes of his paws. Just as neatly as Barbara planting squash seeds.

He went back to the ear, chose another kernel, found another bare spot in the lawn and made another planting. He planted six kernels within a 3-foot circle, then picked up the seed ear, moved a little way, and did the same thing again. He worked the whole side yard, planting, by actual count, thirty-two kernels of corn. By then he had cleaned off the center of the ear, making it look like a dumbbell. I watched carefully and didn't see him eat even one kernel. He discarded several kernels, probably sterile seed, though how he knew I can't even guess. If I were a skeptical scientist I should plant those discarded seeds in a flower pot and see if they germinate. But I'm not that much of a skeptic. I know they won't.

Finished with the side yard, he moved back alongside the woodshed, where the lawn is particularly ratty. There he planted thirty-nine kernels. This I noticed, though: At the back of the yard is a barbed wire fence separating lawn from pasture, and Mr. Squirrel didn't plant one kernel of corn beyond the fence, in the pasture. Don't ask me why. I'm just a human being with limited understanding. But I know that if corn is planted in the pasture the cows will eat it. Maybe the squirrel knows that too. He should. He has watched the cows.

Finished alongside the woodshed, he took his seed ear around the shed and resumed his work back of the house. A crow came and perched in an apple tree nearby, watching. The squirrel glanced at the crow, then went on about his business. And the crow didn't come down to get either the ear of corn or the kernels the squirrel was hiding. I rather wished the crow would make a try, to see what happened.

I lost count while the squirrel was working in the back yard, but he finally had that ear of corn stripped down to half a dozen rows at each end. Then he decided he had done enough for me. He picked up the ear, had a good look around, and went loping across the pasture to a big elm a hundred yards away. I watched him with the field glasses while he climbed to a comfortable crotch and tucked the ear with its remaining kernels into a favorite pantry corner. He ate none of it. He tucked it away, came down, and went off into the woods.

This happened exactly as I have said, on Saturday morning, April 18, between 7:15 and 8. There is only one possible qualification that I can think of, and that is my statement that the squirrel was planting corn rather than merely hiding it. The professional naturalists may say that he was merely caching those kernels for future use. To that I say that there really isn't much difference, except in the matter of intention, between hiding corn in a hole in the ground and planting corn. I do the same thing in the garden, in a somewhat more orderly manner. My purpose may be different from that of the squirrel, but I am not sure. Who can say authoritatively, what is a squirrel's purpose? I can't.

When I appraise this squirrel's actions, several things make me pause. The ear he choose was long, fat and well filled, the kind a farmer considers good seed corn. The kernels he chose to plant—or cache, if you will—were from the center of the ear, not the ends, the best kernels on the ear. And he planted every kernel in the sun. There are some very inviting bare patches under the big spruce, but all are in the shade. He avoided every one of those shaded places. And he didn't plant one kernel, as I said before, in the pasture.

Only one thing really baffles me, his timing. Around here we don't plant corn till mid-May. He was almost a month early. Does that mean it's safe to plant garden corn now? I don't know. I doubt it. But I get my weather forecasts from the Travelers' Weather Service in Hartford. I suspect that the squirrel tunes in on some other frequency.

RED MAPLES begin to liven the damp lowlands with the crimson of their opening buds, and the more cautious, leisurely sugar maples are in fat bud but taking their time. They remind me of a rather tenuous notion that the people of a land partake of their native trees. That the English, for example, are like their oaks, slow to mature, slow to change, endowed with a tough grain and a kind of tannic-acid temperament. That the people of central France are as inclined to elegance as their beech trees, tenacious of life and leaf, able to hold their ground against upstart rivals. And that the Scandinavians are as stolid and stubborn as their conifers.

If one goes by this tenuous theory, New Englanders are like the maples, and though there is a variety of maples here they are most like the dominant ones, the red maples and the sugar maples, both adaptive to a rather stern environment, both firm-fibered and consistent from earliest bud to latest leaf. The red maples have red twigs, red blossoms and rich red leaves in October. The sugar maples tend to a pattern of the sun, faintly straw-colored sap, yellow flowers, and warm yellow leaves, sometimes heightened with flashes of red, in the fall.

The red maples now opening bud along my road will soon be like vivid pastel strokes across the landscape. They love the lowlands, but they reach up the hillsides and thrive along the brooks. All winter long their gray trunks shone against the background of hemlocks, less insistent than the white birches but unmistakable to the eye. Their twigs were like slim, fever-red fingers, and their buds were coral beads. As those buds began to fatten a few weeks ago, the squirrels replenished their vitamin supply by feasting on them.

Now those buds have opened into a crimson mist, a staminate fire in the spring woods, and the bees are feasting, the trees loud as hives with their buzz. Soon the seeds will appear, dainty, flat keys with veins blood-red, nature's original helicopters which will spiral down in a swirl of next year's seedlings. There must be some special fertility in red maple seeds, for a lone tree of the species is rare in nature; the parent is almost always surrounded by a host of offspring. Hence the red maple thickets where there is undisturbed wet soil.

When the leaves begin to spread, their stems will be as red as their blossoms were. And when October comes the flame that was like a bed of coals in spring will become a forest fire of leaves, a leaping flame of color. On a still, blue day it will be breath-taking in its beauty; and when the winds come they will be crimson winds over the red maple groves, winds that celebrate the season with their freight of leaves, claret-gay winds.

There is one phase of New England, both the land and the people. This is the red-maple phase.

Now look at the sugar maples.

Some call them rock maples. The name is apt in a variety of ways, for this is a tree of slow growth, stout fiber, firm substance. It can stand up to a storm. Find a well-crafted chair or table made of rock maple and it will outlive you and all your family. Lay down a floor of rock maple and it will outlast all your footsteps and those of your children. Plant a rock maple in your dooryard and it will be growing when you are gone, casting its shade each summer, offering its sap to those who have the wisdom to use it, proffering a small nursery of seedlings each year for those who appreciate its value.

Its sap is faintly sweet. The sugar concentration is not obtrusive, but it is there, calling for patience and friendly distillation. It is not a quick-riches tree. It is more like a long-term, low-yield bond, secure but not spectacular. It is a comfort in the later years of life, an enduring source of solid substance.

The sugar maples respect this land's late frosts. They will open bud in their own time, come to flower and fruit and spread their leaves. They will sigh comfortably through the summer. I will waken in the night and hear the rain pattering in their leafy branches, and I will hear them talking to the wind and whispering to the breeze. But there will be no moaning from them, and no such clatter as comes from the big popple in the gusts.

October will come, and as the sun moves south it will bestow its own glow on the sugar maples. Most of them will be golden. A few will be orange, a color no other tree achieves. Some will be particolored, some even crimson, aping the maples in the swamp. But mostly they will be full of sun, so full that even on dark days they will cast sunlight on me when I stand beneath them. And when the leaves come down there will be great golden drifts as crisp as beaten foil of gold.

There is another phase of New England, the people and the land. There is the sugar-maple phase. The outlander knows it in the trees, but we who live here know it in the people.

WE STOPPED at a small bogland the other evening and parked the car and went on foot to look and listen. It was just at sunset, and on the hillside beyond the swamp a barred owl was hooting softly. It was quite a way off and at first I thought I was hearing a mourning dove. But it was an owl, all right. Sometimes, at a distance, an owl will sound like a dove, and the doves have been calling so much and the owls so little that I was confused.

In the meadow that sloped down to the bog were a few patches of bluets, *Houstonia caerulea,* which some call Quaker Ladies and some call Innocence. They were like little patches of fog in the grass, for they grew close and bloomed generously. The tiny four-petaled flowers were so white, so sparsely touched with any shade of blue, that I wondered again why anyone ever called them bluets. And down at the wet margin the swamp violets were full of deep purple blossom, one of the richest colors that early May has to offer.

But it was the bog itself we had come to see.

Red-wings challenged us, a small flock of them. They circled and scolded and flashed their crimson epaulettes, and they perched on the stalks of last year's cattails, swaying precariously. The old cattails were fluffed into smoky-looking tufts, ragged out by wind and winter and perhaps by the early nest builders too. But at the base of each stalk rose the bright green of new growth, the blades that will make the bog a green jungle by July. Among them was the darker green of blue flag, the wild iris, which will color the swampland in another month with its big blossoms. At this stage the blades of iris and cattail look much alike, except that the cattails are somewhat narrower and a lighter, yellowish green. And among them were still narrower blades of one of the bur reeds, I couldn't be sure which but guessed at the variety known as *symplex,* the smaller one. The blades looked like rank grass.

On and around the little tussocks that were above the water were marsh marigolds, nearly all of them in bloom. Some were up to their ears in water, the leaves seeming to float and the blossoms only a little higher. They are web-footed cousins of the common buttercups and the Latin name, *Caltha palustris,* means marsh-cup. Botanically, they are also cousins of the columbine; but that is one of those things I have to take on faith. I don't really believe it, though I know it is true. I do believe that the marsh marigold flower is one of the loveliest golden yellows I ever saw anywhere.

And on the tussocks themselves were great masses of skunk cabbage leaves, big as elephant ears, gaudy, extravagant and primitive. And among them I could see others of the *Arum* family, with their dark-striped spathes, a number of light green, plaintain-like leaves of sweet flag, and an occasional dart-shaped leaf of the arrow arum.

On the far margin of the little bog were two tall elms, trembling on the verge of leaf, still lacy in tufts of young seed, and beneath them were clumps of willow brush where the inch-long leaves had already begun to hide the finished catkins. And alder brush was tufting out in leaf, still hung with the little cone-like seed cases from last year. From somewhere nearby a hyla shrilled and I thought he was the last member of the peeper chorus that was so loud two weeks ago. But from down at the other end of the bog came an answer in a voice so high it sounded like falsetto. No chorus, though.

The water caught the glow of sunset and turned from pewter gray to opalescent. The opalescence was fire-dappled with specks of lettuce-green that caught some lively light and almost glistened. Duck-weed, finer than the finest confetti, drifted in the luminous water.

There was a dark movement back among the cattails. As we watched, a big brown muskrat swam into the open, the V of ripples from his nose like long, silvery whiskers. He swam toward the bank where we stood, quietly as a shadow; and suddenly he saw us and dived with a plop and left only a swirling of the opalescent water.

We turned and went back to the car. I always feel close to beginnings in a bogland, especially at dusk, I feel as though I stood on the brink of ancient days when warm seas washed the first land and aquatic life was making its first venture away from the mother element, water. Even here in the Berkshire Hills, bog life has a primitive aspect, a sense of elemental change. The very smell of a bog is fecund and fertile of mysterious and fundamental change.

I get the feeling, particularly at dusk, that anything can happen on the margin of a swampland. Outlandish things. There have been dusks when I was sure that if I waited on such a margin only another hour I would see a 30-foot Stegosaurus, complete with armor-plate scales, come wading out from among the reeds and cattails, trailing a million centuries behind him. I never have, but I still wouldn't bet that I never shall.

I GET INVOLVED in the strangest things. Take the birdhouse.

Russ phoned and said he had invented a newfangled birdhouse and maybe we would like to see it. I said to come along. A couple of years ago he invented a bird feeder that keeps out the jays and starlings, and no telling what he had come up with now.

He arrived with two birdhouses. One was all assembled and looked like a miniature teepee or A-frame ski hut. Very handsome indeed. I said so, and Russ said he was giving it to us to try out. He set it on the table, released the suspension cord, and it collapsed, opened right up. That, he explained, was the idea. Hang it in a tree and it was a weather-tight birdhouse, and maybe bluebirds or wrens would move in. If English sparrows came instead and you wanted to dispossess them, simply take it down, set it on the ground, and it would open right up. You could clean out the mess of trash the sparrows had collected and start over.

He hung the house on the back of a chair and said, "I've got just one problem."

"What?"

"Directions. Instructions for threading the cord so it will close when you hang it up, open when you set it down."

"No problem," I said. "It's all laced up, isn't it?"

"Yes, but . . ." And he pointed to the second birdhouse he had brought. It was four triangles of plywood and a snarl of nylon cord. "Pick it up by this loop," he said.

I picked it up and it became an assembled house. I set it down and it collapsed again. Very simple. But Russ said that it had to be flat to ship, the cord loose. "How do I tell someone how to lace the cord so it will go together right?"

I examined it. The lacing was rather complicated. "There's a simpler way to lace it," I announced.

"Go ahead," Russ said.

So we took out the cord. Then I had those four triangles, each about 8 inches on a side and each with at least two holes in it, and about 5 feet of nylon cord. Barbara was watching. "Do you know how to put it back together?" she asked. It was one of those questions to be ignored. Besides, we still had one birdhouse all assembled.

I started threading the cord a new way. It was very easy. Nothing to it. Except that the pieces weren't labeled. "Better label them," I suggested. "Floor, front, roof." Russ nodded. I went on lacing the cord. "And," I added, "better number the holes." Russ nodded again. I was almost through but I ran short of holes. "Good idea to make another hole here," I said, "and one here and here."

Finally I had it all laced, came out with the loop I had planned, lifted it by the loop, adjusted the cord, and there it was, perfect. Except for one thing. The floor fell out. I tried again, got the floor to stay in place, but the front sagged out. So I took out the cord, started from scratch once more. This time the floor and the front stayed where they belonged, but it wouldn't collapse. You couldn't dispossess those English sparrows.

I do have patience, though. One more try and I had it, perfect. It closed when I picked it up, opened when I set it down. I turned to Russ, who nodded and smiled. I turned to Barbara, and she laughed. And pointed to the birdhouse hanging on the chair. I had finally managed to come out exactly where I started, the pieces threaded together, hole by hole, the way they were to begin with.

After a moment's silence Russ cleared his throat. "Now, about the directions . . ."

"You don't need directions," I said. "Obviously, there's

only one way to do it. A ten-year-old boy couldn't miss."

"How long did it take you?" Barbara asked, another of those rhetorical questions. But it was later than I thought. Russ had been here almost an hour.

"You said something about numbering the holes," Russ said.

"Um-hmmm."

"And labeling the pieces."

"Yes. By the way, is the sap still running up your way? Any geese up there?"

Somehow, we never got back to that matter of directions.

The next day I took the assembled birdhouse out and hung it in the big apple tree. It's a beautiful birdhouse. It hasn't any tenants yet, but I'm sure it will have before long.

THERE HAD BEEN occasional evidence for two or three weeks that a raccoon had put this place on his nightly route, but we didn't actually see anything of him. But one evening when I took Pat out to put him to bed, he bristled as soon as he got outside the back door and seemed to think someone had been snooping around his food dish. I wondered if it was the skunk we surprised there a week or so ago. The skunk wanted none of us, and we wanted none of him, so we waited while the skunk ambled off into the pasture. But this evening it obviously wasn't a skunk. Pat picked up a scent and hurried around the woodshed, found nobody there and came back and dashed around the house.

I thought maybe it was a cat, which would scurry up a maple tree as soon as it heard Pat coming. I shouted at him to come back and forget it. And then a ruckus started around in front of the house, quite a noisy to-do. By the time I got there with the flashlight, Pat had a big buck coon cornered beside the front steps. The coon looked as big as the dog, and it had the tactical advantage of the porch at its back; but Pat was making things hot, darting in and out, carrying the fight to the coon. When I arrived Pat probably felt he had moral backing, for he closed in. There was a flurry of teeth and claws. Pat got one raking claw across his nose and the coon lost a bit of fur.

The nearest weapon was a wooden grass rake leaning against the big Norway spruce. I got it. But a wooden rake is about as awkward a weapon as I know of. Don't ever try to hold a flashlight in one hand and wield a wooden rake effectively with the other. It can't be done. But all I wanted to do was break up the fight before either dog or coon got hurt.

I poked and whacked and thrust, and Pat backed away, and the coon made a rush at me, which I discouraged with the rake. Then he made for the big spruce. Pat bowled him off his feet once, but did no real damage. I dropped the rake, grabbed Pat by the scruff and held him long enough to let the coon start up the tree. It's a big tree, the first branches 15 feet up, and the coon clawed and scratched and slipped and climbed desperately.

When the coon got halfway to the first crotch I let Pat loose, and wished I hadn't, because if the coon slipped and fell there would be a real row. But he didn't fall.

Naturally, all this was rather noisy, though it didn't last long. Barbara came to the front door, opened it cautiously, and shouted, "I hope it isn't a skunk!" I told her it was a coon, and she came out onto the porch. And I hauled Pat off to his own house and locked him in, he protesting rather loudly. He probably had ideas about yapping under that tree until midnight.

I came back, and Barbara wanted to see the coon. So I

spotlighted him, up there in the darkness of the upper branches. She exclaimed, "Why, that isn't a coon at all! That's the Cheshire Cat!" And that's exactly what it was, a disembodied catlike face up there in the darkness, its eyes pinpoints of red-tinged silvery light. All nocturnal animals and most night birds have reflective eyes. They don't shine in the darkness, however, unless there is a light for them to reflect.

Finally the coon became uneasy in the flashlight beam and moved to a higher crotch. Then we could see how big he really was and what a beautiful, blackringed tail he had. Barbara admitted that he was a coon, after all. We left him there and came indoors. I went out and looked again before I went to bed, and he was still there, still so mad, apparently, that his eyes were spitting red sparks at me. That coon had no gratitude in him.

He was gone by the next morning, and I may be sorry, come sweet-corn time, that I let him get away. Dead coons steal no roasting ears, and the coons have held moonlight picnics in our corn patch the past two years. But I have a deep abhorrence of guilt by association, even for coons. And by roasting-ear time he may be a long way from here. He'd better be. If I catch him in the corn patch the story will end differently.

The coon gets its name from the Algonquin word, *arakun,* which means "he who scratches with his hands." It fits. A coon can do almost as much damage as a bobcat if he is cornered by a brash, inexperienced dog. Some wily old coons don't even bother to scratch, though. They lure a dog into the water, grab him by the head and hold him under until he drowns. Tough customers, those old buck coons. Pat was lucky to get off with only a scratch.

UP IN A BRUSHY MARGIN the other day I saw several birds

in deep shadow that I couldn't immediately identify. They were busy in the deep drift of dead leaves, scattering them in all directions. From their actions, I guessed that they were either fox sparrows or towhees. Then one of them paused for a moment and flirted its tail, and there was no mistaking him—it was a towhee. Those white margins to the tail flash at you like a quick flutter of sunlight. A moment later another of them hopped over into the light, and that bright chestnut color, the shiny black head and throat, the white wing bars, were complete identification.

Later in the day one of them came to the dooryard to forage under the feeders, which we are still stocking with seeds. He has been here every day since, and I trust that he and his mate will be nesting nearby. The towhees are a delight to the eye, not as dazzling as the cardinals but always worth a second look.

The towhees are also called chewinks and ground robins. "Towhee" and "chewink" come from the calls; this bird is no real songster, certainly not in a class with either the oriole or the common robin, but it does have a pleasant voice and it sometimes chirps and indulges in a kind of half-trill with rather hoarse overtones. It is primarily a bird to watch, not to listen to.

In size, the towhee is only slightly bigger than a fox sparrow, but its long tail makes it look even larger. Its chestnut sides are about the color of a common robin's breast but seem even redder, perhaps in contrast with the white belly and ebony-black head and breast. Close-up or through field glasses you can see that the eyes are red; not blood-shot, but red all over the pupil. There is a white-eyed towhee, but it is a Southerner, seldom seen north of Charleston, South Carolina.

Only rarely will you see a towhee perched in a tree or anywhere more than 10 feet from the ground. The one who has been here in the dooryard has been up in the big apple tree only once, when a passing hawk sent all the birds scurrying. The towhee followed the crowd, but acted as though he had vertigo as he perched up in that tree, and he came back down as soon as the hawk had gone away. Normally the towhees are not dooryard birds, either. This one comes to our feeders, I imagine, only because there are lilac bushes nearby. They are uneasy in the open.

The towhee belongs to the finch tribe, hence is a cousin of the sparrows. But it eats more insects than most sparrows. Those I saw scratching among the leaves were looking for grubs, and apparently found them. But they also eat weed seeds and small wild fruit. The only tame fruit I ever knew one to eat were gooseberries and an occasional strawberry.

All towhees seem to be patsies for cowbirds. One reason may be that their eggs look a good deal alike, being basically white dotted with brownish lilac. The towhee eggs are slightly bigger than those of the cowbirds, but when the two are in the same nest they are not easy to tell apart. Maybe even the towhees can't tell the difference. Anyway, they tolerate the cowbird eggs unless there are more than three or four. Then the towhees usually abandon the nest and start over somewhere else.

The nest is usually on or close to the ground, in the brush or under a bush or a big tuft of grass. It is made of twigs, leaves, grass, plant fibers, sometimes rather makeshift but at other times neat and compact. It is always well concealed, hard to find unless you almost stumble upon it. Then the female will usually flutter away and put on the broken-wing act. The female is less brilliantly colored than the male, with a dull brown head and back but with those white feathers at the edge of the nervous tail.

They are not even cousins, but the towhee and the redstart are particular favorites of mine, maybe because they both are quick nervous birds of sharply contrasting colors. And neither of them is so abundant or so common in the dooryard that I take them for granted, as I do the robins, for instance. The redstart, of course, is a warbler, most colorful warbler of them all, for my money. But it, too, is primarily a brush bird though it nests in trees. Only occasionally do I see either of them down here in the open. When I do, I want to celebrate. I haven't seen a redstart this year, but the towhees have made the past week rather special. I hope they stay.

PERHAPS because of the unusual warmth of early May, the little creeping mint called ground ivy or gill-over-the-ground is thriving and loaded with blossoms. The flowers are very small, typical mint flowers less than a quarter of an inch across, and light purple in color. They seem to have no fragrance. But apparently they are full of nectar and pollen, for they are the favorite early flowers of the bumblebees.

The gill, as we always call it, is an insistent creeper and this year practically carpets the edges of the garden and makes big patches at the roadside, patches with a warm purple overtone from the multitude of bloom. If it were not so insistent in its weediness, it might be a welcome ground cover, for it lies flat, thrives in the heat of summer, and does very well even in the shade. It is not a native, actually, for the early settlers brought it from England where it once was the early spring equivalent of our trailing arbutus.

I like the gill, which is a beautiful little flowering plant; but just now I am sure it is important to every farmer who grows clover. As I said, the gill's blossoms are host to early bumblebees. When I watch a patch of gill I always see several of the big black and gold bumblers harvesting there. I watched for ten minutes the other afternoon and every bumblebee in sight passed up all the other early flowers, both wild and tame, to reach the gill. They were all big bees, undoubtedly queens who are nesting at this stage and will soon produce their little colonies. Bumblebees are the prime pollinators of clover. Without them, the clover seed crop would be a failure. So the humble little gill, by feeding the nesting queens, helps produce the bumblebees that keep the clover going.

The bumblebee is quite different from the honeybee in many ways. It can make honey, and it collects pollen, but it isn't a honey-hoarder. It makes no combs and it refuses to live in hives. Its colonies are small. Only the young queens survive the winter, and it is those young queens that are so busy now at the gill blossoms. They have passed the winter in some snug hideaway, often a deserted mouse nest. With spring, they aroused from hibernation, found a bit of pollen, chiefly on the willow catkins, and set about making a nursery nest.

The nursery often is in a mouse tunnel, somewhere just under the surface of the ground. The queen lines it with dried grass, builds a simple cell for her eggs, stocks it with honey-moistened pollen, lays her first small clutch of eggs, and closes the cell. In the same hollow she makes a small, rather crude waxen jug and fills it with thin honey. This is her private pantry to be used during stormy weather when she cannot go out foraging.

The eggs hatch and the larvae feed on the pollen she provided, supplemented by fresh pollen and honey when the weather is good. In about ten days the larvae are full grown and enclose themselves in tough papery cocoons. There they pupate, undergo the final stages of change, and in another week or ten days they emerge as winged bees, smaller than the queen but full of vigor. They become the workers of the little colony, and as soon as they start gathering pollen and nectar the queen stays at home and lays more eggs. These first workers are all sterile females.

Later in the season the males and mating females are hatched. Both the fertile females and the males are drones. In late summer the mating females and the loafer males leave the nest, mate, and the males soon die. The pregnant females find places to hibernate for the winter, feed energetically till frost comes, and then tuck themselves in, each by herself, for the long sleep. They are the queens who waken in late April, feed hungrily on such early bloom as that of gill-over-the-ground, and start laying eggs. The old queen and all her workers die with the end of summer.

In England, where the bumblebee is called a humblebee, there is an old saying that spinsters are the support of the British Empire, and this is the explanation: Old maids keep cats; cats catch field mice that otherwise would destroy humblebee nests; humblebees fertilize red clover and enable it to set seed; clover is good food for cattle; and roast beef gives strength to the men who support and defend the Empire.

Using an even better logic, it might be said that gill-over-the-ground keeps our own children healthy. It nourishes the queen bumblebees who rear the broods that fertilize the clover that helps feed our dairy herds.

POKING AROUND on the mountainside the other day I found a gnarled old snag of a lilac bush with a few branches, half a hatful of leaves and three sprays of buds that may be open by now and host to the bees. For a moment that bush baffled me. Then I remembered hearing that years ago there was a house somewhere up there in what is now just a tangle of trees with old stone walls angling across the steep hillside. But now there isn't even a cellar hole. Nothing to recall that vanished house except that persistent old lilac root that sends up a few shoots year after year. I have no idea how old that lilac is, but it must have been there several generations.

I have seen such old lilacs a dozen times in equally unlikely places, and when I inquired I always found that they marked the site of a vanished house. Sometimes there are a few dogged peony shoots, but peonies have not quite the staying power of lilacs. Now and then there are hollyhocks, but seldom around the very old sites. Hollyhocks can't seem to manage even as well as peonies. But the lilacs are as tough as the old-timers were. I have a great admiration for them and wait every year for the week when the whole dooryard will be sweet with the scent of their blossoms.

The lilac, of course, is not a native of America, or even of England, though it came to New England early, with some of the earliest colonists. Lilacs originated, or at least throve, long, long ago in Persia and other parts of the Near East. We can thank the Crusaders for having them in the West. Those old wanderers, who repeatedly found excuse to let off steam in the Near East, had an eye for pretty women, fine horses and beautiful flowers. They brought back all these good things from their belligerent journeys. Go down the list of flowers native to the Near East and you will find that most of them became known in the West soon after the Crusades. That's when lilacs first were known in England. By the time of the migrations to these parts, lilacs were cherished dooryard flowers, so they were brought along.

I always watch the lilacs in early spring, mostly because they bolster my hopes even during dreary March. Those twin terminal buds always look so promising before anything else is really up and doing. By the middle of March, most years, you would think that two warm days in a row would have those buds unfurling. But they bide their time, almost tantalizing. Then the season does change, the lilac buds open, and what a wealth they have inside! Not only a tuft of leaves, which is strongly tinged with purple to start with—as though the flower color was so abundant it stained the leaves themselves—but stems and clusters of flower buds small as pinheads.

The lilac buds open, the leaves begin to spread, and here come the stems with the bunches of flower buds. Then come the days of waiting while those flower buds deliberate the weather, figuratively hunching against the frosty nights, stretching and testing the air during a warm afternoon, huddling against the chill again that evening. Meanwhile, the apple blossoms have begun to open. The peony shoots have come up, blood-red, and grown green and leafed out. And still the lilacs wait. The bees, which gathered hungrily to harvest crocus pollen, then worked the daffodils and the tulips, have a frantic feast at the apple blossoms. But now and then an impatient bee investigates a tuft of lilac buds, senses the treasure in it, paws at it, fails to open it, and goes back to the apple trees.

Finally the terminal buds on a clump of lilac open their petals. Within minutes, the whole dooryard seems to be perfumed. Few other flowers have so much fragrance or send it so far. We seldom bring lilacs indoors because their fragrance, when confined, can be too strong. It belongs outdoors. When the big lilac clump twenty yards north of the house is in bloom, all we have to do is open one window on that side of the house and the whole house is sweet. Besides, who can make an indoor bouquet half as beautiful as a lilac bush in bloom?

I sometimes think of lilacs, like hollyhocks, as typical of New England dooryards. They are, of course; but then I remember dooryards all across the country, richly perfumed and beautifully colored at lilac time. I have even seen dooryard lilacs in the deserts of the Southwest, where some beauty-starved woman with memories of the East tended them like her own children. But the most gallant lilacs I have ever seen were those beside the old cellar holes, like that one I found the other day. I wish the woman who planted it there might know that it still blooms in May.

LAST YEAR an oriole hung her nest in an elm just across the road from the house, from a limber twig that hung out over the river and lower than most oriole nests, only 15 feet or so from the ground. Last week we looked to see if she was nesting there again. No sign of a nest. But while we stood there looking we heard a fuss and two male Baltimores came swirling out of the elm in obvious dispute. They fluttered and beat at each other with their wings, and after a moment one admitted defeat and fled across the river, the victor in close pursuit. They were still in sight when a female oriole rose from the riverbank, trailing a shimmer of white strands, and lit on a limber twig on the other side of the tree.

We moved around to watch her, and saw the first few loops of the nest, in its first stages. It didn't look like anything but a tangle of white fiber, or maybe hair, cow's tail-hair perhaps, salvaged from the barbed wire pasture fence. She flew back to the riverbank. She was still there on the ground when a few strands from her chosen twig blew loose and came floating down. We watched where they fell and went to pick them up, and she flew up to the tree again with several more strands in her beak.

We examined the strands that had blown down. They weren't hair. They looked like fine monofilament nylon, the diameter of coarse thread, and they were a silvery, almost translucent white. They were surprisingly strong; I had to jerk to break a single strand, and three strands together were as strong as my nylon fishing line. I wondered what they were. The only clue was a flake of silvery gray, papery bark that clung to one of the strands.

Five minutes of search on the riverbank identified them. They were the fibers that lie just under the thin outer coat of the old milkweed stems that still stood in the grass. I could peel them off the dry stems in long threads. We loosened a few of them and left them dangling, then went back to watch. The female oriole found them, stripped them loose and flew back to the nest site. How she anchored them is still a mystery to me, but apparently she wound them around the twig and contrived something like a knot. However she did it, she hung a dozen loops on that twig in the next fifteen minutes, all of that milkweed fiber.

We were away most of the next day, but by late afternoon we could see that a pouch had taken shape. Most of it obviously was fashioned of milkweed fiber, for we could identify the color. She was still working at it, and her mate was singing lustily from high in the sugar maple nearby. The male does none of the nest weaving, though he sometimes helps gather material. We saw no such help in this instance, however.

By afternoon of the second day the nest seemed to be practically finished. It was a completed pouch and through the binoculars we couldn't see a hole in it. It had the texture of coarse fabric, almost like burlap. The female was tucking in a few loose ends but she brought no new material. By the fourth day she was nowhere in sight and the nest seemed to bulge. She probably was inside, laying her clutch of eggs and starting to brood them.

Now I know not only what the Baltimore orioles did when tractors displaced horses on the farms, but where those hairlike fibers come from that shape the field sparrow nests I find from time to time. The sparrows, too, know about the fiber in milkweed stems.

The same day the oriole started her nest we had a rare visitor. In midafternoon we were out picking lilacs when we heard a bird call I haven't heard in years. I couldn't believe it, but there it was, "Bob White, Bob-Bob White." It came from the far side of the home pasture. I answered it, got one response, then silence. We came indoors, put the lilacs in a vase and sat down at the open window in the sun room.

A few minutes later we heard the bobwhite again, somewhat closer. I answered, and now there was a steady response. We whistled back and forth a few times and the call came from close at hand, somewhere in the back yard. We finally located it and spotted Mr. Quail, in the big apple tree not 20 feet from the windows. He and I whistled at each other for maybe ten minutes before he wearied of my fraud. He flew off to the pasture beyond the barn and called for another half hour. Then there was silence, and we haven't heard him since. I hope he has a mate, and I wish they would come back and settle here. We are still waiting, hopeful but not too confident.

AFTER WATCHING the oriole who was using milkweed fiber to weave her nest I was talking with a friend who probably knows more about birds than I ever shall and I said she had found a substitute for horsehair. My friend smiled and shook his head. "Orioles," he said, "never use horsehair. They never did. They use vegetable fibers."

I wasn't in the mood to argue, though I remembered oriole nests, some years back and in an area that still had lots of horses on the farms, that either had horsehair or an incredibly good imitation. So I began looking through the books and I came to Forbush's "American Birds." Speaking of the oriole's nest—Baltimore oriole—Forbush says, "The material normally used for the framework is vegetable fiber, gathered chiefly from dried or decaying stalks of the previous year . . . Birds building near the habitations of man also use string, yarn, horsehair, strands of hemp or flax and other similar materials gleaned from dooryards, farmyards or roadsides." And he goes on to say that though they usually choose materials of a white or light grayish color, "I have seen a nest chiefly composed outwardly of jet-black hair from the manes and tails of horses."

I looked no further. Forbush was good enough for me. My friend was mistaken, as most of us are now and then. After several such experiences of my own, I have learned to be wary of two words, "never," and "always."

Some years ago I had an argument with an outdoorsman about porcupines. He insisted that porky can "shoot" quills. I said porky never shoots quills. Then I had an experience with a porcupine in my own woods and had to reconsider. Strictly speaking, that porcupine didn't shoot any quills. But it swished its tail angrily and a dozen loose quills in the tail were flung several feet. Two of them penetrated my trouser leg and jabbed into my calf far enough to be painful to get out. I still say a porcupine can't shoot quills, but under the right conditions it can fling them like darts from its tail.

On the other hand, when someone tells me that a beaver can fell a tree exactly where it chooses I am not only skeptical, but ready with proof. The trees that a beaver fells into the water are, almost without exception, already leaning toward the water. And dozens of times I have seen how a beaver, working on a tree with ample room to fall in the clear, contrived to fell it into the only spot where it could hang up in another tree. When that happens, the beavers never seem to understand that if they cut down that other tree they would have both the hung-up tree and the one in which it hangs.

I have been told by at least half a dozen hunters, one time and another, that if you grab a skunk by the tail and lift it off its feet it cannot spray you. I won't say this is always wrong, but I will say that the only time I knew anyone who tried it, it didn't work. I never smelled anyone more thoroughly skunked. Maybe others have accomplished the trick safely, but "never" is certainly not the word to use here. A skunk *can* spray, even when lifted by its tail.

Time after time, I hear it said that bears hibernate. I hesitate to say they never do, but strictly speaking they are not hibernators. They sleep a good deal during the winter, but they are not hibernating. In hibernation—and the woodchuck is the best example I know of warm-blooded hibernation—body temperature falls close to that of their surroundings, breathing becomes shallow and infrequent, and all bodily processes slow down almost to a stop. Sleeping bears maintain almost normal temperature and respiration; and, as quite a few hunters can testify, they are fairly easy to wake even in their winter dens, and they waken with short tempers and all ready to go into action. A hibernating woodchuck, on the other hand, has to be warmed up for several hours before he shows signs of life, and even then he goes back into hibernating sleep at the first chance.

For a long time I would have said that the trillium is a flower that always is three-petaled. Then, a few years ago, a person whose observation I trust wrote about a four-petaled trillium. I had reservations. My correspondent sent me a pressed flower, definitely four-petaled. I asked that she watch for a repetition the next spring. She did, and a plant in the same spot again produced four-petaled blooms, several of them. This happened three years in a row. So again, "never" is the wrong word. Obviously, on occasion even a trillium can break the botanical law.

THE WHIPPOORWILLS are back. I heard the first one calling a week ago tonight. I wakened at a quarter of three, out of a sound sleep, wondered what had roused me, and lay listening. Everything seemed to be in order. Then, from well up the mountainside back of the house, I heard the whippoorwill calling, faint and distant. It seemed impossible that such a sound, so far away, could have wakened me, but apparently it did. I listened to it for maybe five minutes, then went back to sleep. Every night since then I have heard the whippoorwills, sometimes as many as three at once.

It seemed a bit late for them to arrive, until I looked back in my records. I find that the earliest I ever heard one was April 24, but one year they weren't here—I didn't hear them at least—until the last week in May. So May's second week must be about average.

Our valley always has whippoorwills, every summer, though people who live just over the mountain, on Twin Lakes, tell me that they never hear them. I wonder why. The birds are night feeders and live on insect fare, flying insects such a moths, gnats and mosquitoes, and I am sure there are as many of those insects on the far side of Tom's Mountain as there are here. Incidentally, the whippoorwills probably come down to houses in late evening, and make their outcries, because they find many night insects attracted by the lights in the houses.

Actually, the whippoorwills are good citizens and allies of all gardeners, strange as it may seem. Besides gnats and mosquitoes, they eat all kinds of moths, including gypsy moths, as well as grasshoppers, potato beetles, June bugs, and a variety of garden pests. I have never seen them at work in a garden, but analyses of the stomachs of specimen whippoorwills proves that such insects are a part of their daily diet.

Most of us know the whippoorwills only by sound. We seldom see them. They sleep most of the day, and their coloration is so skillfully blended with the shadows in the brushy woodland where they sleep that one must almost literally kick one out of the brush to find it. And their nests are not worthy of the name. The female simply rearranges a few dead leaves in a clump of brush and lays her eggs there. If someone accidentally comes very close the mother bird will flutter away, making the typical broken-wing gestures, and try to lure the intruder to follow her. She may even cluck angrily. But such discoveries are rare. Only once have I seen a whippoorwill nest and eggs, and that was by pure chance.

When a whippoorwill is close at hand you can hear a kind of *cluck,* almost like a hiccough, ahead of each complete call. This seems to be something like a quick intake of breath, though from a little distance it sounds as though the bird goes through literally dozens of calls without pausing. In the deep of night this can be disconcerting. I have lain and listened, counting the calls and being almost lulled back to sleep by the monotonous repetition, only to be thrown off beat by a hesitation and a break in the rhythm, a kind of half-pause after which the series of calls is resumed on a new pattern. Incidentally, I once counted a sequence of 564 calls by the same bird without more than momentary pauses. This is by no means a record. John Burroughs once counted more than 1,300 calls in such a sequence.

There is a noticeable variation between whippoorwills calling at night. Some have relatively deep voices, some are almost shrill. And the tempo varies, not only from bird to bird but even with the same bird. One night I listened to one of them for ten minutes as he uttered his call in a slow, steady rhythm, as steady as the tick of a clock. Then he paused for a half-beat and quickened the tempo. For another two minutes he called at what must have been three-quarter-second intervals. Then he upped the beat again, almost overlapping one call upon the next. I never did find out the reason for his haste.

The whippoorwill is a cousin of the nighthawk, which also lives on flying insects. But the nighthawk feeds in the daytime and only occasionally at night. And the nighthawk is not really a noisy bird. Both seine the air, in a sense, flying with the big mouth open wide to catch anything in sight. Both are good flyers, but by no means as agile in the air as, say, swallows. But while the nighthawks may persist even in the cities, nesting on the flat roofs of buildings, the whippoorwills are strictly country birds. Which, I suppose, is why we still have them here.

BY THE LAST WEEK in May the green world has begun to catch up with itself. I am always amazed at the way things happen, almost overnight, once the season is really committed and we have three or four warm days in a row. The birches pop into leaf, the aspens flutter a day or two with fine silvery green, then turn green all over, the maples suddenly have leaves as big as a squirrel's ear and before I can turn around they are in full leaf and there are great patches of shade where only a few days before there was sunlight. Apple trees burst into bloom and lilacs are in flower, the whole dooryard flowery and perfumed.

The other morning when I wakened just before five there was a whole chorus of birdsong under way. A whippoorwill had to get into the act, of course, but he only made the songsters sound more musical than ever. As nearly as I could sort them out, there were robins, Baltimore orioles, tanagers and a couple of brown thrashers making most of the dawn music, though there were several others that I couldn't identify.

I had a cup of coffee, pulled on a windbreaker and went out to feel and see the early morning as well as hear it. This is the time of year when every sense a man possesses gets a workout. You don't just see the world; you participate in it.

I went down to the riverbank, and the river was faintly steaming, the thin layer of mist eddying in the air currents and lying only a few feet above the water. The grass was dripping with dew, the trunks of the maples were black with moisture. Somewhere out on the water a fish leaped and splashed, probably a rock bass, maybe a yellow perch. I was briefly tempted to pull the cover off the boat and go fishing, but resisted the urge. If I went I would probably stay a couple of hours, and I had other things to do.

I walked down the road a way, to the middle pasture, and by then the light was bright enough that I could see the individual trees on the mountainside, though the top of the hill was still misted in. Out in the pasture I heard a snort, and when I turned to look there were five deer, all does, standing only about 50 yards away, watching me. I stopped and they turned, flaunted their white flags at me and loped off a little way, then paused and looked at me again. They weren't really alarmed; merely cautious. I stood there beside the fence and they grazed for a few minutes, watching me warily. Then they decided it was time to go and trotted off across the pasture, floated over the fence and vanished in the brush. They looked well fed, I am glad to report. Apparently they came through the winter in good shape.

A red-wing blackbird saw me and made quite a fuss from a roadside willow. Probably his mate—or one of them, since red-wings are polygamous—had a nest in the reeds down on the riverbank. Then a blue jay, the loudmouth of birddom, announced to the world that a man was in sight. It didn't seem to matter to the robins and orioles, who went right on singing.

A cottontail scurried from a tuft of roadside clover and vanished in the pasture grass which has shot up, these past couple of weeks, an inch a day. I stood for a few minutes watching the far side of the pasture strip, hoping to catch a glimpse of the red fox that has a den there, among the rocks just below the big clump of white birches. He sometimes hunts field mice in that area in the early morning. But not that morning.

There's a woodchuck den not 50 feet from the fox den, but the chuck that lives there seldom comes out for breakfast before sunrise. I think that if I were a woodchuck I would sell that den and move to some other neighborhood. But maybe the chuck is the sort of character who thinks he is smarter than a fox.

I turned around and came back toward the house, listening to the rush of Millstone Brook where it comes down a small rapid and spills out across the pasture. I'm still small boy enough to think that some fine day I would like to whittle out a toy paddle wheel and set it in that brook and just sit and watch it turn.

Before I got home the bird chorus tapered off to silence. Only a distant jay had to proclaim his existence, and even he relapsed into silence after a few cries. I have never found the reason for that pause just before sunup, but it happens day after day. Only the light breeze rustled in the treetops, and the brook kept murmuring. I came on home, and just as I got to the front porch I saw the first ray of the sun, which bounced over the horizon like a ball of silvery fire. And suddenly the birds all were singing again, twice as loud as before. The river mist was silvery and glinting, and the dew on the grass was gleaming and the maple leaves were all a-shimmer. It was a brand new day, exultant with song.

HE WAS an outlander, a city man, and he hadn't been here ten minutes before he said, "It's so quiet!" I listened, consciously, and it wasn't quiet at all. The air was full of early spring sound, robins and a couple of grosbeaks singing, a newly freshened cow bawling for her calf, a tractor chuffing in the distance. But I knew what he meant, which was quietness, not silence. There is an important difference, and I suspect that it becomes more important year by year.

The only place one can find absolute silence is in an insulated, sound-proof, locked room, and I understand that those who have spent a few hours in such a place, in experimental research, say that the silence becomes intolerable. But quietness can still be found, mostly in rural places. It is best, of course, in remote places, which is one reason for saving the few wilderness areas we still have. What it is, fundamentally, is the relative absence of the noise of machines, but it is also the lack of loud human voices, sounds that seem to fill so much of our air today and jangle so many of our nerves.

Ours is a relatively quiet valley, but by no means silent. I was reminded of this the other evening when we went to a place about 15 miles from here and parked the car and sat in a field for an hour, just watching and listening to the dusk. At first I thought it was a rather remote spot, but it happened to be less than half a mile from a highway with a hill. Trucks seemed to be coming along that highway every five minutes, and every truck shifted gears and roared up the hill. It was also within range of a small airfield, and two light planes were playing follow-the-leader; every ten minutes they made a pass over the field where we sat. No jets came over, but one air liner did. And several cars on the highway had their radios going full blast.

We saw dusk come, a beautiful dusk, and the half moon brighten and the stars appear. And we heard the vesper songs of the birds and the yelp of the peepers and the croaking of a few frogs. But we never really relaxed into the evening because there was too much noise.

We have all come to expect noise in the cities. That is a part of city life. I can remember, though, when early morning in a city was an almost quiet time. The loudest sound was the clop-clop of the milkman's horse, and you could almost tell the hour by the sounds of the city awakening, slowly. Now when we go to the city for the night there is scarcely an hour when quiet comes. Taxis honk, buses roar, sirens shriek. And dawn is punctuated by the clash of trash cans, the rumble of trucks. And the loud voices. I wonder why so many people in the cities no longer talk—they shout. It becomes a habit, perhaps a defense, and even when they come to the country they continue to shout.

Somebody once said that man was called man simply because the three letters of that word stand for "Make-a-Noise." Maybe so.

We can learn to live with noise. Millions of people have proved that, and more millions are proving it every day. But it eventually deafens when it does not actually kill—and it is possible to kill with the sheer concussion of noise. That is the ghastly prospect, a human race that is deaf to all but the noise its members make. That is one of the penalties of our machine age. We no longer have the din of boiler factories, thanks to welding techniques, and few of our buildings are riveted together now. But every street that is laid, every road that is built, every tree that is cut down, is accompanied by deafening clatter.

The little sounds, the natural sounds, are drowned in the din. And the human nerves are taut and tense, with little chance for rest. Quiet has become a precious thing, something too often beyond the price we are willing to pay. Instead, we pay the doctors who treat our tension illnesses.

Why? Because that is the way things are. This is what we have done to ourselves, and keep on doing.

So my friend from the city exclaims, "It's so quiet!" And after half an hour of the quiet he is restless, uneasy. He doesn't know why, exactly. He misses something, and that something is noise. So he talks a little louder. He laughs. He asks how far it is to the nearest neighbor, and what we do to break the tedium. He hears a cardinal whistle and brightens, thinking it must be some human being whistling, is disappointed when I tell him it is a bird. He says, "Nights must be awfully quiet here. How do you stand it?"

After all, he is a man, a city man, a Make-a-Noise.

III

The first day I saw her, here on the side lawn, I thought this robin was doomed. She was huddled in the grass, neck pulled in, wings half spread, and she didn't move for five minutes. My first thought was that she had flown against a window, knocked herself cold or maybe broken her neck. Only the day before I had found a male goldfinch beside the house, dead and with that small trickle of blood at the beak that usually means the bird fractured its skull by flying headlong against something, often a glass window pane.

I went out to see about this robin. She saw me coming, lifted her head, tensed, and before I got within 10 feet of her, she beat her wings on the ground, got into the air and flew across the road. The only thing I could see wrong was that her legs dangled oddly. I came back into the house, and ten minutes later she was back on the lawn, hunched down just as when I first saw her. But as I watched she turned her head, looking at the ground around her, cocked her head in that typical robin gesture, stabbed with her beak and hauled an angle worm from the grass. She ate it and fluttered a few feet to another spot. There, after a few minutes, she got another worm.

It occurred to me that she might be entangled in a piece of string that had somehow knotted itself around her legs. So I went out again, more cautiously this time, to try to catch her and, if it was string, to loosen it and free her. But she wasn't being caught. I couldn't get within 5 feet of her. Again she fluttered, took wing and flew away. And again she came back to the side lawn within fifteen minutes.

We watched her that evening and the next morning. The side yard seemed to be the only place she came to feed. She came and stayed an hour at a time, flew away, came back. She was there most of the second day. We got out the glasses and couldn't learn much that we hadn't seen with naked eyes. She seemed to be plump, bright-eyed, intact except for those legs. Other robins came and went, and two grackles came. None of them paid her any particular attention, and she seemed neither friendly nor afraid.

The third day I got a better look at her through the glasses. One leg seemed to be all right. She could even stand on it from time to time. The other dangled uselessly. But she didn't trust herself on that one leg. She lay in the grass, peering, thrusting with her beak, feeding; then she fluttered a little way and did the same thing.

Four days and she was still here. She came early, by six o'clock, and she was here off and on all day. Where she went at night or even when she flew away for brief intervals, I do not know. Sometimes she flew toward the maples on the riverbank, sometimes across the back pasture toward the brushy mountainside. But she always came back.

The sixth day she began to stand on that one good leg. She even hopped on it occasionally, balancing herself with her wings. But she still didn't trust that leg. When she wanted to move, even only a few feet, she fluttered her wings and flew. But now she had something of a robin's proud look about her again, head up, alert. Once, that sixth day, I saw her try to haul a big nightcrawler out of the grass. She got a good hold with her beak, reared back, tried to pull. But without two legs to brace her, she couldn't make it. She lost hold, stabbed quickly again, got another hold, then sat back on her tail and flapped her wings. Inch by inch she hauled that big worm out, flapping and floundering, almost falling but never giving up. She got the worm and ate it, every inch. And stood on her one good leg and almost crowed in triumph. I wanted to crow with her.

The seventh day she was hopping about the lawn, but still flying when she wanted to move more than a foot or so. She had begun to learn how to manage on one leg, though. She would never be whole again, for that other leg dangled, useless, and obviously was not going to knit. But she had begun to make her own adjustment. By the eighth day she was getting around the side lawn quite well.

I have no idea what happened to that injured leg. Nor do I know why she chose the side yard as her haven. Perhaps because it offered good hunting, plenty of food. Nor do I know why she never went to other parts of the lawn; she spent all her time here in that one plot, perhaps 30 feet wide and 90 feet long. Other birds came and went all day long, but none of them disturbed her.

She is still here as I write this, the tenth day. She is down there on the grass, active, well-fed, quite normal except for that one leg, which she obviously misses but manages to do without.

JUNE MEANT, when I was a small boy in a small Nebraska town, that school was out and we had a whole summer ahead. Summer was endless. It was June, July and August, and three whole months in a small boy's life was a large part of forever.

I am quite sure, looking back, that we kids were the originators of the do-it-yourself movement, and I feel that today's youngsters are woefully deprived. Every time I go to the village I see youngsters buying things to have fun with. Maybe it's just a part of this vicarious way of life we have evolved, but I say the kids miss half the fun. I doubt that any of us kids had more than a dollar to spend all summer, and we spent most of that for fireworks for the Fourth of July. But we all had jackknives and ingenuity, and what an ingenious boy can do with a jackknife is worth watching. Or remembering.

One of the first things we did when school was out was scatter to the woods down along Nemaha Creek to cut crotches for slingshots. We cut and trimmed the crotches, mooched heavy rubber bands at the drug store, salvaged a few scraps of leather at the shoemaker's waste box, spent half a day assembling parts, and were in business. What we did to the English sparrows, the tin cans and the windows in the abandoned house at the edge of town was a caution. Nowadays, I see, you can buy a ready-made slingshot for a dollar, and you shoot buckshot or ball bearings. We shot pebbles picked up for free.

Or we went in for bows and arrows. Or darts. I haven't seen a good dart in years. To make a good dart you found where someone was building a new house or re-roofing an old one. With cedar shingles. There we gathered a few scraps of shingle and whittled 2-inch strips into the shape of an arrow. The heavy end made the head, the light end the vane, and the middle part was carefully shaped into a shaft. We cut a slanting notch in the shaft, to take the string. Then we made a thrower, a straight stick 2 feet long with a heavy cord about the same length fastened to its tip. With a knot in the free end of the cord, and the cord in the notch of the dart, we could throw those darts a hundred yards.

Or we took a wider piece of shingle, shaped it like a boat, cut out a section of the back to leave two projecting prongs. When we stretched a rubber band between the prongs and inserted a small paddle, either two or four-bladed, and wound it up, the boat would go whooping across the nearest puddle just like the *Robert E. Lee.* Many the races we ran with those toy boats. And what did they cost? Twenty minutes' work with a sharp jack-knife.

Sometimes we picked up thin pieces of board and made waterwheels, morticing two pieces together. That called for a certain amount of skill, but even a small boy could do it, if he had patience. Then we drove a shingle nail in each side at the center, for an axle. After that we found a brook, or a rivulet, some bit of flowing water, and built a dam and a kind of sluice.

Some days were too hot for such activity. Then we found a shady spot and played mumble-de-peg with the jackknives. That could go on for quite a while. But if it palled, we could always go fishing. If we were flush—if it was before July 4—we might buy a brand new cane pole. The best ones cost a dime apiece, but a small boy could always get a crooked one for a nickel. Sometimes the hardware man would throw in a length of string. If not, you usually had one in your overall pocket. And there were always a few hooks on old lines in the woodshed. Old corks for bobbers, too, or you found a bottle cork somewhere. Nobody used lures. We dug worms or caught grasshoppers on the way down to the creek.

There were a few homemade boats around, but mostly we navigated on rafts. An old barn door made a good raft. Or we dragged a few old railroad ties down to the pond and built a raft. With a knife a boy could make a workable pair of oars or paddles in an hour.

For dryland travel we had two good legs. And two bare feet. Night after night I heard the order, "Go wash your feet. Don't you dare put those dirty feet between my clean sheets!" But it wasn't until I was grown that I heard the term "fallen arches."

If one didn't want to go anywhere, one could make music. They tasted terrible, but long dandelion flower stems made wonderful pipes. With beautiful but monotonous tones. So did a blade of grass properly taut between one's thumbs. If there was any ambition left, we made willow whistles which would trill magnificently if we put a dried pea inside. I never learned the trick, but one of the older boys knew how to make a flute from an elder stem with the pith reamed out, a flute that would play four different notes.

How did I get started on this, anyway? Oh, yes, I was thinking that this is June again, and I was wondering if boys still make their own slingshots. I haven't seen one in a long time. Too bad. The boys don't know what they're missing. Maybe I shouldn't tell them.

LOOKING UP botanical information about skunk cabbage, I found that among other common names for the plant is the French Canadian, "tabac du diable," devil's tobacco. And from that I went on into the fascinating world of common names for plants, which always tempts me to spend a whole day. The immediate reason this time was that devil's tobacco is also the colloquial name for two other wholly unrelated plants, false hellebore and giant mullein. The devil apparently used whatever he found when he wanted to smoke a comforting pipe.

Such a start inevitably leads me on. False hellebore is also sometimes called white hellebore and Indian poke. And the giant mullein, common at roadsides all over this area, is also called flannel-plant because of the soft, hairy texture of its gray-green leaves. It is sometimes called velvet-plant abroad, for the same reason.

Another common regional plant is the marsh marigold which we often pick for an early cooked green and even eat raw in an early spring salad. A common name for this wetland plant with the big yellow flowers—it is a big-flowered cousin of the meadow buttercup—is cowslip. It is also known as king cup and Mayblob, though I have never heard either of those names. And the name cowslip is also applied to the wild primrose, or primula, of which we have tame varieties in the flower garden. Cowslip comes from "cow's lip," and I suppose someone once saw some resemblance in the plant's leaves, those of the primula; but how that name got tagged onto the marsh marigold is a mystery.

The wild columbines now blooming in rocky places all through our area have been called five crimson doves. And in Canada they are called meetinghouses and honeysuckles. I can't imagine why the meetinghouse name, but there is some slight resemblance between the deep nectar sacs of a columbine and the nectaries of the true honeysuckle. The "five crimson doves" name comes from the five deep spurs of the blossom, which might be likened to doves, I suppose. There is uncertainty even about the columbine's botanical name, *aquilegia.* It comes from the Latin, and is generally thought to derive from aquila, the eagle, from the resemblance of the curved spurs of the blossom to the claws of an eagle. But some say it comes from *aqua,* for water, and *legere,* to collect, from the dew that collects in the hollow spurs of the flower.

The blueberries that will lure berry pickers this summer have always interested me because I can't make a hard and fast distinction between blueberries and huckleberries. And I am not convinced that the confusion is mine alone. I am sure there will be volunteers to set me right in this matter. But meanwhile I find that blueberry and huckleberry are used interchangeably in many places, and that bilberry is a common name for either—if there is an either—among some people. Some varieties known as blueberries are also called farkleberry or sparkleberry, and still others are known as squaw-huckleberries and deerberries. And one dwarf species is called not only low sweet blueberry but, of all things, sweet hurts. Add cowberry, lingenberry and bearberry and you have quite a list for the fruit of this varying bush of the mountains and valleys.

Among the smaller plants there are at least a dozen that pay tribute to the ladies. I think it is tribute, anyway. Lady's slipper, of course, the common moccasin flower orchid of the woods. Lady fern. Lady's-earrings, which is the familiar spotted jewelweed that grows at almost every damp spot along the roadsides. Ladies'-tobacco, one of the everlastings also known as pussy-toes. Ladies' tresses, one of the inconspicuous little orchids. Lady's thumb, also known as heart's-ease, one of the smartweeds and cousin of buckwheat. And lady's-smock, one of the mustards common to low, wet places.

As I said, I started out to run down an obscure fact about skunk cabbage. I found the fact, which turned out to be of little importance. But along the way, and in the bypaths that led off the way, I found a hundred other things. Just as I always do when I go out to see if a certain flower is yet in bloom. I find what I go after, usually, but what I find along the way is often more interesting, if not more important, than what I went after. Maybe that is the reason the woods and the fields are so fascinating—one never seems to learn all there is to be learned about them.

BOTANICAL NAMES fascinate me, especially the common names, but they can be baffling. Only a couple of weeks ago the shadblow was in bloom along the river here, each small tree looking like a spurt of white steam in the still almost leafless woods. The bloom never lasts long, and the hot spell cut even that brief appearance short. Now the shadblow is in leaf, the blossoms completely vanished. I don't know whether the shad for which it was named have finished their spawning migration or not, but the tree was originally named because its bloom came when the shad came up the rivers. Some call it shad bush. The "blow" part of the name is more obscure, but I finally tracked it down to "blowan," an old Anglo-Saxon term for "blossom."

I first knew this tree, or bush, in the mountain West, and there it is known as service berry, or colloquially as sarviceberry. That was a complete baffler. Then, just the other day, I had a letter from a friend down in Maryland who told me the story of that name, which he says comes from the Southern Appalachians. It seems that in the old days the circuit-riding preachers made their first spring visits to the communities far back in the hills in early May. Until then even the trails were impassable with mud. And on that first spring visit the circuit-riders always held funeral services for all the folk who had died during the winter and been buried without benefit of clergy. The visit coincided with the blooming of the bush, so it came to be known as the "service-time berry," or, eventually, simply as "the service berry."

So the naming depended on where you lived, in the

Southern mountains or along some river where the shad came up to spawn.

Dogwood is in bloom in the woods around here just now, and I have again tried to run down the origins of that name. I haven't got very far, though I have found that in England certain shrubs, cousins of some of our viburnums, are sometimes called dog bush. The name also applies, in England, to some of the alders. Why they are called dog bushes, I don't know. And anyone who says they have bark can go stand in the corner. I do know that one of our native viburnums is known as dockmackie, and the "dock" in that name might possibly be a corruption of "dog." Of course, the corruption could be the other way around, "dog" being a corruption of "dock." But why the "dock" or the "dog"?

We have two small maples here in this area that are commonly called moosewood and elkwood. Moosewood is botanically *Acer pennsylvanicum,* and has two other common names, striped maple and goosefoot maple. The "striped" name comes from the fact that its trunk has lateral stripes of dull white on its dull greenish-brown bark, and the "goosefoot" designation comes from the shape of the leaves, which are three-pointed, shaped much like a goose's foot. The moosewood name interests me because it shows that moose lived in this area, or not far away, in the old days and browsed on it. Elkwood is more generally known as mountain maple, but it shows that elk once were among the native animals even this far east. Incidentally, there are several good specimens of elkwood, or mountain maple, in Sage's Ravine and visible from the Undermountain Road bridge in Sheffield.

There is no question where the name "cat-brier" came from, especially if you ever got caught in a tangle of it. Some call it green-brier, and it belongs to the smilax family, but the thorns it bears are as punishing as any cat claws I ever encountered. Still thinking of cats, I doubt that anyone has any wonder about the name of cattails, the wetland plants of the *Typha* family.

Among the oaks there is one sometimes called basket oak. It is also known as a chestnut oak, because of the shape of its leaves, and swamp oak because of its choice of places to grow. I have even heard it called cow oak, which leaves me baffled. The "basket" name, however, has a clear reason—its wood, when split into splints and soaked to make it pliable, was once used extensively to make durable baskets, not pretty ones but baskets that would last almost forever. Black ash was also used for durable basketry, but I never heard it called basket ash. Sometimes it is called hoop ash, however, which comes from its one-time use in making barrel hoops. It was also used to make barrel staves. But nowadays it is seldom called anything but black ash.

Ironwood must have been so named because the wood is "hard as iron." But another name for it, hornbeam, is obscure unless one remembers that the main part of a deer's antler is called the beam. Hornbeam is as tough as the beam of a deer's horn.

WE BOUGHT a new boat yesterday, sort of. You know how these things go. Barbara said, "Why don't we get a new boat? The old one is pretty shabby. A bright, shiny new one would be lots of fun!" So we discussed it, in odd moments, and decided just what we wanted. Then we had to do a chore over Hartford way and we passed a place that sells boats, and we stopped, went in and were greeted by a nice, friendly man. Told him we were thinking about getting a new boat. He said, "Fine! Come take a look." And he told us about his boat, a fiber-glass job, an 18-

footer with reclining seats and a 70-horsepower motor. He keeps it up in Maine.

We went out to the yard and he showed us one just like his. A beautiful boat, baby blue and white and chrome, or maybe stainless steel. But it looked awfully big. I said so, and he showed us the next size smaller, which was even prettier, but still too big. He said it was a very seaworthy job, and fine for water-skiing. We said we didn't ski. So we looked at the next smaller size, which was just about right, we thought.

Then we talked price, and asked about a trade-in; and he said our boat was a popular make and size and he was sure we could make a deal. So we said we would think about it, and got in the car and went on about our business. And Barbara said, "Well, now that we've got a new boat, where shall we go?" I said Twin Lakes was a little confined, for a boat like that. She said, yes, we would need a big lake, or maybe even the ocean. She likes salt water. So I said, "All right, we'll take it down to the Sound. And maybe go up the coast, taking our time, up to Maine, or to Martha's Vineyard. All we need is a boat trailer." The man had mentioned trailers, too.

Barbara said, "I don't know. The water is cold in Maine. Couldn't we go south?" So I said, "Yes, we'll go south. Down the Inland Waterway." And she said, "I hear there's lots of boat traffic." I said, "We're used to traffic. On the roads, at least." She asked, "When can we start?" I said, "Day after tomorrow." She said, "No. Let's wait till next week. We have to get used to this new boat. And I'm not sure I like the color." I said, "We could paint it red," and she said, "No! I won't have a red boat. In fact," she said, "I don't really like that boat in any color."

I didn't like it either. Baby blue!

So I said. "All right, we'll un-buy that boat." And she said, "Yes, we'll un-buy it."

And that's what we did. On the way home we passed that boat place and, without even stopping, we un-bought that baby blue boat and told ourselves it had been a nuisance anyway, a boat that big. And, you know, the car drove much easier and traffic was much simpler without that big boat on a trailer back of the car. I had been having trouble at every corner, making sure I swung wide and didn't sideswipe the other cars, and I had been dogging it up the hills, with that load. We un-bought the boat and felt free as birds.

And then we remembered the house trailer we bought and got rid of on a trip south some years ago.

We were fed up with hotels and motels, and a cozy house trailer was just the thing for us. So somewhere in Virginia we stopped at a trailer salesroom and looked them over. They had everything we wanted, practically everything. But Barbara said, "Let's think about it," so we got in the car and drove on.

But back of the car was that trailer, and we knew it. We talked about it, gloated over it, told ourselves how wonderful it was to stop when we wanted to, cook meals in that tiny kitchen, sleep on those comfortable beds. It cost a lot of money, but so what? What's money for? And finally I said, "Why don't I stop and you go back in the trailer and whip up a snack?" But she said, "No. You can't stop along here. Too much traffic." So I drove on, and we kept on talking about it. And she said, "I begin to feel all cooped up in this trailer. Maybe we should have got a bigger one." I said, "This size is hard enough to manage on the road." She said, "Watch out! Here comes one of those great big elephants of a truck!" And I swung back into line, just in time. That trailer almost got the whole side ripped off.

I sweated it out another hour, and we came to quite a town, and there was a lot of traffic. I managed things till we came to the main cross-street, where we had to make a right turn, and I made it too sharp and too fast, I knew it was going to happen. That trailer heeled over, the hitch snapped, and the darn thing rolled like a ball. It was still rolling when I gunned the motor and we shot away, down the street, free at last. We didn't un-buy that trailer. We just ditched it, and that was that.

See what I mean?

IN MY YOUTH it was called pieplant and it was grown in every farm garden and most small-town backyards. My grandmother, the one who planted her vegetables "in the phases of the moon," thought her grandchildren would perish of some insidious vernal malady if they didn't have a liberal dosing of pieplant. I learned early to hate it.

Later I learned that its name was also rhubarb, and I began to tolerate it, within reason. Still later I learned that "rhubarb" sounded barbarous because it came from the word "barbarous." But my long-gone grandmother's influence persisted and every spring I ate a helping of rhubarb sauce or downed a small helping of pieplant pie just to quiet the echoes of her scolding. That's why I went out two weeks ago and pulled a dozen stalks of the plant and brewed a panful of the sauce. I kept dabbing at it and finally got down to the bottom of the bowl just last night. Maybe, in justice to the past, I should add that I have had no particular vernal maladies.

I have nothing against rhubarb, nothing at all. Its leaves are poisonous and will kill you if you eat them, I have been told and firmly believe. Its roots are full of bitter essences used in pharmacology, probably to achieve that dark brown taste typical of all effective medical liquids. One of those essences goes into that old-time palliative for the belly-ache called rhubarb-and-soda. Some years ago a doctor friend prescribed it for me and it worked wonders for several weeks. Then my appendix burst and they had to turn to other expedients to save my life. I don't exactly blame rhubarb-and-soda, but I must say it didn't cure me.

As a plant, rhubarb is a cousin of dock and smartweed as well as pigweed and buckwheat. It has been grown as a domesticated plant so long that nobody knows for sure where it originated, maybe in China. Prehistoric man apparently grew it and probably ate it, though I can't imagine why. But prehistoric man ate a lot of strange things. Those stalks we still eat, when we can't avoid it or when, as in my case, conscience drives us, contain a mixture of citric and malic acids, both of which are theoretically good for the blood. Citric acid occurs in citrus fruits, and malic acid is found in apples, grapes and gooseberries. Probably that is why gooseberry pie is such a waste of good pie crust. Or maybe I just have a grudge against malic acid. Grandmother also made gooseberry pie and insisted that it was good for growing children. I don't know why it wasn't good for grown men, too, but Grandfather never ate it. He never ate rhubarb pie either.

The only reason we have rhubarb growing here is that it was here when we bought the place. There were two plants of it, so puny that I didn't bother to get rid of them until we expanded the asparagus bed. Then I dug up the rhubarb roots and tossed them aside, into a perennial weed patch full of wild raspberries, day lilies, Solomon's seal, Joe Pye weed, asters and smartweed. I just tossed them over there and forgot them. That was five years ago.

Last year there was a rhubarb plant among those weeds so big you couldn't cover it with a barrel. This year it looked like a special display in a tropical garden, leaves 2 feet across, stalks 3 feet long. I never saw such rhubarb. Or pieplant either.

So, as I say, I plucked a few stalks, and once I had them I had to do something with them. There are only two things you can do with rhubarb, stew it or make a pie. I settled for the easy way. And as I say, I finished with it last night. So what happens? This morning, with the rhubarb taste still in my mouth, a friend called and said, "I know how you like pie. So I'm going to bake a pie for you, a fresh rhubarb pie! Right out of my own garden."

What can you say in a situation like that and not be an utter, absolute cad? This friend is one of the best pie-makers we know and one of the most generous people in the world. I stammered a bit and finally said, "I've love a pie, one of *your* pies. Nobody ever made a better one. But we've just about had our fill of rhubarb, from *our* garden . . . Yes, it has been a wonderful year for rhubarb. It's very tangy, a lot of character to it. And of course it is very good for tired blood, ha, ha. But let's skip the pie till cherries are ripe."

And I got away with it.

But now my conscience begins to bother me . . .

I have just gone out and down to the far end of the garden. On the pretext of cutting asparagus, but actually to look over into the weed patch where the rhubarb has done so well on its own. And what do you suppose I found? That rhubarb has sent up several big white bud-heads and right now is opening blossom! Everybody knows that rhubarb isn't fit to eat when it is in blossom. I shouldn't be surprised if the stems themselves are poisonous now. Nobody in his right senses would make a pie out of rhubarb at that stage. Or eat it.

My conscience has stopped gnawing. I am safe for another year. Go back to sleep, Grandma.

THE STORIES are countless, and the people in them belong to the legends. I hear them from time to time, as I heard about Charley Fuller the other day, from Morris, who is one of the best story tellers I know.

Charley Fuller died fifteen years or more ago, in his nineties. He was, Morris said, as slim as your finger, a little bit of a man, but still active at ninety-two. He lived just above Schenob Swamp, in the lower corner of Sheffield, in a house set into the hillside and with all the windows on the northwest, so he could look out across the swamp and toward the mountains that are called Plantain and Race on the map. Even in his late years he had phenomenal eyes. "He could see a fly two miles away." He would watch the ledges, and he would say, "I'll be back," and pick up his rifle and just drift off toward the mountain, where he had seen a fox lying up. He might be gone three hours, but he would come back with the fox, for he was a remarkable still hunter.

In the winter he would go out alone, in the snow, with no dog, just his rifle. He would find a fox track and follow it, doggedly, patiently, maybe for half a day, and eventually he would get a shot. One shot was all he needed. He laughed at the hunters who used hounds. He didn't need a hound.

Charley Fuller was a carpenter by trade, and a good one, but when he took a job he warned you, "If it comes up a shower, I'll be leaving." What he meant was that if it rained he was going fishing, to catch them on the water's rise. He was a fabulous fisherman. He knew every nook and cranny of the swamp and its brooks, and he caught trout in there that ran to 3 and 4 pounds. He was a worm fisherman, one of the best. But he never ate fish. He gave them away. He had a tiny tattoo on his chest—a fish!

Those were the days of lake trout, big ones, in Wononscopomuc, the Lakeville lake, and Charley Fuller knew that lake as he knew the palm of his hand. He once caught five lake trout, the limit, in one day, and the smallest ran close to 15 pounds. His biggest one, the biggest he ever took in Wononscopomuc, weighed a bit over 26 pounds. And he told of the time he hooked one even bigger, "Must have been close to fifty pounds," he said. But he never landed it. For those big fish he baited with small suckers or big shiners, 8 to 10 inches long.

He never took a job as a carpenter that would run past the first of November. November, and he started trapping. He knew the swamp, end to end, and he was a remarkable trapper. Hiram Beebe, the Canaan fur buyer, once said he had bought $60,000 worth of fur from Charley Fuller, over the years. Charley knew fur, and his were of the best. He once caught five otters in one day and would have had a sixth if it hadn't gnawed off a leg and got away. Nobody knows how many muskrats he took in his lifetime, but the number must have been unbelievable.

Schenob Swamp has changed now. The beavers have damned the brooks and, some say, utterly ruined the trout streams there. The swamp lies east of Undermountain Road and starts just below the place where Race Brook comes down through Sage's Ravine and cuts under the highway. It is also fed by a little nameless brook about a mile lower down and it extends down to the Connecticut line, just above where Bear Rock Brook comes in, rushing down from Plantain Pond. And Schenob Brook flows through, out at the lower end, past Taconic corner and into the lower of Twin Lakes.

The swamp has always been renowned for its mosquitoes, which keep most people from exploring it. Or trying to. It is a tricky swamp, and the uninitiated have no business there. It's a good 2 miles long, half a mile across at its widest part. Even when Charley Fuller was alive, few strangers ever tried to penetrate it, and those who did try needed help to get out. And Charley Fuller seldom volunteered to show anyone the swamp's secrets. He just smiled and made excuses when his best friends suggested that they would like to have a look at the places he caught those big trout.

It may be that some of those trout are still there. If so, they probably will be there for some time to come. Charley Fuller is gone, and he was the only one who took many of them. And, as I said, the beavers have been busy in the swamp. They have made many changes. Even Charley Fuller wouldn't know it now, probably. But you can be sure he would soon learn it again, if he came back. He was a giant, in his own way. I wish I had known him.

I CONSIDER MYSELF A TOLERANT MAN and I like birds. I will say that I have no affection for English sparrows, who are dirty nuisances, and for starlings, who are noisy vandals. And I am becoming very tired of a certain blue jay who has acquired the habit of perching in an apple tree just outside the bedroom window and yelling at the very first hint of dawn, about 3:45 every morning. But I am on good terms with most birds. However, if that pair of barn swallows doesn't finish the nest they are building in my garage this week, out they go. My patience is fraying.

I am particularly fond of swallows, all kinds of swallows. For my money, they are the most graceful birds that ever laid a wing to the air. And barn swallows are beautiful, glossy steel-blue on the back and wings, cinnamon brown on brow and belly, with long, forked tails. They eat flying insects, especially flies and mosquitoes. This pair I am talking about probably will eat ten times their own weight in mosquitoes before the summer is over. But why must they nest in my garage?

Barn swallows build their nests of mud, reinforced with stray blades of grass. They fly miles carrying that mud, for they carry it in their beaks, less than half a teaspoonful at a trip. How they make it stick to the rafters of a barn—or my garage—is a mystery to me, but they do. They put on a layer of mud about 6 inches square, then begin building on that foundation. They are rather skillful builders, but they are sloppy workmen. By my calculation, every tenth mouthful of mud fails to stick. Since they persist in building their nests almost directly over my car, you know where that mud lands.

If left undisturbed, this pair of swallows will carry 3 pounds of mud and build a nest big as my two fists. Then the female will line that nest with feathers, lay five or six white eggs spotted like Easter eggs with dots of red, brown and lavender. Then she will settle down and brood, and in a few weeks I will have a whole family of swallows. In my garage.

I don't know why those swallows chose my garage as a nesting site in the first place. I have a big old barn not one hundred feet from it, with all kinds of open beams to nest on and all kinds of gaps for entry. But not one barn swallow has ever nested there, as far as I can see. Squirrels nest there. Sparrows nest there. One year two pairs of pigeons arrived from I don't know where and nested there. But no barn swallows.

This pair chose my garage five years ago and I was rather flattered. I let them build, and I washed my car twice a week. They raised a brood and went away in the fall. The next spring they came back, on schedule. Swallows are most prompt in their migration, and this pair arrives on my stretch of the Housatonic within a few days of April 20 year after year. They arrived and I let them clean out the old nest and raise another brood. After all, they had the nest.

They nested there four years, and it got so that I had to wash the car only once a week. Then last fall a visiting boy said he wanted a swallow's nest to take home with him. I was getting tired of swallows in the garage and gave it to him. His mother glared at me, but I thought I had the swallow problem solved.

I couldn't have been more wrong if I had tried. On April 22 the swallows came back, circled the house happily, twittered a greeting to me, and dived for the garage. A few minutes later they came out, perched on the telephone wire and looked at me as though I had just foreclosed their mortgage and thrown their last crust to the dog. I closed the garage and tried to ignore them. But for two weeks they were there, silently accusing me, every time I went outdoors. Then they began building a nest somewhere, and my car began to look as though I had wallowed it through the muddiest lane in New England.

How they got in the garage, I still don't know. They found a gap that I still can't find, maybe a knothole. I looked every day for a week, and they got the nest almost half done. Then I gave up and opened the garage door, hoping they would hurry the job.

Wrong again. They still sulked at me and they loafed on the job. They became more sloppy than ever. I was being punished. I still am. But the nest is now three-quarters finished, and Mamma Swallow has to lay her eggs some time. Maybe she will put the heat on Papa Swallow as her time approaches. I wish she would start warming up.

All I can say at this point is that if you have a pair of barn swallows building a nest in your garage, let them build it and get it over with. Don't think you can discourage them. You can't. They like your company. They love you. Don't let them stop loving you. Take my word for it, you can't win. Besides, swallows eat mosquitoes. Lots of mosquitoes. And mosquitoes don't love you, do they?

I WONDER how many people were as startled as I was to read the headline over the story of commencement exercises at Columbia University. In the *New York Times* that headline read, "Kirk Tells 6,273 Graduates at Columbia That the American Dream Is Over." The reference was to the address by Dr. Grayson Kirk, president of the university. Among the direct quotes were these:

"In one sense the American dream is over. Many of the cherished beliefs of our national youth no longer seem to fit the conditions of life in our time. In consequence it is fair to say that our people appear to be in a greater state of national confusion than at any time in their peacetime history. The future once seemed to be so sure, so certain and so alluring. Now we appear to be unsure of ourselves, sometimes of our course, frequently of our prospects . . . The glow of youthful enthusiasm has faded."

Reading those words, I thought of other headlines. Violence in city streets. Open threats of still more violence. Corruption in national and state capitals. Poverty. Filibuster. Sickness and death. The whole gamut of crime, disaster, cynicism and despair.

Then I thought of the millions of decent, hard-working, honest, self-respecting people who never get into the headlines, and I knew that Dr. Kirk had fallen into a trap to which he made passing reference later in his address, when he said, "Clearly, we must not be bemused by the attitudes of shallow cynicism or rejection so prominent in literature and the arts."

Perhaps it all comes down to a definition of the American dream. And it is important to remember that we are talking about the dream, the hope and aspiration, not necessarily the achievement. Dreams and hopes, to be worth having at all, must be big enough to demand a greater reach, a greater strength than we commonly have. Otherwise they are not dreams at all. The dream must always be bigger than the person or the people.

In the beginning, as colonists, Americans dreamed of freedom from political, religious and economic tyranny. They were not reaching for absolute security, but for a place and a way of life that would allow them to go as far as they humanly could toward a peaceful life of achievement and satisfaction. They wanted justice in their own courts, religion of their own choice, government by their own representatives, and the chance to earn a competence and a decent start for their children.

Fundamentally, it seems to me that is still true of us, as a people. Cynics will deny this, and they will point to the headlines and the stories behind them. I would point to ten thousand unwritten stories of peaceful, hopeful, helpful, honest people for every story of crime and violence and corruption.

True, we are guilty of many failures, many injustices, many wrongs of every kind. But chiefly we are guilty of belonging to the human race, which is both good and bad, worthy and worthless, damnable and exalted. Even so, never before in history has any people done so much to ease pain and suffering, more to alleviate want, more to ease the troubles of the helpless and the aged, more to help other people all over the earth to achieve freedom and physical comfort than we have done and are still doing, day by day. We even dream of making this a world where there will be no more war, with its waste and want and death and destruction. Perhaps we will never fully succeed in all these efforts, but that is characteristic of the dream, to keep hoping and trying and reaching for success in a purpose beyond our present reach.

Here at home we persist in the dream of wiping out want, curing the incurable diseases, making old age secure, giving work to those who want to work, putting an end to bigotry and intolerance, educating all our children.

How can anyone say that the dream is over, even today, especially today? The dream will not be over as long as a people remembers the dreams of the fathers, as long as one man still has a dream. The dream will not be over until we forget that there are ideals which we have not yet attained. And that, I must insist, we still remember.

TIMES CHANGE, and so do places. I am thinking today of the Big Blue River, out in Kansas and Nebraska, and of the Tuttle Creek Reservoir which has just been presented to the people of Kansas by a brigadier general of the U. S. Army Engineers. In the past ten years the Army Engineers built a dam on the Big Blue and created a lake 20 miles long, and now the absurd Kansas admirals, a long-standing joke, have a place where they can sail a cabin cruiser. Officially this is a flood-control project, and it cost 80 million dollars. Hurrah for Kansas. Hurrah for the Army Engineers. Two cheers for both of them. And just forget, if you can, that the floods this dam are supposed to control are results of the plow and the ax, not of an unruly river.

I knew the Blue River when I was a boy, so I am not speaking from a platform of theory. I was born and spent my small boyhood only 50 miles or so north of the new lake. The Blue was a famous stream then, not very big or really rambunctious, but a watercourse of consequence. The big westward migrations of the 1840s and 1850s had to cope with it when they followed the trail that cut northwest from St. Joseph, Mo., to the famous Oregon Trail along the Platte. It was, at that time, a welcome stream with plenty of sweet water and fish and with deer in its thickets. Wagon trains camped on the Blue to rest and prepare for the long drive ahead. It was lined with sycamores and willows and black walnut groves, and the grass grew lush for miles along its course. When the rains came they were sponged up by the grass and trees and floods were rare.

By the time I was a boy the farmers were growing corn all over the valley of the Blue. It was good corn land, deep black soil. They had cut a good many of the groves of timber, but they left the thickets along the river. Rivers, in those days, had a kind of vested right in their trees and men hadn't yet got the idea that they had to "manage" the streams, and the farmers, though they liked big crops, hadn't been prodded into plowing every acre in sight. They even left a good many acres of native grass along the Blue, which provided good pastures and thousands of tons of native hay.

One summer my father and a friend decided to go on a week's fishing trip on the Big Blue, and I begged and wheedled until I was allowed to go along, small as I was. We went in a horse-drawn buckboard, and we camped out. It was a two-day trip to the river, traveling as we did, and we fished a lesser stream the first night out for our supper. Then we had three days' fishing the Big Blue, and we caught channel cats as long as my arm. The Blue was a clear, clean river, clean as spring water, and where we camped there were oaks four feet through and walnut trees 70 feet high. The natural meadows were lush with grass so tall it swept the horses' bellies. Every morning the underbrush was dripping with dew. There were still signs of the spring flood, debris caught in the streamside bushes about 4 feet above the water level when we were there, in late June. None of the nearby fields had been flooded. The dry summer season was at hand, but the river still had a good flow and would continue that way. Farmers who lived nearby said it never got much lower. The slow seep in all the tributary creeks, feeding back the winter snow and spring rain, kept it replenished. It was a healthy river.

But in the next twenty years everything changed. Farmers were urged to plow more land, grow more crops. The natural meadows were ripped up. The groves were cut. The valley of the Big Blue was laid open to wash and erosion, all the way up along its furthest tributaries. Then the floods came. Corn fields eroded. Bridges were washed out. Every year when the snow began to melt there was trouble, for there was no more natural sponge to absorb the water. Then the spring rains came, and they, too, ran off with their heavy load of topsoil. The whole valley became a great funnel down which the water poured, down the Blue, into the Kaw and on to the Missouri, with repeated flood and consequent damage to every town and city and all the farms along the way. It was the old, familiar story.

And the solution? Not the sensible one, of restoring the

grass and the trees, reducing the farmland that had been pushed right down to the water's edge. Man couldn't let nature do the job. Man had to find some other way. Call in the Army Engineers and build a dam. And go right on raising more corn and wheat than we need. And the Engineers, who have to keep busy to keep the appropriations coming, welcomed the summons.

So Kansas has a lake 20 miles long, and Kansas and Nebraska have lost the Big Blue. It's still there, what's left of it. But it isn't really a river any more. It's a drainage ditch, a sad monument to our stupid insistence on "managing" our rivers. But Kansans now have a lake; Kansans can learn to water-ski. Hail progress! Farewell to a river.

RAIN MAY BE a nuisance in the city, especially if it comes on a weekend; but here in the country a June rain is altogether wonderful, especially if it comes as the one did this weekend. The drouth was somewhat eased, but not really broken, by the showers a week ago. They laid the dust and encouraged the fields and gardens, but that was about all. This weekend's rain, however, brought some relief. Best of all, it came gently, without undue bombardment or gusty wind. It was June rain at its best.

It began in the night. I wakened around midnight to the sound of the gurgle in the downspout. Lying there awake, I heard the soft rain-sound in the big apple trees, whose leaves were talking quietly to the raindrops. I listened for a while and went back to sleep, lulled by those welcome rain songs. I can't think of a pleasanter sound in the night than the patter of rain on the roof and the conversation it has with the trees. Especially when the fields are parched with drouth.

Saturday's dawn was late and gray. Around seven

o'clock there were a few distant rumbles of thunder, but I saw no lightning. This wasn't a storm, in the usual sense; it was just rain, without even enough wind to make it gusty. The clouds hung low, making the ridge back of the house hazy and mysterious. The leafy mountainside beyond the pastures was lined with silvery streaks, the slow fall of the rain. The grass in the pastures was already bowed low with a load of moisture. And the lower branches of the big Norway spruce beside the house drooped low, weighted down by the drops, millions of them, clinging to its needles. One raindrop seems to have so little weight that we seldom think how heavy even one tree branch can become when every leaf or needle carries an ounce or two of water on its surface. The spruce was literally forced to bow by the weight of the rain.

In front of the house the river was full of rain, its whole surface seeming to reach up with tiny fingers to grasp the drops. I stood and watched the river for some time, fascinated, as I always am by a rainfall on a river or pond. You can see how the drops fall, see the pattern of the rain itself, there on the surface. Rain, even a quiet rain, almost never comes in a steady, uniform fall of raindrops. There are gaps in the pattern, and waves or surges, and even eddies. Watch the surface of the water and you can see how the rain comes and goes, how it moves, each surge of it passing with a minor pause behind it and followed by another surge. On land you seldom see these variations, these patterns.

Saturday's rain fell most of the morning, easing off soon after eleven o'clock. But it continued to fall beneath the trees for another fifteen minutes, the raindrops on the leaves slowly working down and dripping. It was almost an hour before enough water had dripped off the big spruce for its limbs to begin to lift back to their normal position. Leaves and needles are covered with a kind of natural wax, but they are also covered with an unbelievable number of microscopic pores that give the raindrops a foothold, as it were. The rain lingers, pulled by two forces, the adhesion of water and the pull of gravity. In the end, gravity wins. But some of the moisture is absorbed by the leaves and they all become minutely heavier than they were before the rain.

There was little runoff from Saturday morning's rain. I was surprised at how shallow and how brief were the trickles that flowed in the roadside gutters. The soil was thirsty and this rain came ideally. The earth drank it in. Every grassroot seemed to reach for it, treasure it, and every stalk of young corn in the fields was a tiny green funnel that caught all it could hold, fed it downward, and kept on catching it. When the corn is even kneehigh it can catch and somehow use an incredible quantity of rain, close to one pint in less than an hour. And that is beyond the rain that is absorbed by the roots from the soil.

Up on the mountainside, of course, the rain was being sponged up by the leaf mold and the whole mass of litter in the woods. I listened for the brooks that rise there and flow down across the pastures to begin to chatter, but they never reached the chatter point. There wasn't enough runoff to make them do more than gurgle. The mountainside was absorbing virtually all the rain. It was seeping down the fern fronds into the soil, and going down between the rocks, and filling all the crannies. It was replenishing, somewhat, the sources of the springs.

It was a good rain, a rain that went where it was needed. It was the kind of June rain that a countryman watches happily.

THE MAY DROUTH kept the garden weeds in check, but June's showers have brought them to life with a rush. The hoe has been getting a lot of use, and the back has been bent to the aching point as we have pulled weeds by the thousand. They just lay there waiting for enough moisture to sprout, as they always do in a dry season.

It's an old story, of course. As long ago as 1672 the colonists in New England were having their weed troubles on land that had been plowed only a relatively few years before. For the first few years the virgin soil seemed to be almost free of weeds.

Then weeds the colonists had known at home in Europe began to appear. They had brought them along across the Atlantic, not realizing that the seeds were hidden in their baggage and the litter common to every ship. By the 1670s they were complaining about such immigrant weeds as quack grass, dandelions, shepherd's purse, sow thistle, knotweed, various chickweeds, dock, plantain, groundsel, mullein and a number of others. Every one of those is still with us, and not one was native to America.

According to W. C. Muenscher, at Cornell, one of the top authorities on weeds, 35 per cent of the common weeds of the northern states are of European origin, 39 per cent are native, and the remaining 26 per cent are from all over the world. That means that about 60 per cent of our common weeds were unknown to this land before the first colonists arrived. I am sure I have plenty of company in wishing they had left those weeds at home.

But the early colonists weren't the only sinners, by any means. With the best of intentions, we still encourage plants to grow in new areas and let them escape and become weedy pests. A couple of years ago a well-meaning friend in the Far West sent me a packet of seeds from clumps of a special plume grass that he grows for decoration in his garden and suggested that I plant them. I know that grass and think it is beautiful, but I also know that it produces a great many tufted seeds that are scattered by the wind. In our soil and climate it might invade hay fields and pastures for miles around, and it is useless for forage though it grows vigorously. I burned those seeds instead of planting them.

Somebody long ago set out a few plants of cypress spurge in a graveyard not far from here. Cypress spurge is a low-growing, fine-foliaged plant with greenish-yellow little blossoms, and it is tough and hardy. It spreads both by seed and root. Birds eat and scatter the seeds. From those first few spurge plants have grown patches of the insistent plant all over this area, including several in my pastures and those of my neighbors. Where it grows it chokes out the grass. It is a pest. We have been fighting it for a number of years, but it persists. Clean out one patch and it appears somewhere else. One common name for it is graveyardweed, and now I see it even in dooryards, apparently cherished as an easy plant to grow and a spot of bright color.

Dandelions and mustard, of course, are classic examples of this kind of thing, introduced plants that were first grown because they were useful, but were allowed to escape and became nuisance weeds and pests. So is chicory, of the beautiful blue flower, which has become a roadside weed and a field pest. The hawkweeds, both the yellow and the orange species, are still other examples, beautiful as flowers but persistent and even overwhelming as weeds. I have seen whole hayfields being taken over by hawkweed in New Hampshire and Maine, and I have been waging a war with one patch of them right here on my own lawn. I think they are beautiful as flowers, especially the dark orange ones, but they drive out the grass, choke it to death.

Most of the weeds in the garden, though, are simply weeds—chickweed, pigweed, galinsoga or German-weed, purslane, peppergrass, nettles, round-leafed mallow, lamb's-quarter—and quack grass! Not one of them has a flower worth a second glance, and all of them are tough, hardy and persistent. The frost we had the first week in June scorched some of the German-weed, but it has come back doubly strong. Not one of the others minded that frost. Hence the hoe. Hence the bent back. I just wish that beans and tomato plants were half as vigorous and impervious to frost as those weeds.

NOT LONG AGO I read in a book by George Ordish, a British entomologist, the casual statement that in Tudor England's rural areas there were sometimes as many as 2 million spiders per acre. This seemed a large statement, and as I re-read it I thought that since there are no witnesses from Tudor England around to testify Mr. Ordish might have been a little carefree with his figures. Then, a few mornings ago, when I went outdoors just after sun-up I saw a whole colony of spider webs under the dogwood tree on my side lawn. They were the sheet webs of the common grass spider, and there were thirty-nine of them in a circle no more than 12 feet in diameter.

I came in and got out pencil and scratch paper. A 12-foot circle contains 113 square feet, if I still know how to use the old formula, pi-*r* squared. Since there are 43,560 square feet in an acre, that circle was roughly 1/385 of an acre. Multiplying 39, the number of web-building spiders in my circle, by 385 gave me 15,054, the number of spiders per acre here in Weatogue if my sample circle was typical. That was quite a distance short of 2 million.

But that was only the possible adult spider population at this moment. Big spiders lay eggs which hatch into little spiders. Sometimes a spider lays only a few eggs per cocoon, and sometimes she lays several hundred eggs at a time. And spiders may lay as many as nine cocoons of eggs in a season. Furthermore, spider cocoons have been found with as many as 900 eggs in them, though that seems to be unusual. But if each of those grass spiders in my 12-foot circle should produce even 500 spiderlings in a season, I would have close to 20,000 spiders in that small area. Carry that rate over an entire acre and the totals would come out to more than 7½ million.

Even granting that I had an unusual concentration of spiders under the dogwood tree that morning, here was evidence of the overwhelming numbers of creepers, crawlers, buzzers and chirpers all around us. I put away my pencil and withdrew all my reservations.

Every time I am tempted to take such a census I get enmeshed in more zeroes than there are in an astronomer's distance tables. One reason is the incredible fecundity of spiders and insects. They mature, most of them, in a matter of days, and they lay eggs as plants strew pollen. For example, take the common house fly. Someone else did the paper work, and I have not tried to check its accuracy, but the figures show that if we start with one pair of flies and all their eggs hatch and their offspring mature and in turn lay eggs, in one season that original pair of flies will have increased to 200 million billion flies. This—and again the figures are secondhand—would cover the entire earth to a depth of 47 feet. Fortunately, flies as well as spiders have many natural enemies.

A few days ago the ground-nesting wasps, members of the family called *Sphecoidea* by the entomologists, went to work in the path in our vegetable garden. I tried to discourage them without much luck, and the next day I counted forty-two little tunnels in a space no more than 6 feet long and 2 feet across. Each of those tunnels, as I understand the habits of these wasps, was a nest in which they would stow spiders they had paralyzed with their sting, and among the spiders they would lay eggs. When the eggs hatched the young wasps would eat the spiders. Maybe by the time that colony of wasps is completed the spiders under my dogwood tree will be decimated. Fortunately, there are lots of birds here, too, and some of the birds eat wasps. I wish the birds good hunting.

Ants are not a pest to us, seldom come into the house and thus far have been rather quickly discouraged when they do. Until last summer I thought there weren't many ants on the place. Then one morning I saw a column marching across the far edge of the yard. It seemed to be a long column so I counted the number that passed a given point in one minute and sat down to time them. I watched that column for almost an hour, and still they came. I came indoors and went out to check the column every half hour. They continued to march almost five hours and my calculations set the number at 25,000. They all came from a colony I had never before noticed. I looked for ant colonies and found close to fifty in a casual search around the edges of the lawn. If each of those colonies had as many ants as the one whose members made that march, they housed 1¼ million ants.

Mosquitoes? I doubt that anyone can even estimate the number of mosquitoes in any given area. I know I can't. But late every summer I see sheets, literally sheets of them floating down the Housatonic from backwaters upstream. They are all males, which do not bite, and dead at that; the males can be identified by their bushy antennae. How many millions of them there are, I don't know, but they float down the river for several days, and the fish must have a mammoth feast.

Every time I get involved in such figures I smile at man's talk about a population explosion. And I thank God for nature's balances.

IT WAS 6:30 and a warm afternoon was nearing its close here at the foot of Tom's Mountain. The sun would drop back of the mountain in another three-quarters of an hour, but for a little while the valley was full of long light. A bit of a breeze began to move toward the house, and it was sweet with the smell of curing hay. Albert had clipped the home pasture the day before, mowing the clumps of tall, rank grass that the cows won't eat so that fresh growth would come and renew the pasture. It wasn't a hay crop, but a day in the sun had brought out the sweetness in those clippings.

We were sitting on the sun porch facing the pasture, and Barbara glanced up and said, "What are those out there over the pasture? Aren't they the dragonflies?" I looked, and there they were, a shimmering host that darted and danced just above the grass, flashes of reflected light that seemed to come and go. I remembered the same thing a year ago, almost to the day, so I went out into the pasture to watch and see if I could find the reason I failed to find last year.

The dragonflies, hundreds if not thousands of them, were doing some kind of strange aerial dance. At first I couldn't see any pattern to it. But as I watched, it seemed that the dragonflies were acting a good deal like kingbirds and the other flycatchers—they were making the motions of pursuit, then seemed to dive, make a capture, and go on again. It was quite baffling, for there were so many of them that it was hard to follow any one dragonfly and see what it really was doing.

Then I saw other, lesser flecks of light, some of them small as motes. They winked and were gone, but there were thousands of them. At last I knew what they were—midges. Midges of all sizes were rising out of the grass, for some reason probably connected with the fact that it was newly clipped. Then I knew the reason for the dragonflies and their strange antics. They were hunting. They were feasting on those tiny insects, those midges.

Dragonflies don't capture their prey with their jaws. They cup their six legs into a kind of basket and they seine the air. They are so skillful that they can outfly a midge, scoop it into that basket of legs, then pass it up to their mouths with the two forelegs and eat it while pursuing another midge. That's what they were doing over the pasture that evening. They were chasing midges, capturing them by the score. They darted, dived, sideslipped, almost somersaulted in the air, flashing in the sunlight all the while.

I tried to catch one of the dragonflies to identify it, but a straw hat is a poor substitute for a net. They probably were of the family the entomologists called *Celithemis,* which become adults in late June and are often seen over fields not far from water. My guess is that they were new adults, only a few days old, and that they were from a hatch—actually, a molt—either on the nearby riverbank or along the tiny brook that normally flows across the pasture all through June but this year is dry. The midges probably were newly hatched, too, in that amazing coincidence of timing that one finds again and again in nature. The dragonflies emerge as adults just at the time there will be plenty of food for them. And they swarm over the pasture. The fact that the pasture is clipped just now is not exactly coincidental, though it fits into the whole pattern. Other farm work is done by now and there is time to clip the pastures. So all those circumstances coincide, and the dragonflies benefit. By the next evening there were only a few dozen dragonflies in the pasture, not enough to catch the eye. From here on they will be seining the air over the river.

When I was a boy we called dragonflies "snake feeders," and firmly believed that they fed the snakes. Some grownups called them "devil's darning needles" and said they sewed up the ears of children who did not listen to their elders. And now and then someone spoke of them as "horse stingers" and said they sucked the blood of horses and were a pest that way. All these notions, of course, were false, mere superstition. Dragonflies don't sting or bite anybody or anything. But they are remarkable fliers, some of them swift as birds and all of them unbelievably agile in the air. And they consume tiny insects in vast quantities. So do their close cousins, the damsel flies.

The annual aerial dance of the dragonflies over the pasture has baffled me for several years. Now I know the answer.

SUMMER ARRIVED, by the almanac, yesterday afternoon. And, sure enough, someone said to me, "Summer is a-comin' in. Loud sing the cuckoo." That, too, is a sign of the season. It seems to me I have heard it every year of my life. But when I asked where the saying came from, I got the wrong answer. It isn't from Chaucer, as most of my friends seem to think. It is from the anonymous

"Cuckoo Song," which dates back to the middle of the thirteenth century, almost a century before Geoffrey Chaucer was born. It comes from the song's first stanza which reads, in the old spelling:

> Sumer is icumen in,
>   Lhude sing cuccu!
> Groweth sed, bloweth med,
> And springeth the wud nu—
>   Sing cuccu!

I first heard it from my grandmother, who didn't know a cuckoo from a meadow lark. But, like most of her generation, she was full of old quotations. For quite a while I thought that she, or maybe her own grandmother, had made them up. She had a saying for practically every occasion. "Give the devil his due," she would say. Or, "It's plain as the nose on a man's face." Or, when someone jumped to the wrong conclusion, "He's got the wrong sow by the ear."

Then I discovered Shakespeare, and after him I read Chaucer, and finally I got around to Cervantes and *Don Quixote*. And there I found almost every one of those pithy sayings of my aphoristic granthers. I know my grandmother never read Cervantes, and I doubt that a good many of her generation did. But somehow the old Spaniard filtered down into the common language, though he died four years before the *Mayflower* arrived on these shores. And it wasn't a regional way of speech, either. I have heard Cervantes quoted, unwittingly, all my life and all over the United States.

Here are a few Cervantes quotes, more or less at random:

One swallow doesn't make a summer . . . Can we ever have too much of a good thing? . . . The proof of the pudding is in the eating . . . Time out of mind . . . As ill-luck would have it . . . I don't know that I ever saw one in my born days . . . A peck of troubles . . . Thank you for nothing . . . I know it all by heart . . . Murder will out.

More? All right, look at these:

Raise a hue and cry . . . Nor do they care a straw . . . Why do you lead me a wild-goose chase? . . . Without a wink of sleep . . . Bell, book and candle . . . A finger in every pie . . . Every dog has his day . . . You may go whistle for the rest . . . I find my familiarity with thee has bred contempt . . . Ill-luck, you know, seldom comes alone . . . Thank your stars . . . Harp on the same string . . . She made a virtue of necessity . . . Birds of a feather flock together . . . Fore-warned, fore-armed . . . Even a worm when trod upon will turn again . . . 'T will do you a world of good . . . The pot calls the kettle black.

All of them are right out of *Don Quixote*. And these, too:

Many count their chickens before they are hatched . . . Every man was not born with a silver spoon in his mouth . . . An honest man's word is as good as his bond . . . Ready to split his sides with laughing . . . Honesty's the best policy . . . 'T is good to live and learn . . . Out of the frying-pan into the fire.

But there's no need to go on. The list could be doubled easily, and what I would come out with would be a short lexicon of what we sometimes call folk-wisdom, the pithy sayings that have been handed down by word of mouth for many generations. They were as common in New England as they were in the Midwest, and I still hear them, in one form or another, every day. Just as I hear that "Summer is a-comin' in" every June. They are a part of the language, and they persist because they contain nuggets of truth or because they are colorful statements put in a few words. Most of them have now become clichés and their color is no longer as vivid as it once was. But I wonder if many of them weren't almost clichés when they were first put on paper. Maybe Chaucer and Cervantes and Shakespeare are classic because they used the language and the current aphorisms of the people. None of them was really trying to be "classic." They all wrote for the public, not for some small group of esoteric admirers. The old lady who dismissed Shakespeare's plays as "just a lot of old sayings strung together" may very well have had her counterpart when those plays were first performed.

Anyway, we live and learn, thank our lucky stars for such writers, know the old sayings by heart, and listen for the cuckoo when summer is a-comin' in. That is as plain as the nose on a man's face.

WE HAVE BEEN HAVING cotton-thick fog these past few mornings, here in the valley, and I like it. I wouldn't care to live in a place where such fog was a daily occurrence, as it is along parts of the Pacific Coast, and I wouldn't ask for fog here more than a week at a time. I'll even settle for a few days of it. But the fogs we have had recently give me a feeling of adventure, of living for a few hours each day in a brand new place. Strangely, the fog also makes me appreciate this valley as it is, for it is a kind of agent of revelation. It makes the familiar contours, even the trees with which I live every day, seem new and fresh.

Perhaps this feeling comes from the way that fog can blank out the background. I remember a day two years ago last fall, when the color was magnificent. I prowled the hills and valleys for a few days, marveling. But somehow the expanse of color under full and brilliant sun was too much for the eye to take in except in the large. The details were lost, the individual trees.

Then the fog came, and when I went out on some errand I saw that color as I had never before seen it. I drove down the valley, and the hillsides were nowhere in sight. The fog—actually a vast cloud that lay on the hilltops and flowed and eddied down all the hollows—was a backdrop for the nearby trees. A particular soft maple that had been just another splash of color in the sunlight became a vivid individual tree, a mass of crimson. I had seen that tree a thousand times, spring and fall, but I had never really seen it before. It had always been lost in the woods, a part of the big picture. And, thanks to the fog, the same was true of dozens of trees. That fog had sharpened my eyes, given them focus.

Now I have been seeing the same thing happen on these foggy, early summer mornings. The big sugar maples in front of the house have been muted by the background of trees across the river. They lost their identity. Then the fog lay over the river, thick as smoke, and there were those maples against that silvery background, each one standing out as an individual. Their gray trunks and big limbs were black with moisture, and their leaves almost shone. I felt that I could count the leaves, if I only tried. The eye had lost its confusion and now could absorb details.

And when I looked the other way, out across the pasture, the mountain had vanished. In its place was a cloud, that thick gray bank of fog. I couldn't even see the fence and the brush beyond, only a hundred yards away. There was the feeling that somehow, overnight, the whole mountain had been swept away and the pasture, with its lush grass, stretched for miles, if I could only see that far. I lived on the edge of a vast, grassy plain instead of in a snug valley at the foot of a mountain.

It's an uncanny feeling, as though one went to sleep in one place, firmly rooted and among familiar surroundings, and wakened at dawn in a new, strange area. Yet close at hand are all the familiar landmarks, the old apple trees, the woodshed, the big gray barn. And those sugar maples beside the river. Yet even the river is gone, replaced by a billowing mass of softly glowing mist.

Then the sun comes up. It can't be seen as the sun; it is only a shimmer, a glow, a warmth of silver light that seems to come from everywhere. The cloud that displaced the mountain is as brilliant and full of light as that gently surging, slowly billowing cloud that lies where a river flowed last night. The leaves on the maples begin to glow, then to twinkle. Spider webs on the lawn and among the roadside weeds are patches of frost, incredibly white.

Minute by minute, as the sun rises and strengthens, the fog thins. On the mountainside it rises like smoke. I look up, and there is a rift in the fog at treetop level. Through the rift I see a patch of blue sky as blue as the flax flowers in the corner of the garden, blue as a blonde baby's eyes. Then the fog closes in again. The sky is gone. But I had one glimpse of the day's promise.

The fog lifts from the pasture. I can see the far fence and the line of brush beyond. Somewhere off there two orioles sing, then a robin. In the fog bank that has displaced the river a duck quacks, another duck answers. Now I can see the white pines on the mountain's lower slope. But they have no tops; they were cut off 15 feet from the ground.

The river is steaming like a boiling pot in a cold room,

but the sunlight begins to cut through. I can see the top of the towering cottonwood just up the road. It wasn't there twenty minutes ago. I look at the fog beyond the pasture again, and there is my mountain, all but the very crest. And overhead is a vast expanse of blue.

I am at home once more, here where I went to sleep last night. Everything is where it belongs. Another hour and I will take it all for granted again. But for a little while the fog came and took it all away. I was a stranger in a strange land.

A HIGH SCHOOL TEACHER of botany and biology recently wrote to me from another state asking for advice. Somehow—he didn't explain the miracle—his school had acquired 10 acres of land near the school which was to be used as a nature area, a kind of outdoor laboratory for his natural history classes. How, he asked, should he go about "developing" it? Summarized, my answer was, "Leave it alone and watch what happens."

Even if he likes that advice, I am quite sure he will have difficulty following it unless the donor of the land has a good deal of patience and foresight. The fact that he asked how to develop the tract proves that. Actually, you don't develop such an area. You "un-develop" it. Start developing and you make it into a park. Parks are pleasant places, and we need parks; but if you are going to have a nature laboratory you have to let nature have her way. You can't run things or you change the whole aspect and lose what you set out to achieve.

Anyone who ever tried to preserve a natural area, or let nature create one, knows the problems. Even here on my own land, where I decided fifteen years ago to let the wooded mountainside become a natural area, I have had my problems. People have wanted to spray the woods to control gypsy moths. They have said that if I didn't take out a couple of diseased pines I would lose every pine on the mountainside. They have wanted to trap the foxes, shoot the partridges, kill the bobcats. They even urged that I reopen a couple of old woods roads, "for access."

Instead, I let the old, gullied roads go back to grass and brush, which eventually stopped the gullying. I let the diseased pines die, and nothing happened to the other pines. I refused to spray, and the birds and other natural enemies have kept the moths and other leaf-eaters pretty well in check. Leaf mold has hidden most of the old scars. In all but drouth seasons, the springs are live, and several seep springs have appeared where there were none twelve years ago.

Birds and animal life thrive up there. Wanting to give them a chance, I posted the land, which had been heavily hunted in the past. Partridges came back and scattered from my woods to the whole ridge, having a haven here. Bobcats and foxes take their natural toll, of course, but the bobcats seem to have checked the porcupines. The untrimmed trees, including a few old apple trees from some forgotten orchard, offer nesting places for woodpeckers, owls, flying squirrels and, when we have them, bluebirds. And the wild flowers are everywhere.

It still isn't a completely natural area, but it is steadily moving toward a natural balance. It is beginning to be what I hoped it would become. Nature is making it over in her own pattern, and if I am both wise and observant I can see what is happening and how. I can begin to understand basic lessons in ecology.

But it took fifteen years of studied neglect to achieve even that much. And that is why the natural science teacher will have his problems with his 10 acres. If he lets them grow up to brush and weeds, which is the first natural stage, he will be asked what in heaven's name he is doing. If he says he is watching what happens when man keeps his hands off, someone will call him a crackpot. But if he, or anyone else, wants to create a natural laboratory in which to study nature, he should keep his hands off. And he must be patient. Most of all, his sponsors must be patient.

You simply can't "develop" a natural area, whether it is Bartholomew's Cobble, or Mount Greylock, or a private mountainside. You have to leave it alone, keep human interference at a minimum. We say we love the woodlands and the wildlife in them, and then we do things to them that change the whole aspect. We make conditions intolerable for wildlife, then wonder where it went, and why. And when it is gone we wish we had it back again. Instead, all we have is a raw, new road, or a raucous amusement park, or a ski run, or a picnic ground.

START BY ADMITTING that there are puzzles we can't solve. One of them, for me at least, is the way the feminine mind works. I do my best to get a glimpse of understanding. Then I come up against something like the fan.

Ours isn't a particularly hot house, even when the outside temperature is something to be wary of. But when we get the combination of heat and humidity it can be a mite uncomfortable. We have had several unhappy experiences with air-conditioning, not here but elsewhere, particularly in hotels and motels. I am sure air-conditioning has much to recommend it, for some people and in some places, but both Barbara and I like air, fresh outdoor air, even when it is hot air. So we rely on fans to relieve the occasional discomfort of a blistering afternoon.

Being a man, and having had some training long ago as

an engineer, I know at least the theory about fans. The whirling blades drive the air from one place to another, on the same principle the propeller uses, or even the windmill, though the windmill is the fan in reverse, if you follow me. A man will follow me, anyway. But Barbara has no such background in aerodynamics. To her a fan is a thing with a switch that somehow makes you feel cooler. Those whirling blades have something to do with this, but mostly they are what you keep your fingers away from and don't let the curtains get tangled up with. Understand? Quite simple.

Well, this year we decided to install a window fan. I explained that it would drive out the warm air from the living room and most of the downstairs and let the cool outside air flow in from the other end of the house. It would work best if we kept all the doors and windows closed except those at the opposite end of the house from the fan. Barbara listened, nodded, then frowned and said, "It would work better, wouldn't it, if all the windows and doors are open?" So I tried again.

"It blows out the warm air," I said. "It creates a kind of vacuum, and the cool air from the shady side of the house flows in to fill the vacuum. That's what makes it cool. Leave the windows open on the sunny side and you get hot air instead of cool."

She seemed convinced, though still baffled. I turned on the window fan, explaining that it was reversible and could suck cool air in when the sun got around to the other side of the house. That, of course, was a mistake on my part. It left me wide open to the question, "How can it suck cool air in and drive hot air out at the same time?" So I said, "Just take it on faith, please." And the fan began cooling the place, and Barbara smiled and said, "I like it. It even *sounds* cool." I pointed out that you open the window before you turn on the fan, and that seemed to be that.

It worked very well for a week. I thought we had the whole problem solved. Actually, we did, though the solution is still somewhat beyond me.

One of those blistering hot days I had to go to Canaan and do a couple of errands. Before I left I said, "If it gets hot in here, turn on the window fan. You know which way to turn the switch?" Of course she did. Switches are things you turn things on with.

So I did the errands and came home. The house seemed rather warm, but Barbara said, "It's very comfortable. I turned on the big fan right after you left. Can't you hear it?"

I did. It seemed much louder than usual. I went into the living room, and the fan was really roaring, turned up to its highest speed. But there was a peculiar rattle. The window behind the fan was still closed and the fan threatened to blow the glass right out of the sash.

"Hey!" I exclaimed. "You didn't open the window." And I started to open it, let the fan begin to do some good.

"No!" Barbara exclaimed. "No, don't open it! I tried it both ways, open and shut, and with the window open it hardly makes any noise at all. This way it sounds almost icy. It's much cooler this way. Aren't you glad I found that out?"

I just stood there, speechless.

"Sit down and cool off," she urged. "I'll bet it was broiling in Canaan."

So I sat down and cooled off, sort of. And that's the way it has been ever since. On a warm afternoon we open the window and turn on the fan. On a really hot afternoon we leave the window shut and turn the fan on full blast. It shakes that whole end of the house, but Barbara says it cools things off beautifully. And who am I to argue? A fan is just a thing with a switch to make you feel cooler, isn't it?

IV

VI

The weeks and months go too fast. Only day before yesterday it was April and I was watching for the first swallows to arrive. Last week the catbirds that nest every year in the big lilac bush brought off their brood of nestlings and now they are all in flight, every one of them. Catbirds all over the place. And more brown thrashers this year than I can remember. Two pairs nested here in the yard, though I haven't found either nest. One of the parents came and sat on the porch ledge every afternoon for a while, talking to itself. Now it seems too busy gathering food for such intervals. A few days ago one of these thrashers plucked a caterpillar out of the grass, flew to a wire with it, and I was sure that caterpillar was on the way to a gaping mouth in the nursery. But I was wrong. After a few moments the thrasher opened its beak, gulped, and the worm was gone. A mid-afternoon snack. Definitely not baby food.

One of the few rewards of mowing the lawn is the opportunity to sit and watch the birds on the newly cut grass in the early evening. They all come, robins, catbirds, thrashers, even the various sparrows. They stalk about, watching, probably listening, and they find dozens of worms and insects. A picnic, probably, with even the ants welcome. And, for once, very little squabbling. There seems to be room enough and food enough for all of them. By the next morning there are grackles in the yard, taking their share of the harvest. Incidentally, there has been a good-sized flock of purple grackles near Dutcher's Bridge on Route 44 for some weeks now. They appear to be nesting there and making a good living in the nearby alfalfa fields. And there is a sparrow hawk who has a lookout in a white ash just down the road. I see it every few days. I have seen a sparrow hawk there, probably this same one, every summer for the past four years.

There is one particular red-wing blackbird that comes and calls every day here at the house. I know him because his epaulets are dull yellow instead of red. All red-wings have a yellow edge on that red shoulder patch, and in winter it often is so wide that it conceals the red; but this fellow doesn't reveal any red at all, even when in flight. His voice isn't particularly good, I must add. He has friends, though, who come around early in the morning and sound rather musical. Several pairs of red-wings are nesting along my pasture brook.

I really shouldn't have said that "pairs" of red-wings were nesting. They don't nest in pairs. The males are polygamous, have several wives who do the nesting chores, each with a nest of her own. At that, the arrangement seems much more commendable to me than the habits of the cowbirds, who never nest at all. They lay their eggs in other birds' nests and get away with it, let the enforced foster-parents do all the work. Last year we had several big flocks of cowbirds here in the valley, but I haven't seen half as many this year.

Howard Baine, up in Ashley Falls, tells me that he had a pair of bluebirds nesting in his dooryard this year and that they have brought off their brood. Good news indeed. I haven't seen a bluebird down my way in two years. Mr. Baine also reports hearing a bobwhite the other morning.

Maybe the same one that Gelston Hardy, not far from him, heard a couple of year ago. I hope that quail has a mate, and a nest, and a family. But even if he has, some fool may shoot him down, some idiot who will shoot anything on wings.

Quite a lot of flickers around this year, but not as many, it seems to me, as there were last year. Three or four of them come into my dooryard, especially when the lawn is newly cut, and especially in the heat of the day, and act almost like robins, working the short grass for worms and insects.

A friend down in Princeton, N.J., writes me that they have lots of mockingbirds this year. The range of the mockers moves steadily north. Twenty years ago they were rare in the Philadelphia area. This friend also says that he thinks a Baltimore oriole has a nest in a Japanese quince in his dooryard. I had my fingers crossed on that one, but he says he will make a full report later. That would be one for the book.

Another friend tells me a story about house wrens and English sparrows. He put up a wren house a few years ago and it was happily used by the wrens until this year. This spring the wrens moved in again, but the sparrows began harrying them. They couldn't get into the house, but they sat on the perch and made life miserable for the wrens. Finally the wrens gave up, moved out, nested somewhere else. But the papa wren made sure neither the sparrows nor anyone else would use that wren house. He stuffed it full of twigs, so full that nobody else could get in. Smart boys, those wrens.

THERE WASN'T MUCH WIND and it was blowing down the valley, so we didn't smell the smoke. Then the rural mail carrier arrived, honked insistently and, when I went out, said, "There's a fire in the woods just down the road. Albert is there, but he may need help." I got out the car and went right down. Fire strikes the fear of disaster into the heart of any countryman, and a fire in the woods in time of drouth can be devastating. Our wooded ridge was bone-dry.

The fire was just below my far pasture. A tall, dead tree was in flame from bottom to top and the brush around it was ablaze in a circle 20 yards across. Albert and his hired man were trying to check the brush fire, watching the malevolent flaming tree, which was showering brands, setting new fires. I shouted, and Albert said, "I'm afraid we can't hold it. Better turn in an alarm." He was calm, but grim. His barn, full of new hay, was only a few hundred yards away, and if the flames leaped the railroad tracks and got into the pines they could race all up and down the valley.

I came home and phoned in the alarm, and the Canaan siren began to wail almost before I had hung up the phone. Barbara said she would call the neighbors, and I went back. The first pumper arrived less than fifteen minutes after I called. Volunteers came right in its wake, and then a second pumper. Hose was put out, the pumpers built up pressure, a dozen men surrounded the flames. Ten minutes and the flames were confined, though the blazing tree still was a menace. Its hollow trunk was a chimney, drafting the fire upward.

The brush fire was tamed and quenched in less than half an hour. Albert went for a chain saw, and the dead tree was brought down in a shower of sparks and ashes and embers. It, too, was quenched. Then the firefighters checked for latent embers, made sure there weren't hidden patches of smolder that would burst out again. And finally the hoses were reeled and the pumpers went back to the village. The firemen waited a little longer, just to be sure, then got in their cars and went back to their stores and shops and homes, a job well done. And we folk here in the valley were grateful beyond words. We tried to say our thanks, and had to let it go at that. You can't really say all the things you feel at a time like that.

How it started, nobody knows. There were half a dozen theories. Bottles sometimes act like burning-glasses; but nobody found such a bottle. Lightning fire can smolder in a tree for a week, but we have had no recent lightning. It was too far from the road to blame a carelessly tossed cigarette or match. Maybe a passerby sat under that dead tree and failed to snuff out a cigarette; but there were few passersby yesterday. Like so many fires, it remains a mystery.

But it drove home again two lessons. We were cautious before about fire, and now we are fanatically careful. And we knew the value of friends and neighbors before, but now we know they are priceless. Cities have their paid fire departments, but in the country it's a matter of volunteers, men who answer the siren, day or night, because their neighbors need help. Because fire is one of the most ruthless enemies man can face, especially in the country.

In a sense, ours was a little fire. But no fire in the woods is unimportant. It isn't a little fire when hundreds of acres of timber are threatened. It isn't a little fire when a farmer's barn is anywhere within reach, or a house, or a garage. Little fires grow swiftly, as any countryman knows and as all volunteer firemen know only too well. Fire is fire, and that's the sum of it. And only a fool would set a fire in any place where it might spread. We were doubly lucky in having the river close beside the road, where the pumpers could draw water all day, if need be.

Visitors sometimes think country folk are unduly cautious about fire. But they never saw a fire racing through the woods or destroying a barn and threatening a whole farmstead. Perhaps one has to see such things to have a proper respect for flames. That's one reason country folk don't go in for bonfires, or even for cook-outs unless they have a proper fireplace or a tested grill. That's one reason so many farmers aren't smokers. They know. That's the particular reason a countryman sniffs nervously when he smells smoke and doesn't rest until he knows its source.

And that's the reason country folk watch hikers who are also cigarette smokers, and are suspicious of anyone who takes a shortcut through the woods. That's why they get indignant when roadside picnickers start a fire, "just a little one to roast a hot-dog." That's why, if I see a motorist flip a cigarette from a car along this road I'm going to take his license number and call the cops.

JULY'S ARRIVAL always surprises me, and I'm not sure whether that is a sign of protracted youth or premature age. July means that the year is half gone, that we have passed the vernal equinox and the summer solstice and that the days have begun to shorten again, as we say. Fall is already there in the offing. Where does time go?

But I suppose that time gets away from all of us. The problem is how to keep up. I know a farmer who got hopelessly lost in time some years ago. The first year I watched him he seemed to be two weeks behind all his neighbors. He didn't cut his hay until July, when the grass was all headed out, and he ran into rain with it and never did get it all in. His corn wasn't particularly late, but we had an early frost and he lost most of his crop. The next year he fell a few days further back, and that kept on year after year. This year he didn't get his corn planted until last week, when all the corn roundabout was knee-high, and I don't know when he will get at his hay, if ever. By now he is so far behind that I said to him the other day, "Why don't you take a year off and get a fresh start?" He shook his head. "I haven't got time to take a year off. But the way I'm going the seasons will catch up with me one of these days."

Man, however, seems to be the only living thing that gets tangled in time. The trees never fall behind, nor does the grass. They put out their leaves and send up their shoots on schedule, and as far as I can see they seldom miss the season by more than a day or two. Maybe they have better clocks than man has ever made. Or maybe they get along better by not depending on such contrivances as man has devised to split the days into hours and the hours into minutes and seconds. I sometimes wonder just what advantage man ever gained by tying himself to a little machine that goes tick, tick, tick and counts one, two, three up to twelve and then starts all over again.

Nature does miss the time now and then in minor matters. The other morning there was a big to-do on a limb of the big spruce just outside my study window. An oriole chick was perched there, desperately yeeping for adult attention. As I watched, the mother oriole fluttered close and clucked and scolded, then flew away. Trying to climb the steep limb, the chick lost its footing and fluttered to the ground on inadequate wings. I went down and put it back in the tree, noting that its tail feathers were just sprouting. It yeeped and fluttered there most of the morning, in the tree and out, too young by a week to have left the nest. It yeeped and fluttered away its precarious life, and by late afternoon it was dead. A few more days in the nest and it would have been safe. Something went wrong with its time schedule.

But for every perishing chick, here along the river, there probably are a thousand that achieve flight and song. And nature persists by the averages. How many maple seeds fall and fail to sprout, and how many acorns never become oaks? Some mathematician once calculated that if all the offspring lived, a single aphid could produce 5 tons of aphids in forty-eight hours. Or was it twenty-four hours? I forget. It doesn't matter, for aphids are expendable, and ladybird beetles, among others, eat them by the thousand. And what is time to an aphid?

When we planted the garden back in April we said that we would have peas by late June, the first week in July at the latest. We had them on July 2, but it wasn't the calendar that brought them to pod and pot; it was a clock there in the soil and a clock in the sun and still a third time element in the seed itself. All we could do was cooperate and let nature take its course. The same thing will happen with the sweet corn, the earliest of which is now beginning to tassel. Oh, if we were hybridists we might see that the proper pollen reached the right silk and somewhat maneuver matters. But even then the essential process, the mating of sperm and germ, would take place hidden beneath the husks, out of our reach. Neither clock nor calendar has a thing to do with that . . .

I have just killed a wasp on the inside of my window screen, a wasp that emerged only a few days ago from an egg that probably was timed 50 million years ago. The wasp has practically no capacity for thought, yet somewhere in its instinct must be the equivalent of a time sense. It knows when to lay its eggs, and in the egg is the urgency to hatch in due time. The egg hatches and matures and, if it is a female, lays eggs in turn. Thus the tribe of wasps persists, unaware of time and yet inexorably tied to the dictates of time itself.

July, the midpoint of the year, as man knows each turn around the sun. Out there in the garden a lavender blossom falls and a tiny pod appears on the bean vine. Yellow petals wilt and a tomato begins to take form. And man watches his ingenious clock and his makeshift calendar and ticks off the days, wondering where time goes. Cherishing life, metering it out for himself in bits and pieces, hoping thus to control it. Cherishing life, never quite understanding it, and resenting life's one inevitability, which is mortality.

TOMORROW is the Fourth of July, and we shall abide by some of the traditions. At the dinner table, at least. We will have new potatoes, fresh peas, beet greens, and all the head lettuce we can eat, all from our own garden. That's the way it should be.

We've had our own lettuce for several weeks, and we had the first beet greens and baby beets last week. First sweet corn is just showing first sign of tassel, thanks to a May without late frost and the fact that Barbara always plants a couple of rows of corn two weeks before it's safe. When she is lucky, as this year, we have early corn. The main crop, for the freezer, was planted the last week in May, and we will plant the late corn, two more rows, this afternoon. This time we will be taking a chance with early frost. With luck we will have roasting ears the third week in September. Those late ears are special, as tasty as the very first ones of the season. The middle crop is just sweet corn, though the same variety—it isn't *first* corn, and it isn't *last* corn. Two years out of three we get it.

The traditional Fourth of July dinner should have fried chicken, too, from the home flock. But we don't raise chickens. I cleaned my chicken coops long ago, and now we get our friers and broilers from the market, by way of our own freezer. We'll probably have a broiler, but if it's as hot as today I'll gladly forgo that. Menus change, over the years.

Another item on that old family Fourth of July dinner was home-made ice cream, but we won't have that either. I see that you can still buy those old-style handpower freezers here and there; but you can buy an electrified one almost anywhere. We have adopted the idea that muscles are obsolete, apparently, even such lesser muscles as those once used to open cans, whet knives and brush teeth. But even the power-driven home freezers appear still to have a dasher, the agitator that stirred the mixture inside the can and was taken out, once the cream was frozen, all covered with the most delicious ice cream ever made. The woman of the house spooned it off somewhat, but left enough to reward the younger generation that had turned the crank. It was a great privilege to lick the dasher. While that was going on, the finished can of ice cream was packed in ice and salt and set in the shade till time for dessert.

Sometimes there were fresh strawberries with the ice cream, but it was a little late in the season for the best berries. Always there was cake, and usually there was pie. In a way, that Fourth of July dinner was an early model for Thanksgiving. Maybe one reason was to fill the kids enough to keep them out of noisy mischief most of the afternoon. They had made enough noise all morning. That, of course, was in the dangerous age when you could still buy fiecrackers and other such explosives. Now we ban firecrackers and kill and maim the celebrants, far, far more of them, with automobiles.

Firecrackers came in all sizes, from the tiny "lady crackers," not much bigger around than the lead in a pencil, to "giant crackers" that could blow up a barn. Practically all of them came from China, where they had been bombarding the air with black powder for centuries and seemed to survive and multiply rather well. As a youngster, you began hoarding pennies and nickels right after Christmas and if you were lucky you had a dollar to spend on firecrackers. If your luck held on the Fourth you still had a few left for the afternoon. The most horrible Fourth I can remember was the one when I had a whole dollar's worth of firecrackers in a shoe box and carelessly dropped a lighted piece of punk into it about ten o'clock in the morning. I escaped with both hands and both eyes by some miracle, but my day was ruined.

But nothing so disastrous ever happened at the family dinner table. Folks, grownups as well as kids, just sat down and ate and ate and ate. The portly uncle kept saying, "It's too hot to eat please pass the fried chicken." Mother, who was the hostess, said, "I guess there's too much salt in the peas and the potatoes are overdone, but maybe you can find something else to eat." Aunt Mabel said to my father, "I don't see why you have to put both sugar and vinegar on your lettuce." And mother, who didn't "get along" with Mabel, said sharply, "I guess we can afford sugar as well as vinegar, even if some folks can't." That was the nearest thing to an explosion, and the portly uncle covered that by saying, "It's too hot to eat please pass the chicken I got a neck the last time."

After the cake and ice cream the women folk cleared away and the kids began shooting off their last few firecrackers. The portly uncle took a nap in the barrel-stave hammock and the other men played a game of horseshoes. And by evening everybody was ready to eat again. all except the portly uncle, who said, "It's still too hot to eat but it's a shame to let that cold chicken go to waste."

Then it was dark and everybody went home. And Mother always said, before we went to bed, "I wonder if everybody had enough to eat."

NOISE. That's the way the day began, half a century ago, at least in the small town where I was born. A dozen of the town's young men got up at dawn and "shot the anvil." It made a blast that jolted the whole town. Nobody slept after that. It was the Fourth of July, and no mistaking it.

I don't know whether shooting the anvil was a common custom, but it certainly was an effective one. I never saw it done, but the way I heard it described made it both awesome and perilous. They took a blacksmith's anvil, set it in the middle of Main Street, and poured gunpowder into the hole that took the colter. It would hold at least half a pint of powder. The load was fused and wadded. The fuse was lit and everybody ran. When the blast went off it sometimes hoisted the anvil ten feet into the air, they said. On occasion it blew in a window or two in one of the stores nearby. It was like a cannon blast.

After the anvil was shot, the big firecrackers, giant crackers or cannon crackers, were set off, maybe a dozen of them. They were a foot long, as I remember them, and sometimes 2 inches in diameter. Awesome things, and full of maiming and injury. Even the daredevils respected them. Sometimes one was put under a barrel, and the blast blew barrel staves in all directions. One year one was set off under a lumber wagon someone had carelessly left handy. It blew the wagon bed right off the running gears.

By then the youngsters in their early teens were up, dressed and swarming toward Main Street. Someone with a little common sense ordered an end to the cannon crackers. Smaller firecrackers, four inches long and big around as a man's thumb, had their turn. They could tear a hand off, of course, but somehow they never did in my town. They merely ripped the air and raised the dust and wakened the deafest man in town. And had most of the dogs cowering in dark corners and under beds, and all the horses in the livery stables were quivering and neighing in fright.

By breakfast time the air over the whole town was rank with that unmistakable odor of burned powder, that special firecracker powder whose smell is one of the long, long memories of my generation.

After breakfast things got off to a new start, equally loud in total but composed of relatively minor blasts, the everyday size of firecrackers, the kind that came in packages with the fuses braided across the top. And torpedoes, of course, those vicious little bombs that one hurled at the sidewalk. And caps, in pistols and canes and detonators of all kinds. It was a continuing fusillade, on almost every street in town.

By noon the worst was over. Supplies were almost exhausted. Ears were ringing, patience among the elders was worn thin, and picnic fare began to lure. Fried chicken, potato salad, deviled eggs, home-made ice cream, cake, pie, watermelon. There were picnics on almost every front lawn in town, family picnics with hordes of aunts and uncles and cousins and grandparents. People gorged. People drank gallons of lemonade, and maybe some of it was spiked, for all I know. Tired, sated people tried to nap, and when the last of the explosives were brought out, frayed tempers and ragged nerves snapped. A good deal of the noise was vocal.

Dusk, more food, and then the fireworks. Roman candles, sky rockets, whiz-bangs, pin-wheels, colored lights, sparklers, sky bombs. Now and then somebody got scorched by a sky rocket or burned by a Roman candle. Things did happen, of course. Over the nation there were injuries and deaths, maybe as many as a hundred deaths in one year, though I don't remember the figure that high. Anyway, fireworks were banned here and there, finally over whole states. The slogan, "A Safe and Sane Fourth," took hold. The Old Fourth became a memory.

It probably was a good thing, to be done with it. But when I hear that slogan now I cringe. I think of the statistics gathered by the National Safety Council. Nobody shoots the anvil any more, and the firecrackers big and little are outlawed. Now the noise comes from crashing cars and bellowing outboard motors. And if we could get the annual fatalities down to even three hundred we would be exultant. We haven't yet achieved safety or real sanity, as the figures we will read day after tomorrow will show.

But when I wake to the silence tomorrow morning I shall remember. And I hope I will be pardoned for a nostalgic twinge. I do wish I had been big enough to watch them shoot that anvil.

EVERY TIME I hear the apologists for poison sprays say that the loss of a few songbirds is unimportant compared to the protection of growing crops I want to say, "Hey! Wait a minute." If it was that simple there would be little argument. But it isn't that simple. Songbirds aren't merely beautiful singers that please both ear and eye. They are allies in the age-old war with the insects. They save more crops than all the chemical pesticides put together. Every time a bird is killed the insects benefit and we are the ultimate losers.

Take a few examples.

One flicker will eat more than 5,000 ants in a day, besides all the grubs and borers it consumes.

The brown thrasher's diet consists of one-third fruit, berries and grain, two-thirds insects. At the time of heaviest insect infestation the thrasher's insect consumption rises shaply. But all summer long the thrasher eats beetles, white grubs, army worms, cutworms, tent caterpillars, wasps, grasshoppers. And most of the fruit it eats is wild fruit.

Almost half the diet of a robin is worms and insects. In addition to earthworms, robins eat flies, cutworms, army worms, cicadas, spiders, grasshoppers, weevils, borers, gypsy moths.

The wood thrush of the beautiful contralto evening song eats 62 per cent worms and insects, 38 per cent vegetable products. Among the insects they eat are spiders, caterpillars of all kinds including gypsy moths, potato beetles, grasshoppers, weevils, crickets. Most of their vegetable diet is wild fruit.

The bluebirds eat both vegetable and animal food, but prefer an insect diet. Among the worms and insects they eat are predaceous beetles, caterpillars of all kinds, and grasshoppers. Virtually all their vegetable diet is wild seeds and berries.

House sparrows, which can be such unwelcome residents with their noise and untidy habits, habitually eat seeds and can be a pest in the fields. But when there are hordes of insects they switch diet and consume vast numbers of aphids, Japanese beetles, inchworms and locusts.

Red-wing blackbirds are normally seed eaters, prefer weed seeds but sometimes raid cultivated fields. However, when there is an outbreak of insects they gorge on caterpillars and other insect larva. In the South they are a pest in the rice fields, but here in the North they eat few cultivated crops.

The orioles, both Baltimore and orchard, have a diet of about 90 per cent insect, 10 per cent plant products. Caterpillars make up more than one-third of their diet, and among them the chief ones are gypsy moths and tent caterpillars. They also eat weevils, plant lice, grasshoppers, borers.

The noisy grackles are omnivorous birds, sometimes raid cornfields, eat acorns and beechnuts as well as quantities of weed seeds. But they also eat vast numbers of insect grubs, especially the grubs of Japanese beetles.

Cowbirds have a bad reputation because they lay their eggs in the nests of other birds and refuse to hatch or raise their own chicks. But they eat weed seeds by the peck and insects by the pound—grasshoppers, locusts, beetles, flies, wasps, mosquitoes.

Of all the birds that visit the garden, the rose-breasted grosbeak is one of the most helpful. It eats potato bugs, cucumber beetles, leaf beetles, tent caterpillars, scale insects, plant lice, stink bugs, and the caterpillars of gypsy moths, army worms, tussock and brown-tail moths.

Practically all our native sparrows are known as seed eaters, and they consume literally tons of weed seeds each year. But they also eat vast numbers of insects, particularly beetles, grubs and caterpillars of all kinds.

Audubon Society estimates indicate that 12 to 15 billion birds spend a part of each year in the United States and Canada. That averages almost 2,000 birds to the square mile. Most of the birds are in the country, where food crops are grown. Considering the diet of the typical birds just cited, one may imagine what would happen to those crops if the number of birds were materially reduced. Add to this the fact that almost all birds feed their nestlings exclusively on insects, and that nestlings are hatched when the insects are emerging in incredible numbers, and the situation becomes even more significant.

No, the death of a few songbirds—as singers of song—is not vital. But the death of birds as destroyers of the insects that plague and endanger all the plant life on earth would be nothing less than disastrous to all of us, no matter where we live.

A COUPLE OF YEARS AGO a photographer out for the afternoon took a picture of our old barn, captioned it, "Deserted Farm," and won a competition with it. I didn't know anything about the incident until I saw a story about the contest and a reproduction of the picture, and though I thought it was all amusing I was just enough nettled to say I wouldn't do anything about that barn, no matter how it looked. I did go out a few weeks later and remove the old wooden-wheeled hay rake that had been there, broken down, for years, and I persuaded someone to drag off the old hay loader that looked like a junk dealer's trademark. But the sway-backed old barn with its doors that had to be propped shut wasn't going to be touched, I said. Not till the doors fell off.

They never fell off, quite, but pieces of them did, and when it got so that Pat could chase woodchucks in and out as though the doors weren't there, I began to weaken. And when a skunk and a raccoon both moved in I gave up. We had to put new doors on that barn.

There was some discussion about whether the barn was worth it, but I ordered the lumber just the same. Carl brought it down from his sawmill in Ashley Falls and while we were unloading it I asked Carl how much longer the barn would stand up. He went inside, looked around, and said, "Probably as long as you live, at least." And he seemed to think I was in average health, so we discussed barns and their construction.

I don't know what you call it, but my barn is built the old way, with a framework of hand-hewn beams and round rafters that are pegged at the peak and adzed flat for the roof boards. Most of the framing is of oak and the rafters are white oak. The beams are a good foot square in cross section and they are morticed together, and the old siding is put on vertically. The beams are very old, must have come out of some earlier barn, and are hard as iron. Some of them have been spliced, probably when the barn was built.

Carl said that when he was a boy he saw lots of barns built that way, the only way to built a good barn, folks thought. There were carpenters then who could lay out the framing, cut the mortices, shape the tenons, get every piece ready without raising a stick. Then there would be a barn-raising. And all the pieces went together perfectly, though the carpenter who designed the barn didn't have a blueprint or a plan of any kind on paper, just the overall dimensions and that clear picture in his own mind. They put up the beams and rafters, and there was the framework of the barn, square and plumb, every mortice matching every tenon. Then all they had to do was roof it and side it, and it was there for years to come.

We agreed that those old carpenters were geniuses, and we swapped a few barnyard jokes, and Carl said that now we had something to do the next rainy day and went back to Ashley Falls. So the next rainy day Albert and I started building the doors. Now they are all ready to hang when we get around to it, and for a long while they will stand out like sore thumbs because they are new lumber and the barn is gray with years of weather and no paint. I thought of painting the doors gray, trying to match them up a bit, but decided it couldn't be done. So they'll just have to weather, with a coat of oil to keep them from warping.

While we were building those doors, I saw an odd-shaped stick in one corner and picked it up and found that it was the handle of a flail. On one end was the old wooden loop, hand-carved to shape and probably steamed to make the curve, a fine piece of handwork though the handle itself was not too well finished. I thought I had looked that barn over from nook to cranny, but there was that flail handle, right in plain sight, back of the old hand-power cornsheller, and I had never before seen it. I looked for an hour for the rest of the flail, but it wasn't there. Probably the handle was set in the corner when the rest of it broke, years ago. I doubt that it is as old as the small millstone I found in the bed of the brook at the foot of the mountain a few years back, a stone only 15 inches in diameter. But I am sure it's been a long time since anyone used a flail here on this farm.

Anyway, the old barn is going to have new doors, when we get around to hanging them, and though it may look strange it shouldn't invite wandering camera folk to take pictures and call them "Deserted Farm." Why, do you know, a year or so ago some woman who said she was an artist stopped and asked if she could go out and just touch that barn, feel its texture? Well, she did. She said, "It's beautiful!" So she went out and ran her hands over the old boards and came back to the front door and thanked us. I don't know her name, but she appreciated that barn.

BARN SWALLOWS are remarkable birds. On the wing they make flight as beautiful as a song, and they do it without the slightest sign of effort. They make it look as though the air were made specially for a swallow's wing. And the way they built their mud nests is almost incredible.

But of all the jittery, neurotic, screaming-meemie birds there are, the barn swallow takes the palm. Their jitters start when they choose the nest site, increase as they build the nest, become acute tensions as the eggs are brooded, and become something close to frenzy when the chicks are ready to fly.

I had thought it was a matter of parental nervousness, let's say, until the other evening. Now I am not so sure. I began to wonder if it isn't someting innate, something in the very egg.

It had been one of those scorching days and Barbara and I were out on the porch just after sunset, cooling off and watching the clouds build up toward a thunderstorm. We heard swallows chittering. Two adult barn swallows were circling in front of the house, swooping at the telephone cable. Then we saw four swallow chicks perched on the cable. They probably had left the nest only that day, and they seemed scared stiff. Two of them clung to the cable and huddled to each other like a pair of love birds. The other two were a little distance away, each by itself.

The parent birds circled and dived, obviously trying to lure the chicks into the air. The chicks wouldn't lure. Finally one parent brushed one of the lone chicks with a wing, flying past, and it lost its balance, fluttered, began to fall, spread its wings and flew desperately. It circled once and came back to perch on the cable. The other lone chick was likewise brushed off, flew awkwardly, and circled back to perch a foot away from the two chicks still huddled side by side. And the two that had been forced to fly for a moment ducked and dodged as the parents made passes at them.

This went on for ten or fifteen minutes. Then the parents flew out over the river and the two lone chicks moved, inch by inch, along the cable until they reached the two huddled against each other. There were the four of them, wing to wing, hunched down like baby rabbits. The parents came back, tried again to force them into the air. But somehow the four of them, perhaps by sheer force of numbers, couldn't be budged.

Dusk deepened and the thunder clouds rolled closer. The parent birds chittered desperately, seeming to beg, wheedle, threaten as they kept trying to force the chicks off the cable. Then they flew away again.

It was almost dark and the storm was close at hand. A first fierce gust of wind struck. The chicks, barely visible in the gathering darkness, clung to the cable, weathered the wind. Then the rain began, and the lightning.

We came indoors. It was a vicious lightning storm and the rain came in drenching bursts, but when I went out on the porch after another fifteen minutes I saw those four chicks still there when a flash of lightning opened the sky for an instant. The thunder made the hills shudder. The rain beat down, eased, beat down still harder.

The storm continued half an hour before the lightning bursts dimmed. Then it settled down to a slow rain that came and went. I was tempted to get out the big flashlight and have a last look before we went to bed, but the rain was falling so heavily the beam couldn't reach the cable. We told each other that those four swallow chicks were going to be victims of the storm.

We were up by six o'clock the next morning to a bright and sunny day. Barbara said, "How about those baby swallows?" and we went out on the porch to look. I gasped. They were still there! They still clung to that cable right where they had been when we came indoors the night before. It was incredible. While we watched, one chick lifted a wing and seemed to shrug off the cold and the raindrops. Then it settled back, motionless again.

We came back in, made the morning coffee, both of us marveling. And a quarter of seven I went out onto the porch again. The chicks were gone. They weren't on the ground beneath the cable. They had flown away. And we haven't seen them since.

MID-JULY, and now come the Dog Days when, by the old traditions, ponds grow scummy and poisonous, dogs go mad, and snakes are doubly venomous. Actually, the Dog Days were only casually related to summer's frothing dogs in ancient Roman streets. The time was named for Canicula, the Dog Star, which the stargazers found to be in conjunction with the sun and thus responsible for all seasonal ills. Now we have inoculations to prevent rabies, we know that snakes are blind and touchy when they shed their skins, and scummy ponds are poisonous primarily in the mosquitoes that hatch in their tepid water. But the old name persists—Dog Days.

Had the traditions come from Egypt instead of Rome, the Dog Days probably would be a time of thanksgiving. The Nile rose in flood at this time of year, fertilizing the fields with silt and insuring an ample harvest. Egyptian stargazers knew about the Dog Star and its conjunction with the sun—they called the star Sirius, as we still do—but to them it was a time of benison, not bane. They probably had mad dogs and blind asps too, but they took them in stride, grateful for the fertile flood.

We haven't seen a mad dog in years, and though a couple of rattlesnakes were killed recently down at Lime Rock we have seen nothing more frightening than a couple of garter snakes and a very small milk snake. So we will go along with the Egyptians, even without a flood. We did get a rain, at last, and the drouth has been partially broken. Some pastures are as brown as October, but here in the valley we had a heavy first cutting of hay and the second cutting is now under way. Since the rain, field corn has shot up incredibly fast, and the first planting of sweet corn in our garden is in tassel and showing silk. Tomatoes are loaded with fruit and summer squash is being eaten. So are snap beans. And our peas, a bumper crop, were all gone before July 4, onto the plate and into the freezer. We never had such a crop of peas.

But the weeds that lay dormant during the drought have also sprung to life. This is the time the true gardeners are sorted out from the planters and yearners. You can tell a gardener now by the kink in his back and the callouses on his hands. The hoe handle is polished with sweat and the blade is bright with daily use.

Basswood has bloomed with its pervading sweetness. Milkweed is perfuming the evening air, fragrant as tuberoses. The sumac has its red fruit heads on display. The apple trees are loaded, the heaviest crop I can remember, on our trees at least. Little blackcaps, the wild raspberries, also had a heavy crop and in many places are still bearing. Red baneberries are gleaming at the roadside, a great display of them just up the road toward Bartholomew's Cobble, pretty enough to eat but sure to make the eater sick with their poison.

Birds still sing, though in a minor chorus, just before sunrise and maybe an hour afterward. If the afternoon has not been too hot they sing again at dusk. We hear wood thrushes every evening, and I heard two of them in competition at ten o'clock the other morning. One house wren has been singing almost every morning in the big spruce just outside my study, and now and then a catbird tries to fool me into thinking he is a brown thrasher or a song sparrow.

We have had more robins than usual. The other evening I counted eleven of them in the freshly mowed backyard, all finding plenty for a late supper. That was the evening Barbara saw the beautiful skunk. It came from the upper pasture in broad daylight and it moved with the grace of all the weasel family, seeming to flow in ripples that ran from its black nose to the tip of its tail, glistening black and pristine white. It was, as she said, strikingly beautiful. It went to the compost heap back of the woodshed and foraged there for half an hour. I was out in the yard the next evening when it came again, and it paid me no attention though it passed within 20 feet of me. I made no attempt to catch its attention, either. But we haven't seen it since.

Black-eyed Susans dapple the roadside with brilliant orange petals, Queen Anne's lace seems pinker than usual, and the streaks on the petals of some of the Bouncing Bet are almost crimson. Day lilies are fading. Daisy fleabane is everywhere, masquerading as early asters. Joe Pye weed has bluish-purple terminal leaves, forecast of the bloom to come.

Dog Days are right on schedule.

WE WERE playing around with words this afternoon, because it was too hot to do anything else, and we came up with some real singdingers. A singdinger, of course, is something with more oomph and bounce than a humdinger. I forget what started it, but it may have been a cramp Barbara had in her leg. We decided it was just a spasm in one of her legaments. You know, a ligament in her leg. Of course it may have been nothing more than the heat.

Anyway, we mentioned someone who was so liberal we decided he just had to be hideloose. And that led to the conclusion that, since he was quite outspoken, he was usually sidious in his comments and opinions because everyone knew what he was up to. And, because his appearance is by no means nondescript, he had to be described as descript.

These, of course, were onhand opinions, well considered.

Then we remembered the girl who, at age ten or so, said of a boy who was out of favor at the time, that he was "positively repungent." Asked what she meant by that, she said he was not only repugnant but that, in the language of her generation, he stunk. She was the one who, when she found a hard-shelled animal she couldn't quite identify, decided that it must be either a tortle or a turtice. At least those names had to suffice until she knew that it was either a tortoise or a turtle.

After that we got back to a few of our own. There was, for example, the banhee who howled in the night. We knew, from the bass voice, that it had to be a male, because a banshee always howls soprano, or at least alto. There was the drinkard, the fellow who drank a lot but never seemed to get drunk. And there was the bibulouse, the bibulous louse.

There was the fellow who took disaster in his stride, actually throve on it, and we decided he always was crestrisen. And there were all those uptrodden people who haven't a complaint about anything. Actually, they usually are upcast in their attitude toward life. You might even say they are socially jected, though you couldn't say that anyone is rejected who hasn't been repulsed more than once. That, of course, led to the possibility that you have to be pulsed before you can be repulsed. And of course you can't be rebuked until you have been buked.

We both know a certain gossip who always gets her news wrong, so we decided she must be an eavesdripper, not a full-fledged eavesdropper. Or maybe she was just a half-fledged eavesdropper. And since another person we know is always talking about her very dull ancestors, it seemed inevitable that all her grandparents must have been forebores.

We seemed to know a lot of odd-balls—and odd-belles. There was the man who spent most of his time thinking up hopelessly shady business deals, so we labeled him an abyssness man. Far-fetched, maybe, but I can't think of a more near-fetched way to describe him. There was also the fat man who was always making unqualified statements in a loud, firm voice. Obviously an adipositive fellow. And there was the baffling grandparent, the anagrampa.

These, of course, were all datements of our imagination. We don't care for figs; the seeds get in our teeth.

Then there was the bridegroom-to-be who lectured his friends on the merits of marriage on the eve of his wedding. He became almost poetic as he delivered a bacheloreate sermon. And there was the woman who never lost her aplomb, no matter what happned—she was always plussed, never nonplussed. There was another woman who decided, for the first time, to take off a few pounds. So she went on a ducing diet. Eventually, of course, she would put it all back on, and then she would have to go on a reducing diet.

There were the guests who arrived unannounced and unwanted and had to be outvited at the door. There were the stray cats with high-piched voices who were caterwailers. There was the non-stop talker who was very hard to checkmute—checkmate, yes, but not really checkmute. And there was the shiftless fellow who had no enterprise at all. He was one of those people who seem to be endowed only with exitprise.

And when the power goes off in one of those failures that the power companies insist are nothing but outages, why not call it an illuminot? Or, if they insist on the word "outage," then why can't we call relatively normal operations innages? That, after all, is what the power company officials, and their press agents want, isn't it—a good innage, publicity-wise? Some of their announcements, of course, are publicity-stupid.

But by the time we got to that one we decided that the heat had got to us, or the drouth, or maybe just plain summer. Simmer, of course, is a better word for it, but that takes no imaginotion whatever. Or, since it's a pretty broad area, maybe it should be imaginocean. Anyway, it was almost time for the evening meal, so we turned to guesstronomical matters, that summer afternoon game called "What shall we eat?"

I HAVE BEEN doing a little homework. A man asked how many florets there are in a head of Queen Anne's lace, the wild carrot, and I didn't know. Somebody must have counted them, but I never saw the figures, so I decided to find out for myself. Now I know the answer, for one head at least, and I suspect that it will do for most heads of Queen Anne's lace. The figure? I am tempted to wait for guesses; but I doubt that many guesses would be very close. I found 2,450 florets in the head I counted.

The head I chose was a typical flat-topped head, an umbel as the botanists call it, 3 inches across. Actually, it consisted of seventy small individual clusters or umbels, each on a curved stem that brought it into the big head in the proper place. At the base of the whole head was a whorl of fourteen sepals, each one a long, flat, leafgreen spear divided into three prongs.

To count the florets in this head I plucked off one of the individual clusters and counted the florets on it. There were 35. I counted the florets on five such clusters and came out with the figures 35, 36, 35, 34. The average was 35, and probably the variations were errors on my part. Then I counted the total number of such clusters in the head, plucking them off one by one. They totaled 70. Seventy times 35 comes out to 2,450 florets for the entire head.

Having made my count, I examined a few of the individual florets under a 10-power pocket magnifying glass. Each floret was less than ⅛ inch in diameter, but under the glass I could see that they were five-petaled flowers with a greenish yellow center, a miniature ovary topped by a stamen. The petals were pure white, though the head of the blossom gave a slightly gray appearance. Those petals were all odd-shaped, much like the mitten-leaves of a sassafras tree. Each petal had a "thumb" to mar its symmetry. There was no order about these thumbs; some were on the right, some on the left. But I found no symmetrical petal, no matter how long I looked.

When I had removed all the individual clusters from the head, all the white blossoms, I found at the center four individual flowers. One was a fully opened deep purple-red floret, five-petaled like the individual white florets, and the petals mitten-shaped. One was an unopened bud of such a purple-red floret. Two were white buds with purple-red splotches on them. The fully opened dark floret was the "jewel," as it is sometimes called, at the center of the head. The unopened buds may have been alternate "jewels." I don't know. Nature sometimes does things that appear to be plausible but really aren't, in human terms at least. Perhaps those were stand-by "jewels." Perhaps they were mere accidents. Accidents happen in nature.

Anyway, there are the results of my homework with a head of Queen Anne's lace. Now I know that one head can produce at least 2,000 seeds. Often a single plant will have four or five heads. Ten thousand seeds from one plant certainly insures perpetuation of the species, though it is not exceptional.

The mathematics of this count interest me. I am not sure that there is significance in the figures, but I suspect that there is. Start with the individual floret, which has five petals. There is the figure 5. Take the fourteen sepals. Multiply that 14 by 5 and you get 70, the number of individual clusters that made up the whole flower head. Arbitrarily divide 14 by 2 and multiply the 7 you get by 5 and you get 35, the number of florets in each small cluster. And there were twice as many clusters as there were florets in each cluster; both numbers, 70 and 35, are multiples of the basic 5.

In the plant world there is a persistent basic number in each kind of plant, occasionally two of them. Five is a common number, five-petaled flowers being very common. Seven is less common, though it is occasionally found in stamens, infrequently in petals.

In Queen Anne's lace there appears to be an insistence on fives, sevens and their multiples. All of which merely points to the habitual order in plant life, a habit of organization that persists through all the members of each plant family. Members of the pink family, for instance, nearly always have five petals, five sepals and five stamens. In the poppy family there are four, occasionally twelve—3 times 4—petals. The mustard family is characterized by fours—four petals, four sepals, four long stamens and two short ones. There is nothing new about this. Botanists have known it for many, many years. I never saw it explained. I am not sure there is an explanation any more than there is an explanation of why dogs have four legs. Nature has her own reasons, and most of them add up to a system of order.

Anyway, I chose to count the florets on one head of wild carrot, and I have new reasons to respect the ways of nature. Some of those ways I'll never understand, but even the mysteries demand respect.

FOR SOME YEARS I have wondered whether the ornithologists who say that the birds stop singing by early July are perpetuating an old myth or whether the birds around here just don't know about that rule. If I listen at the right time of day I can hear bird songs all through July and even into August.

I am reminded of this because at this moment, at 8:30 in the morning of what has been forecast as another hot day, a house wren is singing like mad in the pear tree at the edge of our vegetable garden. He has sung like that, even at noontime, for weeks. And, though I do not classify the whippoorwill as a songbird—some do, simply because the whippoorwill's calls have a certain variety of notes—I have heard those monotonous fellows calling every evening for the past ten days. They were relatively silent for almost a month, probably during nesting, but now they are very vocal indeed from late dusk well into the night.

The actual songsters, however, are best heard now at dawn. There is still a dawn chorus around 5 A.M. It is neither so varied nor so long as it was back in May, but I can recognize the songs of robins, tanagers, orioles, cardinals, and grosbeaks. Not one of those birds sings more than an occasional snatch of melody after 6 or 6:30 now, which may be why they are supposed not to sing at all. It could be that those who say they don't sing at this time of year don't get out of bed in time to hear them.

In the evening, just before the whippoorwills start calling, I still hear the wood thrushes calling. They are the thrushes with the lovely, resonant contralto voices, and they still sing beautifully. I don't hear them every evening, but I hear them often enough to say that they haven't quit for the season.

I also hear the mourning doves, both morning and evening. They, too, are supposed to have retreated into the silence by now, but apparently the word hasn't reached them. They aren't as vocal as they were two months ago, but they are just as melancholy when they do call.

The best midday singer here in the valley is the catbird. We have two of them that prefer perches in low trees on the riverbank from which to sing—and jeer—half an hour at a time. One of them has fooled me repeatedly with his imitations. Catbirds, of course, are cousins of both the mockingbird and the brown thrasher, and are splendid mimics when they really want to sing. This particular catbird seems to take special delight in imitating a brown thrasher, repetitive phrases and all. I have listened to him for several minutes and would swear it was a thrasher; then the catbird goes into a typical flurry of squeaks and squawks as though laughing at himself, and there is no doubt of his identity.

I seldom hear a real brown thrasher now, but twice within the past week I have heard one sing for five or ten minutes. Both times were in midmorning and the day was hot and humid.

There are also several song sparrows around here who

sing, usually in midmorning but occasionally in the afternoon. I don't know whether the exuberant wrens inspire them or not, but when they do sing it usually is just after the wrens have put on a specially long and loud performance.

The late Aldo Leopold once made a study of birdsong and its relationship to light intensity. He found that the morning songs almost invariably begin later on cloudy days. He also found that a bright moon still in the sky would hasten the time of first morning song. And among the unexpected and unexplained findings Leopold made was that birds living in the city begin their morning songs at least ten minutes later than the same species living in the country. This had no connection with light intensity. Apparently the urban birds just got up a little later than their country cousins, maybe following urban habit.

This all agrees with the observation, made long ago and often confirmed, that during solar eclipses the birds that sing in the daytime stop singing and the evening singers start singing. I have even heard whippoorwills call during the darkest period of an eclipse. So obviously there is a relationship between the volume of birdsong and the intensity of the light, and the actual clock time has little to do with it.

But this doesn't explain why birds in our valley—and possibly elsewhere—are still singing after mid-July. All I know is that they do sing, and that they have sung year after year, when the old rules say they shouldn't. Maybe our birds don't read.

HOLLYHOCKS are in bloom and they, of all flowers, are typical of New England to me. That is in part because almost thirty years ago, on my first trip to New England, I seemed to see hollyhocks in every farmhouse dooryard and growing wild along many roadsides.

That first trip was made in July, on a vacation from a daily job in Philadelphia. I had two weeks in which to wander, and I drove up the west bank of the Hudson to Poughkeepsie, then turned northeast into Connecticut, not knowing that I was seeing the country I would some day call home. It was a strange land, placid in the July-hot valleys, green and cool on the hills. I came up through Salisbury and Canaan, on north through Great Barrington and Pittsfield, marveling at the maples, the stone walls, the plain farmhouses—and the hollyhocks. I went east along the Mohawk Trail, turned south on back roads, by-passed Springfield, Hartford, New Haven, and returned to Pennsylvania. I had seen a land new to me, old to American history. I knew I would come back eventually.

Remembering now, I think it was the tumbled hills of the Berkshires that most fascinated me. The hills, the stone walls, the small farms, the quiet villages, and the ubiquitous hollyhocks couldn't be forgotten. Now I know that these are only a few of the thousand things that are, to me, special to New England, and particularly to the Berkshire country, though not exclusively here.

The white church spires, the elms, the gracefully proportioned old houses, are traditional New England. Yet I have seen villages in Ohio, in Illinois, even in Oregon, that could be set down in Connecticut or Massachusetts and look completely at home. That is no accident. The early settlers in all those places were from New England and they took with them their village patterns and traditions. Early Oregonians even shipped pre-cut houses, complete with doors and windows, around Cape Horn so they might have the familiar homes of their tradition in that alien land. And I have seen towns in Kansas—they are called towns, not villages, out there—complete with central greens, white clapboard churches, classic houses, and hollyhocks in the dooryards. Free-staters, abolitionists, who went to eastern Kansas in the "Bloody '50s" of a century ago, established those towns in the pattern of their home villages here in Connecticut and Massachusetts.

But nowhere else is the combination quite the same. The snug farmhouses in the narrow valleys are different here—even though now so many of them have been taken over by summer folk or retired year-rounders from the cities. The stone walls are unique to New England, man-made monuments, actually, to the debris scattered over this land by the glaciers of twenty-five thousand years ago. The brooks, some of them unpolluted and relatively natural, hurry down the valleys and dawdle across the meadows in a particular rhythm and pattern. The maples and oaks thrive on the shallow topsoil and color in October as nowhere else in the world. Dandelions in spring, daisies and hawkweed in summer, goldenrod and asters in autumn, try the patience of New England farmers who cherish a clean meadow and a profitable crop of corn and oats. And hollyhocks bring a special glory to our dooryards in July.

Barbara, who is a Connecticut Yankee from away back, tells me that hollyhocks are not really special. Others try to tell me that hollyhocks are common because they are easily grown and persistent, and because they will tolerate neglect. The early farm wives, they say, had little time to pamper dooryard flowers. But I insist that hollyhocks were brought to New England for the same reason they were taken to Old England, for the sake of beauty, for the satisfaction of seeing those crinkled silken petals spread their color in midsummer. Hollyhocks, originally native to the Near East, were probably taken back to England by the Crusaders, who had an eye for beauty, floral as well as feminine. And they were brought here to New England by the very early colonists, not to eat or to provide an infusion to cure a fever or a bellyache, but just for beauty. Those settlers were tough and practical, but like all successful pioneers everywhere they had a streak of sentiment in them, thank goodness.

So here are the hollyhocks, New England as a stone wall or a Seth Thomas clock. They still come in the fine old whites and pinks and honest reds, as well as the newer shades. They are gnawed by Japanese beetles, infested with rust, get crown rot and root diseases, but they persist. If the year should ever come when they fail to bloom, something will have gone from New England, something lovely, something beautiful. But I doubt that such a time will come, for hollyhocks, like old New Englanders, are of a tough, enduring strain.

BOUNCING BET is in bloom along the roadsides, great banks of it, pale pink and sometimes almost white. We know it as a weed, but it came here originally as a garden flower and useful herb. Its botanical name, *Saponaria,* indicates that it can be used for soap, and at one time its roots were in demand as a shampoo, particularly by our pioneer women. In the South, it is often called My Lady's Washbowl.

Bouncing Bet belongs to the pink family, and every time I look at the pink family in a botany handbook I am struck by the number which are "escapes," plants brought here originally from Europe and now gone wild in great numbers. The dainty little Deptford pink and the Maiden pink were garden flowers originally. I don't know whether bladder campion, another of our roadside weeds today, was originally a garden flower or not. Bladder campion and corn cockle and ragged robin and even the pesky chickweed were imports originally.

Go through any wildflower handbook and see how many common weeds of meadow and roadside are not native here. For example, we have only one native American mint, *Mentha arvensis,* which, oddly enough, has no common name except wild mint, as far as I can find. All the others, pennyroyal, horse balm, wood sage, spearmint, peppermint, bugleweed, hyssop, horehound, the bergamots and all the rest, were originally imports.

Queen Anne's lace, already showing flower along the roads, is another import, though you would never suspect it from the way it has taken hold and spread. So is its cousin, the wild parsnip. Go on through the parsley family, to which they both belong, and you find close to a dozen more than were originally strangers here. Toadflax or butter-and-eggs, actually a wild snapdragon, came originally from Europe. So did the plantains, which are now persistent weeds in practically every lawn in the land, not to mention their hold in less conspicuous places.

The wild asters are our own, but feverfew and tansy both escaped from Colonial gardens planted with seeds from Europe. Nobody has yet, to my knowledge, pinned a foreign origin on burdock, but the common thistle *Circium lanceolatum,* wasn't here until Europeans came. The same is true of the Canada thistle. And chicory, of course, was brought here from Europe because its roasted roots were added to coffee to make a brew that was, and still is, a libel on the word "coffee." Hawkweed, sometimes called king devil or devil's paint brush, came from England in the 1880s, and see how it has spread since then!

Plants travel with man, as well as with animals. The first European settlers here brought weed seeds with them inevitably. They came in their crop seeds, and they came in straw used for animal bedding or feed aboard ship. They even came in the settlers' clothes, probably some of them such tiny burs and stick-tights as those we know as begger's ticks. Now and then the incoming ships were cleaned up and swept out, and the dust and litter in their holds had alien seeds among it. We know this because the old records show that a good many plants from Europe were first seen here around the docks and landing places. From there the seeds were scattered along the paths and roadways, and in due time they appeared all along railroad right-of-ways, carried by the trains themselves. I have no doubt that botanists are now finding strange plants from far away on or near the airports to which the transoceanic air liners come.

In the old days, travelers, even Marco Polo, noted how plants from far away gradually spread along the caravan routes. The seeds were carried by the animals as well as by the men in every company, unnoticed members of the caravan. Here and there a few seeds were shaken off or discarded with the litter, and when they found soil and climate that suited their needs, they grew. No doubt the Crusaders brought back a good many weeds with them, unwittingly, as well as the assortment of flowers and useful plants they brought by intention. Many of the wild plants in European meadows are said to be more closely related to natives of Asia than they are to known European native plants.

Betty Flanders Thomson, associate professor of botany at Connecticut College, says that the list of native New Englanders, the common and conspicuous field flowers, includes only milkweed, cranesbill, robin's plantain, steeplebush, asters and goldenrod. All the rest came from across the seas, even the daisies and most of the buttercups.

So when I go out and see Bouncing Bet at my roadside, and when I walk half a mile along that road looking at the wild flowers, I am seeing a record of immigration. Most of those plants came from somewhere else, originally; like the rest of us immigrants, they liked it here.

THANK THE INDIANS. They were the ones who created corn from some obscure Central American grass, by a process of selective breeding that still amazes those who try to trace its origins. The specific name, maize, comes from the old language of the natives down Guatemala way, and there is little doubt that the corn we know was brought to this northern part of the continent from Mexico and the West Indies, though nobody knows when. It was long ago, long before Columbus blundered onto Hispaniola.

So eat up now, as sweet corn comes to its prime, and thank the Indians.

When Jacques Cartier, the first European to enter the St. Lawrence, arrived there he saw huge fields of maize cultivated by the Indians at what is now Montreal. That was in 1534. In 1604 Champlain found maize being grown almost everywhere from Nova Scotia to the upper Ottawa area. When Marquette, Joliet, La Salle and the other early French explorers made their way down the Mississippi Valley they saw the Indian equivalent of today's cornfields in Iowa and Illinois and all the way down to the Gulf, from Minnesota to Louisiana and Texas. When Coronado made his mad trip in search of legendary Quivira in 1540 he saw cornfields from Mexico to present-day Kansas and Nebraska. And the Indians of New England were famous for their corn.

Praise Massasoit. Remember him in your prayers.

"Plant four grains in a hill," the Indians told Thomas Hariot, inquiring of their methods in 1586, "and be sure the grains do not touch. Plant a fish with the grains. Tend the maize with care, and when the kernals on the ear are full of mother's milk, pluck it and roast it in the fire." If they roasted more than they could eat, they dried the roasted corn and saved it. Often they had special cooking pits for corn, and sometimes they had special ovens. Corn was so special that they had gods who looked over it, gave it their particular care. The corn gods were very special beings.

When it was left on the stalk to mature, corn was used in many ways. It was leached with wood-ash lye and became hominy. It was ground into meal for ash-cakes and pone and mush. It was parched and ground into meal for special occasions. It was stored, whole and in the ear, in bins set on posts to keep it from the dampness and the mildew of the ground. From the Indians we learned the simple principle of the corn crib.

Pluck it prime, cook it reverently, be generous with the butter and judicious with the salt. And remember that wise and helpful Indian who was named Corn-Planter. He was a great man.

When the white men came to New England the Indians were growing four varieties of corn. One was for roasting ears. One was for storage and for meal. One was popcorn. And one was specially grown for succotash. There are various recipes for succotash, but basically they are all a combination of corn and beans, which the Indians grew together. "Plant the corn," they said, "and when the corn has grown to the height of a man's knee, plant the beans beside it. They will grow and give you succotash, loving each other." Some say the beans were green, snap beans as we call them now, when used in succotash. Some say they were ripe, dry beans, though it is hard to understand how one could have dry beans and roasting-ear corn at the same time. Some say they were lima beans; but limas were not common this far north.

Succotash is for later. Now eat the green corn from the ear, standing not on ceremony. And remember whence it came.

August was the Moon of Green Corn. August was a favored time, and there were Green Corn festivals. In July there were festivals to the pollen of the corn, especially in the Southwest. Corn pollen was holy, and the corn tassel was a symbol of fertility. In autumn there were other festivals, East and West, and among the symbols were the baskets of meal, corn meal, which represented plenty and the favor of the gods. Now we buy corn meal in a box and sometimes use it to coat fish before we fry them. The Indians, planting fish to nourish the corn, were away ahead of us and no doubt wiser. Somewhere along the way the relationship of corn and fish was reversed.

Among the Indians, especially those of the Southwest, there were many songs and chants about corn, and there were corn maidens and cornsilk women. We have seldom listened to those songs, and the loss is ours, for we, too, are a Corn People. Listen now, in August, when the green corn is ripe, and hear the echo of those songs.

Celebrate the roasting ear. Feast! And while you eat this food of the gods, this blessing of the earth, thank the Indians.

PECULIAR THINGS seem to have happened in the world of small animals this year. I keep hearing of unusually large populations of field mice, moles, chipmunks, squirrels and woodchucks, and I know that we have more woodchucks and somewhat more chipmunks here in the valley than at any time I can remember.

Only a week or so ago a friend near Pawling, N. Y., wrote to me that his farm is overrun with chipmunks. "They are digging holes everywhere. They remind me of the prairie-dog towns I knew as a boy in Dakota." And he added that in the past two weeks there has been an unusual influx of gray squirrels, for no reason that he can even guess.

The other evening a man only a few miles from here phoned to say his lawn was being riddled by moles. The grass, he said, is dotted with small mounds of fresh earth and the whole lawn feels spongy underfoot, heaved and tunneled with mole runs. Our lawn seems to be relatively free of moles, but I know of half a dozen places where they have become a plague.

Ever since late May we have been having woodchuck problems all up and down the valley. All the farmers have the same story—more woodchucks than ever before. Here on our place there is an unwritten law that the 'chucks can live in peace as long as they stay a hundred yards from the house and garden. Normally only a few break the law, but this year they have come down from the hill almost in squads. Some took up temporary quarters under the outbuildings and had to be dispossessed. Some days I can't look out a window or step outdoors without seeing anywhere from two to six of them in the home pasture. We have had to take steps, but at times it seems that when we get rid of one invader, two take its place.

Thus far we have had no particular increase in the

number of squirrels. And the field mice are still out in the fields. But this is a boom year for the other rodents.

Such population explosions of small animals occur from time to time. Those who have studied such matters have found definite cycles, basically ten-year cycles but often with three lesser cycles within the ten-year spans. We probably are in the ten-year period, when populations seem to reach a peak. There are other factors, of course, but drouth doesn't seem to be one of them. The major factor is predators, and even among the predators there are these cycles.

For most of these small rodents, particularly chipmunks, field mice, voles and woodchucks, the most effective of the predators are foxes, skunks, weasels, bobcats, hawks and owls. If these predators are killed off or sharply reduced in numbers, the rodents increase doubly fast. Normally such an explosion in numbers is followed by disease, which eventually cuts down their population. But it may take a couple of years for diseases to thin them out. If the natural predators, the foxes, bobcats, hawks and owls especially, are not killed off they reduce the excess numbers much more quickly. The balance between foxes and woodchucks in any area has been studied many times. Kill off the foxes and you are almost certain to be overrun by woodchucks.

It is basically the same situation they have in the West, with coyotes and gophers and ground squirrels. The stockmen say the coyotes are killing lambs and calves, and they put on a campaign to rid the area of coyotes. The coyotes are decimated. Within a few years the area is overrun with ground squirrels, gophers and rabbits. Then the stockmen say these animals are destroying the grass, and they start a campaign to get rid of them. Had they let things alone to start with, the coyotes would have maintained a healthy balance, kept the rodents in check.

It may be that we are seeing something of the same sequence. Bounties on bobcats have encouraged their destruction. The foxes have been thinned out. Hawks have suffered both from the stupidity of some hunters, who will kill anything that flies or runs, and from the effects of DDT. So we now have a cyclic explosion of the other rodents, possibly including rabbits, and the natural predators that would help keep them in check are missing. The rodents will overpopulate, and we will have to wait for disease to thin them out again.

Meanwhile, here they are—and at this very moment I see a woodchuck in the vegetable garden . . . Well, that woodchuck paid the penalty. But I wish we had a few more foxes on the hill. They would be a great help. Anybody got a few spare foxes I could borrow?

THE CHANGE always comes about mid-August, and it always catches me by surprise. I mean the day when I know that summer is fraying at the edges, that September isn't far off and fall is just over the hill or up the valley. This year it happened yesterday.

Three evenings ago we had a storm that broke the August humidity, vicious lightning and a couple of downpours that lasted well into the night. The next day was a clearing day, clouds scudding and the sun, when it broke through, not as blistering as it had been. By evening the sky cleared, it cooled off and I heard the first katydid.

We never are overwhelmed by katydids, thank goodness, but we always have a few. I went outdoors to listen. This obviously was a katydid new at his fiddling. He was still tuning up, missing a few notes, rehearsing for noisy nights to come, but finally he got going right and kept rasping long after I came indoors.

I had my warning. But I couldn't quite accept it. But yesterday, while having my first cup of coffee about 5:30, I looked out and saw the sun lighting up the whole mountainside and knew the change had come. I exclaimed, "Look at that light! Fall is here."

Actually, it wasn't much different from the light the morning before, and yet it was brand new. The way the light fell, the sharp shadows, the deep blue of the sky, the clean green of the pasture, the deep green of the trees—it was all there, a brand new season. I went outdoors, both to look and to feel. The temperature was 56. It got down to 48 one night a few weeks ago, but it didn't feel like anything more than a chilly midsummer night. This time it felt like fall, a fall morning.

A couple of jays began to scream. They flew up the valley, looking gray against the blue sky. Not another bird made a sound. Then a crow cawed in the distance, the autumn caw. Quite different from the summer caw, though I can't explain it. Something in the intonation. I went over to the riverbank. The water has been brown for days. That morning it was deep blue-green. A few day lilies were still in bloom, but they already looked out of season. The sumac, with its red fruit clusters, looked right, though. So did the milkweeds, with their fat pods. Without thinking, I looked across the river at the dead popple that is twined to the top with Virginia creeper. I expected to see it fiery with color. It was still green. It won't turn till mid-September, another month.

I came back indoors for another cup of hot coffee. Barbara, still in her robe, said, "It's chilly." Then she began worrying about the winter squash, which aren't ready yet, of course. And about the limas, which took quite a beating in the storm. Then she caught herself, just as I had, and said, "Why, it's only the middle of August!" And we started breakfast.

It was that way all morning. It was a wonderful day, a beautiful day. It was early autumn at its best. But we couldn't quite accept it, quite believe it. You know how it is when you meet somebody you know and like but where you don't expect that person to be? It takes a moment to adjust. Things are out of context. Well, that's the way it was with yesterday. We kept thinking about September and October and fall, and talking about it, and feeling halfway into next month. And then catching ourselves, saying, "It's still August."

But that didn't change the day, or spoil it. Nor did it completely contradict our thinking. We like to get out and go in the autumn, and though we didn't go anywhere we kept thinking we should. We wanted to. Our blood responded, our very bones. A few big white cumulus clouds came drifting up and across the sky, and we envied them. Their big, cool shadows drifted across the pasture and up the mountainside, tantalizing. Even the wind, which was just a breeze, was restless. It never really set in. It just went up the valley a little way, then came back.

So we went out and looked at the garden, and checked the corn, which had to be rescued after the storm and which was standing up quite well. At the beans, which had taken hold again. At the tomatoes, ripening fast after the first crop. At the fall lettuce, transplanted ten days ago and coming nicely. The garden knew what time it was. The garden knew it was still August, mid-August.

But all day I kept thinking of next month. I had one foot in summer, the other in fall. And no matter how hot it gets from now on, I'll not be able to get both feet back in summer again. The change came, the foretaste. I saw, and smelled, and heard, and felt autumn up the valley yesterday morning.

IT SEEMS IMPOSSIBLE that Labor Day is just around the corner, and then the autumn equinox and frost. What happened to summer? It seems only a couple of weeks ago that we observed the Fourth of July, and a week or so before that was Decoration Day. What happens to time?

The fact is that nothing at all happens to time. Time is the same as it always was. It is we, and our lives, that have changed. I sometimes think that the whole web of modern communications has entangled us in a speedup of life.

But that isn't quite true either, for we created that web and we submit to it. We participate in so many things that we complicate our lives to a point of frustration if not confusion. And that, I suspect, is one reason we keep reaching for instant solutions and immediate answers. Lacking them, we find the flood of new problems and new questions filling our days and robbing us of time. At least of the sense of time, of the margin we reach for in our lives.

It is like saying water is wet to say that life is complex. In one sense that is true, but life itself is not any more complex than it ever was. We have complicated living, the routines of our days and weeks. And the ironic fact is that while we have steadily reduced our working hours and increased what we call our leisure time, we seem to have lost the leisure itself. We can't go back, obviously, but I am sure there are many who remember with sweet pleasure the time they ate a leisurely evening meal, on an August day, then sat and talked or went out and sprinkled the lawn and let the dusk and darkness come, and the twinkle of fireflies and the first stars. Those days are gone forever, apparently.

There were weekends then, too, when families went on picnics or went to the lake or the shore and had a pleasant afternoon without having to fight traffic for three hours to get home. Weekends now seem to be hurried from Friday dusk till Monday dawn, and it is something of a relief to get back to the job and the routine where at least one knows the degree of haste demanded. Weekends now are more tightly scheduled than the week itself. Recreation has become an industry, and play is harder than work. Or maybe we have forgotten how to play and have to work at it, organize it, plan it, make it an organized chore.

I haven't the figures handy, but I suspect that what we call the service industries now rank right up with manufacturing in economic importance. Service, which theoretically does the things that take the work out of living and gives us more leisure. Household services, restaurants, laundries, lawn-care services, service stations for automobiles, travel service, hotels, motels, resorts. And labor-saving machinery, all the way from vacuum cleaners and electric can openers and electric toothbrushes to golf carts and power mowers and rotisseries for the home terrace. Timesavers. And what happens to the time saved? I know one thing that happens to it. A part of that time is spent taking the machines to the repair shop, begging someone to fix them, and going back to get them.

Meanwhile, we have all those problems and worries of everyone else thrown at us, every hour on the hour. If it isn't the problems of some other nation, it's the plight of the Red Sox or the Yankees. Or of some other area that is in a bind because of the drouth or the floods. Or another brush fire in Los Angeles. Or a strike in Detroit. Or a school of sharks off Long Island. We are not only allowed to participate; we are commanded to take part. We aren't allowed the time to think maybe this particular problem or personal crisis will be settled by tomorrow noon; we are told to bleed for it now, fill our lives with it, concentrate on it.

Curious, I just looked in the fat annual Almanac for the extended summary of August, 1965. The important happenings of that month, both national and international, were summed up in thirty very brief paragraphs, fourteen for national events, sixteen for international. Among the notable national events were opposition of physicians and surgeons to the Medicare program, a Ku Klux Klan march in Americus, Ga., a conference on the drouth in the Northeast and Senate approval of the foreign aid appropriation bill. Actually, the one memorable event of that whole month was the five-day riot in Watts, Calif. Internationally, the war in Vietnam continued to escalate, Singapore seceded from Malasia, the Soviet Union bought wheat from Canada, India and Pakistan squabbled over Kashmir, Egypt and Saudia Arabia agreed to cease fire in Yemen. Most of the entries are footnotes now, but we bled for them, or were commanded to, at the time.

What has happened to time? Nothing. There still are sixty minutes in every hour, twenty-four hours in every day. But it's sometimes hard to remember that, living the way we do.

I WAS WONDERING what ever happened to the barefoot boy, and I went to the village and there on the street, hopping painfully along the hot sidewalk, was the first barefoot youngster I'd seen in years. I don't count the barefoot teen-agers; I'm talking about kids too young to grow beards and sing phony folk-songs of protest. Kids like this one, who was only about five years old. The whiteness of his feet proved he wasn't habitually a bare-footer. Someone else noticed him and said, "That kid's going to blister his toes before he gets home and puts his sneakers back on. And if his mother catches him he may get a blistered bottom too." And right then I knew what happened to the barefoot boy. Somebody caught him about thirty years ago and put sneakers on him, and that was the end of an era.

I guess I must be getting along in years because I still remember the delight, the utter sense of freedom, when those first warm days came in May and I could take off my shoes and stockings and go barefoot. I lived in a Nebraska village, and I was less than ten years old because when I was ten we moved to the plains of Colorado where there was lots of cactus and one didn't go barefoot. But in that Nebraska town not far from the Missouri river, every kid in town, even including a good many of the girls, shed shoes and socks—long black cotton stockings, really—about the time the first violets bloomed. And they didn't get back into shoes, except for Sunday school and very special occasions, until September.

It wasn't for any economic reason, though it did cut down on the outlay at the shoe store. And kids' shoes cost a dollar or a dollar and a half a pair in those days. If you think that was cheap, just remember that eggs cost a penny apiece and butter sold for about 15 cents a pound. A man making $20 a week was in the chips. My father was in the chips, but I went barefoot just the same.

Maybe I am talking about a time that passed in New England somewhat earlier, because there was an east-west lag in customs in those days. Whittier's "The Barefoot Boy" was published in 1856, but I doubt that it marked the end of an era; more likely it was the heyday. And my casual research indicates that the rubber-soled, canvas-topped sneaker didn't come into general use as children's casual footwear until the 1930s at least. So some of my readers will remember, as I do.

The feel of hot dust between the emancipated toes was downright sensuous. So was the squish of roadside mud after an early summer rain. Lawn grass was wonderful, and we wore paths alongside the sidewalks in our goings and comings. Cement sidewalks were hot and board sidewalks were a bother because they often had slivers. But there was little blacktop or other paving so one could walk in the streets with little discomfort. There were boards with rusty nails, and there were horses, but somehow we managed to escape lockjaw—it wasn't tetanus to us; it was lockjaw.

We prowled the woods and fields barefoot. A clover patch was sheer delight, and even the bumblebees there were an exciting menace. Tough kids proved their mettle by stomping bumblebees with their bare heels. Of course, a fresh-cut field of oat stubble was a test of fortitude, but when one played follow-the-leader with the big boys one went through the stubble, or else.

And we went fishing. I keep seeing references to small boys who caught fish with bent pins and kitchen string, and every time I want to shout, "No!" I could be wrong. Maybe New England kids *did* catch trout and bluegills with bent pins, but if they did they were well behind those of us who were much closer to the limitations of the frontier. We used any string at hand, but we always used regular fishhooks. Why not? They cost only a nickel a dozen, and when you hooked a fish with one you landed it. Every kid I knew carried two or three fishhooks stuck in a big bottle cork in his pocket, and he usually had a hank of hard-twist line, too. Thus he was equipped for fishing anywhere, any time. For premeditated fishing we used cane poles, but for impulsive fishing we cut willow poles from streamside brush. I never saw anyone fish with a bent pin.

But there we were, free as rabbits from May till September, dressed only in bib-overalls, sometimes a shirt, never shod. There were barefoot penalties, of course: Slivers, thorns, sore toes, stone-bruised heels. And one had to wash his feet before he got in bed. But what rewards we had! I wonder that no psychiatrist has come up with a theory about the damage done to the juvenile ego when his feet were clapped into sneakers for the summer.

"THIS LITTLE BEAST," my friend said, "looked like a mouse except that it had a long, tapered nose. It jumped right at my cat and hung on the cat's face until she clawed it off. Then it got away. The cat couldn't catch it, or didn't at least. Could it have been a shrew?"

It undoubtedly was a shrew. A shrew looks something like a long-nosed mouse, it wouldn't hesitate to attack a cat, and it has musk glands that make it distasteful to cats. Cats occasionally kill shrews, but they almost never eat them. Owls, bobcats and weasels do eat them. But owls eat skunks, too, which proves more about the strength of an owl's stomach than the discrimination of its palate.

My friend knew something about shrews though she had never seen one before. She had read about them, but never thought that they might be right in her back yard. Actually, shrews are in a great many back yards as well as in the open meadows and woodland, but they are so busy and so furtive that few people know they are there. I am sure there are a good many shrews here on my place, especially along the riverbank—they like damp places; but I have seen only three or four in the years I have lived here. Every winter I see their runways in the snow and in the summer I can spot their paths in the leaf mold and litter at the damp edge of the woods.

Ounce for ounce, the shrew is probably the most ferocious animal there is. One reason is that shrews are always hungry and seem always to be hunting for something to eat. The shrew's rate of metabolism is more than twice that of a human being, and it needs to eat often. Shrews have been known to eat three times their own weight in twenty-four hours, and they have been known to starve to death in a few hours when deprived of food.

Fortunately, shrews are small animals. The pygmy shrew is the smallest mammal in America, only about 3 inches long from nose to tail tip, and weighing about one-twelfth of an ounce, about the same as one dime. The masked shrew, common in our area, is somewhat bigger and will weigh twice as much, as much as two dimes. And the short-tailed shrew, also common everywhere east of Nebraska, is as much as 4 inches long and may weigh almost an ounce.

One of the largest shrews, but still well under an ounce in weight, is the water shrew. It lives near ponds, brooks and streams in southern Canada and into our area. It has rather large feet, and the feet are fringed with stiff hairs. So equipped, it can actually walk on water, apparently supported by surface tension. It also dives and swims, and it lives on all kinds of small aquatic life.

The first shrew I ever saw, the first live one, had just captured a monarch butterfly. I was out in a field and saw the butterfly in the grass, fluttering frantic wings. I leaned over to see what was going on, and I looked right into the face of a shrew. It wasn't what you might call a friendly encounter. The shrew was crouched on the butterfly, sleek, gray-brown, the size of a very small mouse. Its nose was long, pointed and shiny-black. Its eyes were tiny and beady. Its mouth was open in a snarl, and that mouth was full of sharp little teeth. It uttered a high-pitched kind of growl, definitely a warning; which was absurd, for I had no notion of challenging that little demon. I straightened up and the shrew nipped the wings from the dead butterfly, looked at me again with that defiant snarl, and gulped the body of its prey. Then it darted off into the grass. Not running away from me, but looking for something more to eat, a cricket, a grasshopper, a beetle, any live thing, even a baby bird.

I once saw a shrew chase a field mouse down a cowpath in the home pasture. The mouse was so frantic and the shrew so intent on the chase that neither saw me though they practically ran over my feet. And once I saw a shrew emerge from a mole-run here in the dooryard. It was a new run and I was standing beside it, wondering if I should take measures; and suddenly the earth heaved and this shrew popped out, glared at me, seemed to decide I wasn't worth killing, and dived back into the run. I suspect that he caught up with the mole, somewhere down there, for the run was never extended another foot.

I have no grudge against shrews. They eat a lot of insects and other vermin, and as far as I know they do me no damage and are not in any sense nuisances. All I insist is that they stay the size they are. And I am quite sure that my friend's cat, if she were capable of such thought, would agree with me. Shrews are not only aggressive and incredibly vicious; their saliva is poisonous, as venomous in a way as snake venom. It can kill a mouse or a bird, and it can cause a painful but not really dangerous wound if a shrew bites a man. If shrews grew as big as house cats, they would be more dangerous than man-eating tigers.

CITY FRIENDS stopped past a few days ago and said, "How restful it must be up here in the summer! Nothing to do but relax and get a good tan and eat your fill of garden-fresh vegetables." I said, "You don't know the half of it," but I didn't try to tell them the other half. It would have taken the rest of the afternoon, and I still had a whole day's work to do after they went their leisurely, relaxing way in midafternoon.

The lawn needed another mowing, and before I could mow it I had to pick up three bushels of windfalls under the apple trees. When that was done I had to get out the duster and give the cabbages and Brussels sprouts another dose of rotenone, because the cabbage butterflies are still busy. There were summer squashes to pick, and snap beans. And the corn was prime for freezing. The sonic booms which shook the living daylights out of the house yesterday broke two windows, and I should replace the panes; but that meant a trip to the village, so I let the windows go for now.

That's the way it has gone. The flower garden has become a weed patch, and if I don't get at things there it will be a weed patch next spring and all next summer. The bushes beside the house need a drastic pruning if we are going to be able to see out the windows much longer. The birds—and maybe the chipmunks, too—are nipping the tomatoes and must be discouraged if we are to get any tomatoes to can. The lima beans are fattening pod, will demand a picking in a few more days, and that means shelling and blanching and freezing. There's a patch of young poison ivy that should be given a dose of ammate before it's too late. The German weed, as we call it—the botanical name is *Galinsoga,* and it is a pest if there ever was one—should be pulled before it takes over the whole garden. There is jelly to be made. We shall skip the pickles this year. No time.

The other evening we dropped everything and went out and walked in the pastures for fifteen minutes, just to look. It seemed only a week ago that we saw the bloodroot in bloom, and now the goldenrod was gilding the fencerow and the milkweeds were in fat greenish-silver pod, ready to pop in another three weeks or a month. The crow's nest in the clump of white birch at the edge of the woods is now empty. The fledglings grown and on their own. The flickers are getting restless. I haven't seen a cowbird in two weeks, and the swallows are scarce, most of them already gone south. We heard a barred owl the other evening.

"How restful it must be up here in the summer!"

I haven't even had time to go up and see if the wild plums are ripening a crop this year. I saw them in bloom, from a distance, and I said that I would gather enough to make jam when they were ripe. I may yet, but the prospects aren't good. I may have to go up on the mountain to see why the spring line isn't delivering its full quota of water, and if the trouble is simple, no more than a couple of hours' work, I may get to the plums. But I distrust that spring line. Meanwhile, we are "on the pump," which keeps water from the well in the lines. And the pump hasn't thrown a tantrum yet. The woodshed lost a few shingles in one of the windstorms, and they should be replaced before winter. But the roof doesn't leak, so I've let it go. The front porch steps need a coat of paint. The compost piles need turning.

We thought we could get over to the Cape for a couple of days. Friends there insisted. Now we'll be lucky to get there by October. We had plans, back in May, to spend a few days in New Hampshire before the summer was over.

And we haven't been away from home half a day up till now. When the wanderlust hits too hard we drive over Cooper Hill and back, maybe 10 miles in all, and watch the long light of evening.

I did take time the other afternoon to cut back the mulberry tree that insists on growing beside the garage door. It was scratching the car every time I drove out or in. Some day I'll get time to kill the root of that tree, maybe, or dig it out. And I pulled down the wild grape and woodbine that are fighting for a foothold on that end of the garage. Last spring I made a brief campaign against the plantain on the side lawn, but it recovered and I haven't got at it again. Maybe I can resume the battle next spring. If I'm not too busy fighting the cypress spurge in the home pasture.

There's no doubt about it, summer in the country is restful, even relaxing—for visitors. Not for those who live here the year around. When the phone rings you can spot the transients, if not by their voices, then by their invitations. "Come on over this afternoon. We haven't a thing to do and we'd love to see you." The others say, "Won't keep you a minute. Just wanted to know how you are. We'll get together in the fall. After things quiet down a little."

A CORRESPONDENT from over in New York State tells me that she found three or four trilliums last spring that had four leaves instead of the usual three and bloomed with four petals, freaks in any man's language. She carefully dug up a couple of them and moved them to her dooryard to watch them next spring and see if they persist in their violation of the family traits.

Those trilliums are mutations, of course. All forms of life seem to have them occasionally, and there seems no doubt that mutation plays an important part in evolution. Something happens to the genes and an offspring takes a sudden leap off in an unexpected direction. Sometimes the mutant reproduces the same changes, and a new variety is produced. Sometimes the mutant is sterile, and sometimes its offspring revert to the original pattern.

Last summer a friend of mine who had a light heart attack was told to walk every day, so he took to roaming the country roads around this area. He had a latent interest in natural history, and here was botany at every roadside. He began to see plants, really see them, for the first time, and he began to find odd flowers, especially on the black-eyed Susans. Watching for them, he turned up a surprising collection of freaks before the summer was out. He found black-eyed Susans with double rows of rays, some with double centers, some like Siamese twins—two flowers merged but with their individual identities still evident. He found Susans with only half a dozen petals, Susans with quilled petals like dahlias, Susans with no petals at all, like outsize tansy blossoms.

Why all these variants, all of them freaks, should have appeared among the black-eyed Susans that year, I have no idea. He walked the same roads again this summer, his eye as keen as ever, and he found only two or three such freaks. The mutants didn't reproduce true to their variations, apparently. And some condition that distorted them last year wasn't present this year.

Every year we have a few freaks among the yellow crookneck squashes in the vegetable garden. Some of them are Siamese twins, joined their full length but still recognizable as two individual squashes. This year I found at least half a dozen such freaks. I have no idea why. None of the other squashes showed the same tendency. And the yellow squash vines grew from seed Barbara had from last year, the same packet of seed that produced only a couple such freaks last summer.

Among the sweet corn rows this year I found several freak ears. I have seen them occasionally before, ears that had a rudimentary tassel at the tip, a kind of hermaphrodite ear. I found at least four of them this year. Why, I don't know. I don't even know whether they grew on stalks from last year's seed or this year's, since we planted some of both. But there they were.

I hesitate to say that atomic fallout has anything at all to do with these strange things. Such freakishness is not new, by any means, and it is quite possible that my discovery of more this year than ever before was sheer coincidence. I have no explanation for the freak black-eyed Susans of last year, either. It doesn't even seem likely that the sprays that have been used as weed killers and insecticides should have been the cause, though we do know now that some of those insecticides have radically changed the form and tolerance of insects and have impaired the fertility of birds and possibly animals. It is conceivable that the weed killers, now used so generally by farmers, have an effect on the genes of plants they aren't supposed to affect, but I have seen no statements about that.

And, of course, it could be that we are in a sun-spot cycle that is doing unexpected things. There is biological evidence that animal life and probably plant life, as well, responds to those sun-spot cycles in ways we do not yet understand. Durward L. Allen, in his book *Our Wild Life Legacy* of a few years back, dealt with this in several exciting and provocative chapters. But he hadn't the answers either.

All we know, really, is that nature's balances are precarious and dependent on matters that we still don't understand fully. If we keep tinkering with the atmosphere we may provoke nature into creating two-pronged mosquitoes and twin-headed cabbage worms. Four-petaled trilliums are mere curiosities, but it could be that that gun we are playing with is loaded with really terrifying things.

NOW a zoology professor, Dr. Richard V. Rovbjerg of the State University of Iowa, finds that crayfish get tense and jumpy when they have to live in the midst of a crowd. Without a little elbow room, they and other small aquatic animals, the zoologist has found, have trouble with their nervous systems. And the crayfish haven't yet evolved their own psychiatrists, apparently.

What Dr. Rovbjerg has discovered sounds very much like the "shock disease" other researchers found among animals some years ago, when they were studying overcrowding of squirrels, rabbits, deer and other game animals. Their reports make the kind of reading that should make man stop and think, but the reports were printed mostly in scientific journals and didn't get much widespread publicity. Anyway, the prognosticators who were getting the headlines at the time were talking about human population explosions and living space and farm crops, and reviving the theories of Thomas Malthus of 150 years ago. The Malthus idea, roughly stated, was that man reproduced so fast he would eventually starve the whole race to death.

Well, this "shock disease" was a new approach, fundamentally, and it still deserves attention. To my mind it has implications that man ignores at his own peril. It applies to every crowded area on earth, including our own cities and the whole urban complex, as the planners call it, that is spreading along both coasts of this country and in many inland areas.

At a certain point of population density, the animal researchers discovered, certain physical changes occurred. Most of these changes were in the glandular system, particularly the pituitary and adrenals. Those are the glands more directly affected by such emotions as fear, anger and pain. When an area became crowded, many of the animals in that area showed a shortage of blood sugar, enlargement of the adrenals, reduction of sugar storage in the liver, degeneration of the liver, and definite changes in the whole chemistry of the blood. These changes made the animals prime targets for diseases that normally would have been of slight consequence. Many of them died of those diseases.

But others did not die that way. They simply went mad. Not rabid mad, but frenzied mad. They ran in circles as though blind, bumped into objects, injured themselves without seeming to be aware of the injury. Their nervous systems degenerated. Sometimes, even with food at hand, they failed to eat. Sometimes they just went into a kind of lethargy and lay down and died, and sometimes they had a sort of screaming-meemies and died. And when they were examined after such death, their bodies showed no fatal disease except that disintegration of the nervous system. They died of "shock disease." They couldn't stand living in the crowd any longer; that was about the sum of it.

This condition was found first among fox squirrels in Michigan. They had fatal seizures when they grew excited or when they overexerted. Some became too weak to climb trees. Some failed to eat. Some just didn't run when a predator appeared. Then, also in Michigan, similar symptoms were found among crowded skunks. They acted crazy and irresponsible. Some died in their dens. Examination showed that their nervous systems had gone to pieces and they had a variety of encephalitis. Then it was found among snowshoe hares with symptoms much like those among the fox squirrels. The hares simply went crazy, didn't know enough to come in out of the cold or even to eat their meals. They, too, had "shock disease," enlarged glands, bad livers, shortage of blood sugar, all the rest of it. They couldn't take life in the midst of a crowd, so the nervous systems gave way. And finally someone remembered a report on the Kaibab deer when they were so overcrowded, in 1926–27. The actions of the deer tallied—they too obviously were suffering from the "shock disease."

And now this researcher in Iowa finds the same kind of thing among the crowded crayfish, though he doesn't call it "shock disease." The symptoms seem to match right up with all the other cases.

There is no need to draw elaborate parallels. They should be obvious. Whether man admits it or not, nature has all kinds of ways to keep the populations in check, and this is one of them. We have, all around us, examples of crowd madness of one kind or another, though we use other names for the malady. There isn't much doubt that "shock disease" is afflicting mankind right now. If you doubt it, look up the statistics on sales of tranquilizers. Or look at the totals of the highway kill on any long holiday weekend.

V

We had the last full moon of summer last night. The next one will be the Harvest Moon. I have to say this fast and right away quick, to get my say, because a lot of people want to argue about these things. Statisticians, who are more interested in figures than in moonlight, insist that the Harvest Moon is the full moon nearest the autumn equinox and can occur as early as September 7 or as late as October 7. That's all right as mathematics, I suppose, but lacking in back-country logic. To my mind, the full moon isn't the Harvest Moon unless it comes between mid-September and October 1. Before that, it's just the last full moon of summer. After that, it is the Hunter's Moon. End argument.

Anyway, the moon will soon be in its last quarter, and according to venerable moon-lore it will be a good time to cut chestnut, because chestnut cut then won't snap and spit embers in the fireplace. Yes, I know all about the present shortage of chestnut trees to cut for firewood or anything else, but it's still true. Something to remember if we ever have chestnut trees again.

This is also a good time to cut hemlock and split it, if you have any particular need for split hemlock. And it is a good time to set out young trees, according to the old lore. And, finally, it is a good time to go fishing. That makes sense. Any time in September, or when a man can get away in any comfortable month or moon's phase, is a good time to go fishing. I do wonder, though, if fish study the moon's phases.

There is also the old belief about the moon's effect on the weather, expressed in this doggerel:

The moon and the weather
May change together.

To which some meteorologists, sticklers that they are, have added these lines:

But a change in the moon
Does not change the weather.

All of which adds up to about as good an equivocation as anyone could ask. I have heard it said during a drouth that it will rain when the moon changes. And during a wet spell I have heard it said with equal certainty that it will stop raining when the moon changes. Both sides in this argument have about equal chances of being right. Or wrong.

The moon, to be sure, does create the tides in the ocean, and those who set store by the moon's effects on the weather say that it also creates tides in the air. Maybe so, but those who have checked carefully tell me that the moon's phases do not alter the barometric pressure by more than 1/1,000 of an inch. They also say there is no connection between the moon and the progress of high and low pressure areas across the land.

Another of the old folk sayings was that you should slaughter live stock three days after the full moon to be sure of getting the best price per pound. So day after tomorrow would be a good day for butchering, I suppose.

But show me the farmer who would risk blow-flies now! Or the farmer who does his own butchering, for that matter. Nowadays beef goes to market on the hoof. And as for meat prices, I would say, judging by the prices we have to pay, we have been in this three-days-after-the-full-moon phase for months and months. Have you priced lamb lately? Or even sirloin steak.

Another bit of advice was to dig potatoes just after the full moon. That one makes sense all around. Wait for the next full moon, the Harvest Moon, and those potatoes may get frosted. We dug the last of our own potatoes last week, not because of the moon but because we were out of cooking potatoes. I may add that it wasn't a particularly good year for potatoes, in our garden at least. Others, I hear, had better luck.

One year we had our first frost on September 17, frost that whitened roofs and killed all the tender plants. That was the day after the September full moon, last year's Harvest Moon. We had frost again on September 19, down to 28 degrees. After that it warmed up, into the 70s and even the low 80s, for several weeks. I had to mow the lawn on October 15, in fact, which was ridiculous. We didn't get the next really hard frost until October 19. Then the chilly nights began. That was just three days after the October full moon, the Hunter's Moon.

Maybe there is some connection between the full moon at this time of year and the weather, despite what the statisticians say. I sometimes think we need a little more mysticism and imagination in these matters, a little less reliance on charts. Heaven knows that weather forecasting is a hazardous task at best in New England, but I have my doubts about the charts, which add up to climate, not weather.

In any case, we have now passed the last full moon of

summer and the next one will be the Harvest Moon. Look out for frost when it comes. Take in your late tomatoes and tender squashes if you want to save them. And if you have any butchering to do, take my advice and wait till then. Remember, three days after the full moon.

WELL, MAH FRIENDS, Ah'm happy tu say Septembah is heah, and even the gahden knows it. Ah'm specially happy to say the okra knows it. Ah've had mah okra, Southern style, and maybe now we can get back to the blend of Western-New England cooking that usually prevails around this house. Not all at once, though, because there are a few other culinary oddities that will have to be disposed of.

Let me hedge a bit before I go one word farther. Barbara is a wife of diverse talents, and among them is unusual skill as a cook. She is also a vegetable gardener of high talent and intuition. And she has a refreshing sense of adventure. All these abilities, and others, I cherish and admire. But when you combine cooking skill, gardening enthusiasm, and a sense of adventure, you sometimes come out with surprising results. Such as okra, Southern style.

When she was planning and planting, back in April and May, she said she was putting in a short row of okra. I raised an eyebrow. "For the blossoms," she said. "They are lovely!" Which is true. So she planted okra, for blossoms. The okra liked our soil, throve, came to lovely blossom. And the blossoms became pods, okra pods.

My wife is a practical person. She gardens to eat as well as to admire. True, we plant flowers in the vegetable garden, glads and single dahlias and zinnias, and we never eat them; though she did once wonder if zinnia buds would taste like nasturtium buds. I said no, and made it stick. But when a plant is an outright edible, she hates to waste it. So when the okra pods appeared she watched them a few days, then began gathering them. I asked what was going on. "I'm freezing them," she said. "For what?" I asked. "For soup next winter. Just a bit of okra in a pot of soup . . ."

I let it pass, thinking to handle that one come winter. I was busy picking green beans.

The other day she said, "I've frozen enough okra." And went on picking it. She chose a panful of tomatoes. She got out a recipe from her big file box and went to the kitchen. Don't ask me how she did it—I'm just a second-rate short-order cook; but come dinner time and she put okra, Southern style, on the table. I looked, asked what it was, sniffed, and reminded her that I once spent some time in Texas, in Georgia, in Louisiana, and in North Carolina, and never learned to like grits, let alone okra. She said, "Try it." And I tried. I really did.

"Cad" is an old-fashioned word, but I guess I am one. But I plead for a hearing, if not a full pardon.

The first Thanksgiving after we were married Barbara said we would have delectable New England viands for Thanksgiving dinner. I asked what delectable viands, and she said, "Turnip, and creamed onions, and giblet gravy, and oyster cocktail, and plum pudding, and—" And I said, "Turnips?" She said, "Yellow turnips!" I said, "You mean *rutabagas?*" That was what she meant. I said, "Look. Where I come from rutabagas are cow feed. *People* don't eat rutabagas!"

We had rutabagas—pardon, yellow turnips—for Thanksgiving dinner. And the way she cooked them and seasoned them they were almost tasty.

But okra! Okra, Southern style! I can't prove this, but I suspect that cheap mucilage is made from an okra base.

So are the worst of gelatine mixtures. And the queezy gravies that slattern cooks serve. Okra is a flower, not a food plant.

So I am glad that September is now in its ninth day. When I went out to look this morning the okra was beginning to fade, with only two incipient blossoms and not a pod big enough to harvest.

Then I looked around the garden. And saw the salsify. Barbara planted salsify last spring, "just for fun." I raised no vigorous objections, though I once tasted salsify. It wasn't until the salsify was well up that I knew what was happening. Barbara dotes on oysters, and salsify is also called oyster plant. Thus far I have avoided digging any salsify, but I can't temporize forever. We shall yet have salsify on the table. She has a recipe.

All right, so I am not a gourmet. So I am a plodding person at the table. But I like corn and beans and lettuce, and pickles and relish and stuffed peppers, and baked beans and chile con carne, and bread and butter, and meat and potatoes—and, so help me, rutabagas. I like young milkweed, and boiled dandelions, and wild cress, and marsh marigolds. But there is a limit to this fun in the garden. For four years we grew peanuts, the first year for fun, the remaining years because we had the seed. We didn't eat a dozen peanuts, because Barbara doesn't like them. But, she said, it was a shame to waste the seed. I just hope she planted all her okra seed this year. And I hope she doesn't get the notion to plant castor beans next spring, "for their lovely flowers."

THE OTHER DAY I was talking to Albert, my neighbor down the road, about his corn crop, and he said, "When I was a boy we used to put corn into sows and husk it out later in the fall."

I said, "Put it into sows? What do you mean by that?"

Surprised, he said, "Why, just put it into sows. Bundles. Shocks."

I'd never heard the word used that way. To me, a sow was a female hog. But I finally ran it down in the unabridged Webster, where it is listed as a Scottish or dialectical English word for a stack or a heap. And I found that it is an old New England word, too, though little used nowadays. It probably went out of use with the arrival of the silage cutter and the mechanical corn picker, another victim of the machine age on the farm.

Probably any Yankee of middle age or older, particularly one with a rural background, would know the word "sow." But I am only a Yankee-in-law, as it were, and my ear perks up at many of the old regional words and expressions. They often have color and usually they make logical sense if one stops to puzzle them out.

When we first came to this lower Berkshire country Charley, my neighbor up the road, spoke of a barway. It baffled me, until I saw that what he meant was what I had always called a gate. But his word for it was logical. Most of the gates, as I called them, were closed by long cedar poles, bars, slipped into slots on each side. I had half a dozen barways on my place, and now they are barways even to me. The gate to the garden is still a gate—it is hinged; but there are no gates in the pastures, only barways.

Another word that baffled me at first was "sluice," sometimes lengthened to "sluiceway." A sluice, I learned, is what I used to know as a culvert, a pipe to carry water, usually from a brook, under the road. According to Webster, a sluice really should have a valve in it; but that is technical. Now I know that both the brooks on my place flow under the road and into the Housatonic through sluices.

"Brook" is another regional word, but no longer limited to New England. In the West a brook is a creek, and in the South it is a branch or a run. In many parts of the Midwest, however, a small stream is a brook, just as it is here and for the simple reason that most of the early settlers in Ohio, Indiana and Illinois came from Massachusetts and Connecticut. They took the word with them and it became native there too. But in the Mountain West, where a creek is definitely a creek, fly fishermen never catch "creek trout." They catch brook trout, or brookies. Which indicates who caught the first of those trout—New Englanders, of course.

Talking with a townsman just the other day I heard him say, "We sent a truck out to draw a load of sand." I constantly hear the word "draw" in that meaning among farm folk, a meaning for which I instinctively would use either "haul" or "drag." But "draw" is one of the old words, deeply embedded in these New England hills and valleys. It goes back to the days of oxen. It goes all the way back to England, to the Anglo-Saxon, and even has a root in Latin. I like it, though it still comes unfamiliarly to my tongue.

"Popple" is another native word with a fine old ancestry. The first summer I lived here a man spoke of the row of sugar maples on my land and said, "How do you suppose that maverick got in the row, that popple?" I had to smile, for in that one sentence he had used a cow-country word, "maverick," and an old New England name for the poplar tree. But he was right on both counts. That popple, a towering poplar, is a maverick, a stranger of another breed in that row of maples. But now it and all the other poplars on my place are, in casual conversation, popples.

I hear the word "piney" only occasionally, but it is a good old word that has Massachusetts roots. I have a whole row of "pineys," which more pretentious gardeners than I am call peonies, at the back of the flower garden. Piney, however, is not a strange word to me. My grandmother used it, in Nebraska. We often smiled at the word, though it was quaint and old-fashioned. But I learned, after my grandmother was gone, that she was more right than I was, for the name comes from a Latin word, *Paeonia,* which is much closer to piney than to peony. And my grandmother came by the word honestly. She had a grandmother from Massachusetts.

The regional words dim out, which is too bad. Radio and television have done them in, except in exaggerated regional skits. But they were good words, most of them, colorful words. I hate to see them go. In fact, I am going to bundle my sweet corn stalks into a sow this fall and tell all comers that it *is* a sow.

MAYBE this isn't an unusually prolific goldenrod year, but I can't recall one like it. Everywhere I go I see goldenrod. Roadsides are lined with it, neglected fields are covered with it. And something about the season makes it specially spectacular. I don't think it is merely the fact that the big purple New England asters are coming into flower right now in the midst of the goldenrod, though aster-purple always makes goldenrod-gold look twice as golden. The asters certainly haven't anything to do with the spectacle of three or four solid acres of goldenrod that I saw the other day on one side road. And they aren't responsible for the way the goldenrod has infiltrated my raspberry patch. It is beautiful there but I don't really appreciate the way it now advertises my neglect of the berries.

Out of long habit, I always think of goldenrod as strictly a fall flower. And I am perennially surprised when I see it come to blossom, the very earliest of the species, the first week in August. But there it is, year after year, and by September it is well along. If I kept a bee I probably would pay more attention to the goldenrod schedule. On a sunny September afternoon the goldenrod patches are as loud with honeybees as the clover fields were in June. A beekeeper friend once told me that he preferred late honey for his own table because it was so rich with goldenrod. There is always a generous touch of aster in it too, since the asters are also rich in nectar. Without goldenrod and asters, the bees would be out of business by early September.

The old notion that goldenrod causes hay fever has been pretty well disproven, though I now and then still meet someone who insists that it is sheer punishment to go near a patch of goldenrod. The allergists say this just isn't so unless the potential sufferer bends down and sniffs the blossoms. Goldenrod pollen doesn't reach anyone through the air. It is heavy and waxy, so heavy that even when it falls from the flowers it simply falls to the ground. The allergy comes from wind-borne pollen such as that of the grasses and that particular villain, ragweed. The allergic person usually is safe with any plant that the bees are working on because its pollen is too heavy to drift on the air.

Most of the goldenrods are native Americans. We have about a hundred species, and all Europe has only ten. Britain only one. Here in the Northeast we have about twenty-five species, ranging from the dwarf Alpine goldenrod, only about 9 inches tall, to the Canada, late, and rough-stemmed species that grow 7 or 8 feet high. There isn't much fragrance to any of them, but I often pluck a few leaves of the modest sized sweet goldenrod and crushed them just to get the scent, which is something like anise.

The Latin family name is *Solidago,* which means to strengthen. It refers to the longstanding reputation of goldenrod as an all-purpose herb. The herb folk used to gather the leaves and brew various concoctions with which to dose folk who were feeling poorly. Like many of those old herbal brews, but by no means all of them, goldenrod tea probably strengthened one's resolution to get well and escape further dosing with the stuff. Anyway, it must have strengthened something.

The old-timers, the healthy ones at least, used more goldenrod for dyeing—cloth, that is—than for medication. It was once known as "dyer's weed," in fact. It provided a rather strong yellow dye, not as rich as the color of the blossoms but good enough to brighten the winter garb of a good many pioneers. I once owned a patchwork comforter made of homespun, and the old lady who gave it to me never tired of explaining that the yellow pieces in it were dyed with goldenrod. By the time it came to me the yellow was a bit faded, by sunlight and soapsuds, but it was a reminder that goldenrod made a pretty good dye.

This same old lady told me that her mother had the notion that the fiber in goldenrod stems was valuable, and she even retted some of them and tried to spin the fiber, like flax. It didn't work, so she had to give up on that notion. She also tried to spin milkweed floss and make silk out of it. That didn't work either. No twist in milkweed fiber.

Curious, I once spent a couple of hours counting the florets on a plume of goldenrod. If you want to test your patience and your eyesight, try it some time. That one plume had 3,023 individual flowers, and each flower was made of five to ten florets each of which would produce a seed. A total of 15,000 to 20,000 individual florets which would produce enough seed to plant half an acre. That's one reason there's so much goldenrod this year.

A NEW WORD, to me at least, recently popped up—"bionics." As I understand, it is being used by some engineers to describe the application of knowledge about living organisms to the solution of engineering problems. For instance, researchers at Lockheed Aviation are exploring bionics to find out how mosquitoes can communicate with each other 100 feet away despite overtones of jet planes, thunder, sirens and other sounds that do things to human ears.

What this means, of course, is that the slide-rule and beaker boys are coming around to some of the matters that the nature folks have been dealing with a long time. They now even admit, in public, that the helicopter is a rather primitive contraption when compared to the flight skill of the hummingbird.

I have no intention of belittling the work of the engineers. But for too long the laboratory folk, some of them at least, pretty well alienated themselves from life outside the door, where there actually are answers to a whole raft of questions and even more questions that are worth finding answers to. Nobody yet knows why or really how birds migrate or navigate. I see that one scientist, at least, is now trying to find out how wasps, for instance, can navigate on cloudy days. The theory seems to be that the wasp has a kind of built-in celestial guidance system. Maybe so. Maybe the wasp has some contact with terrestrial magnetism, some innate sense of direction. I see too that they are now looking into the mechanism, or whatever it is, that enables some snakes, which have notoriously poor eyesight, to detect warm-blooded creatures nearby. Apparently it is some version of infra-red detection.

So far it seems that only naturalists have done much in solving the question of how bees communicate with each other. A bee returning to the hive with news of a specially rich patch of nectar can tell other bees what and where it is. The method seems to be a kind of dance, circular motions which have been charted and, to a degree, analyzed. But there may be more to it than that. It could be worth looking into.

Nobody to my knowledge yet knows a great deal about hibernation. I wouldn't care to indulge, myself; life is too short as it is. But I would like to know, and maybe others would too, how a woodchuck manages to go to sleep for six or seven months, and wake up full of life. How the whole series of bodily processes, from heartbeat to respiration, can be slowed down to the degree they are is one of the big mysteries. When we say, as we sometimes do, that the woodchuck reverts to a primitive, cold-blooded state during hibernation we aren't explaining anything. We are just saying that this happens.

In the same area of speculation, how come that some fledgling birds are "primitive" in the same way, cold-blooded and susceptible to death by exposure? Unless they are hovered carefully by a warm-blooded parent during that period, they perish. But after a few days the fledglings establish warm-bloodedness, and that danger period is past.

Or take the instance of the moth and the butterfly. Why and how do they go through such totally different stages, winged, egg, crawling worm, mummy-like crysalis, then winged stage again? And how does the woolly bear, to take one example, survive winter as it does? The woolly bears simply crawl up onto a beam or some such place, curl up and freeze solid. Then spring comes and they thaw and crawl out and find a plantain plant and are as good as new and twice as hungry.

Maybe somebody will be interested in the kingfisher's eye, eventually. It is a very strange eye, pear-shaped and with two sets of lenses, or a divided lens, maybe, I don't know. I do know that the kingfisher's eye can see under water, making just the right adjustment to account for the refraction, and it can also see in the air just as well as any bird's eye, which is very well indeed. Maybe somebody can find out how a hawk flying at 1,000 feet can see an object as small as a dime on the ground, and in the next instant can see a kingbird about to attack him from 10 feet away.

There are so many things—how a seed lives as long as it does, how half a dozen leaves and a big blossom can be packed into a hickory bud, how grass renews itself after it is mowed or eaten off, how a lizard grows a new tail. We don't know more than a minute fraction of the wonders that exist all around us every day. Some of them might be useful, if we could find the answers. A good deal more useful and important, it seems to me, than putting a man on the moon. I hope more good minds and intellectual discipline get to work on bionics. The whole idea leads back to fundamentals that cry for attention.

THIS IS WRITTEN on a Sunday morning, a dark morning with a slow rain falling. It began in the night and I wakened and heard it gurgling in the downspout and lay and listened, thinking what a pleasant sound it was. We need the rain. Then I slept again, content. And it was still raining, a slow, gentle rain that will soak into the ground and renew the springs and awaken the autumn brooks.

And now I wonder how soon we will hear complaints that the rain has spoiled the weekend, a weekend when there might have been long lines of travelers out to look at the color in the trees. The color is early, not yet at its peak but maturing fast, and it lures the visitors. But not in the rain. I can hear the complaints now: "Why does it have to rain on a weekend, when people want to get out and go? When they are willing to spend money for meals and gas and all the things we have to sell."

We are a strangely perverse species, aren't we?

A few years ago Walter Gropius, in a speech at Williamstown, said that we live in a "slip-cover civilization" based on "a Gallup poll mentality of quantity over quality." He was making a plea for the artist, for the creative mind and temperament, and he said sharp things about "our era of expediency and mechanization." He had dreams of a beautiful world, and he had ideas about what it should be.

Listening to the rain, I think of Mr. Gropius and his dream of a beautiful world. "The vast development of science," he said, "has thrown us out of balance . . . over shadowed other developments that are indispensable to the harmony of life." Then he went on to say that it is the obligation of "the form-giving artist, the creative architect or designer" to control "the visual manifestations of our productive life, that is, of our whole physical environment." And there he became the special pleader for one phase of art; and there he lost me. Beauty and balance, yes; but control of our whole physical environment, no. That, to me, leads to imbalance, to the arrogance that has upset the apple-cart time after time.

What is more beautiful than a raindrop, or a snowflake,

or the inconceivably complex patterns on every weedstem and bush on a morning glittering with hoar frost? And neither science nor art can improve upon any of these things. Or the beauty of an autumn leaf.

One autumn day a few years ago an industrial chemist who was visiting me went with me for a walk in the woods, and he stooped and picked up a swamp maple leaf and examined it. He asked about the color, and I explained as best I could about the sugars and the acids, the anthocyanins and the xanthophylls. Finally he asked, "What is the function of the colors? What use are they?" And I had to say that they really seemed to have no particular function or use except to create beauty, and no leaf was conscious of that.

"Then the color is sheer waste," he said. And, from the chemist's viewpoint, he was right. But from the viewpoint of a professional host or one who caters to travelers in color time, he was wholly wrong. The color is a commodity, transient as it is, a tourist attraction that draws business. And when it rains on a color weekend, rain is unwelcome. Color is sheer waste, to my chemist friend; to my friend who sells food and gasoline, color is dollars and cents in the till.

Are we out of balance? Definitely. We have been for a long, long time. Even in terms of rain we are out of balance. Otherwise there would be no drouths or floods, no deserts, no tropical jungles. If we really were in balance, scientific balance, it would rain every Thursday, say, and in prescribed amounts, no more, no less. It is this lack of balance that makes life livable, at least as far as rain and weather go. And I suspect that this may be true in other matters, too. A completely predictable future, a controllable environment, a man-made order of life, would be as dull as ditch-water.

And that would be the fundamental flaw in any world completely dominated by either the artist or the scientist. Life is not something that can be confined to a chart or a set of statistics; and life is not all esthetic perfection. The ideal, from either viewpoint, is as elusive as absolute truth. For that we should all be grateful. Given the ideal, what would we have left to dream about?

It looks and sounds as though it might rain all day. It is a sweet, gentle, benevolent rain, even though it does keep the color-watchers at home. I wonder what my chemist friend thinks about on a rainy day, and I wonder if Mr. Gropius had a really rainproof raincoat.

MAYBE it is because I just had my annual physical checkup and have been thinking about cancer, ulcers, blood pressure and all kinds of dire possibilities that didn't turn up in my own carcass. Anyway, a report from Purdue University's College of Agriculture caught and held my eye because it mentioned gastric ulcers in hogs.

Somehow, I never thought of hogs as being ulcer-prone. There was a time when I knew hogs at first hand, as most farm boys do, and I knew they can be temperamental, stubborn as mules, mean as bears with sore paws, supercilious and independent as cats. I also knew they catch all kinds of disease, on occasion. But I never thought they were worriers. Why should they be? They are pampered from birth to butchering; and anyone who has ever tried to make a hog go where it doesn't want to go knows what an uproar a frustrated hog can make. No hog I ever knew remained frustrated more than a few minutes—the human ear just can't stand the noise, and the only way to stop it is to stop frustrating the beast.

But the Midwestern hogs apparently do get ulcers. They first showed up about six years ago, and the vets who treated them thought it was a strictly local condition. Then hog ulcers were reported from Ohio, Wisconsin, Iowa, Kansas, Indiana, all the major hog-producing states, and the scientists went to work.

The first thing they found was that hog ulcers seem to follow the same seasonal pattern as human ulcers. They occurred most frequently in February, May, September and December. Why that particular cycle, I don't know. I didn't even know that human gastric ulcers followed that pattern, but apparently they do.

Then they found more ulcers in male hogs than in females, again following the human trend. There was no explanation for that, either. Maybe male hogs, like male people, worry more and keep more of the worries to themselves. Anyway, the research then centered on the male hogs. And finally a scientist at the University of Wisconsin department of Veterinary Medicine suggested that hog ulcers were related to psychosomatic stress. What causes that stress? High-pressure feeding and quick preparation for market, maybe.

With that theory for a starter, they tried easing the pressure on the hogs in the control pens. Once the pressure was off, the incidence of ulcers declined. Presumably, that psychosomatic stress was the villain. Given time to eat and not too much to eat, the hogs stayed well. At least their intestinal tracts didn't ulcerate. Under pressure, similar hogs in other pens developed bleeding ulcers that killed them.

Nobody drew any moral from these hog studies. The scientists were out to run down the cause of ulcers in hogs, not to draw parallels. So maybe nobody else should either. But it does seem in order to suggest that it fits into a pattern of stress and the consequences.

A while back another researcher found that crayfish

can't stand crowd pressures. As far as I know, nobody ever force-fed the crayfish for market, and nobody checked them for gastric ulcers. Maybe if crayfish were as financially important to as many producers as hogs are, they would have gone deeper into the matter. They might even have run cholesterol tests on crayfish. But they didn't. They just said, "Crayfish can't take it in a crowded environment," and let it go at that.

But now there is that matter of hogs, and maybe they can't take it in a crowded environment, either. They obviously can't take being pushed at the feed trough and hurried toward maturity.

Far be it from me to point a finger, but when I see the kids who are being pushed toward maturity ahead of their years, and when I see the way ulcers and other stress diseases are creeping down into the ranks of the younguns, I do wonder what we are doing. We aren't in the habit of listening to crayfish or even to hogs, but they just might have something worth hearing. A psychosomatic hog sounds funny, and quite possibly it is. But ulcers aren't, even in a pig-pen. And a crayfish with a nervous breakdown is incredibly droll, offhand. To a noncrayfish, at least. But crowd pressures and social stresses aren't.

Maybe I should be glad I'm not a hog, or a crayfish. I am glad, of course. It's lots more fun being more or less human. But every time I run across one of these reports I wonder how long we can continue to laugh them off, we fun-loving, gregarious, high-pressure, ulcer-prone, thrombotic, two-legged animals.

THE WOOLLY BEAR caterpillars have been hurrying across the lawn, on warm afternoons, obviously on their way to my garage. I don't know how many of those fuzzy, black-banded brownish-red fellows hibernate there, but I know that every fall I see at least a dozen of them curled up on the horizontal beams, tucked in for the winter. If I look around I usually can find twice that many. It seems to be a kind of Woolly Bear Haven. Why they prefer that place rather than the big barn, which should offer better and more numerous retreats, I never could understand. But then, I never could understand why the barn swallows insist on nesting in the garage and completely ignore the barn.

The woolly bears are the caterpillar stage of the small pinkish-yellow moth known as Isia Isabella. As caterpillars they feast on the common plantain that grows so insistently on my side lawn. I often wish there were more woolly bears to eat that plantain, but I suppose they do their best. Anyway, in late spring the woolly bears pupate and, about the time plantain comes to bloom, emerge as lovely little Isia Isabella moths. The moths feed at the plantain flowers, on pollen and whatever nectar there is, and soon lay eggs—on the plantain, of course. The eggs hatch, the moths die, and the new crop of woolly bear caterpillars fattens on plantain leaves till mid-September, when they hold convention and march off toward my garage.

There is an old belief that woolly bears foretell the coming winter. I am not sure just how one reads their forecast, and every year I hear at least two versions of the method. One insists that the breadth of the black band around their middle is the key—a broad band, a long, hard winter; a narrow band, a short, mild winter. The other version insists that it is their reddish-brown end-bands that hold the secret. This seems to me ambiguous, because a wide black band means narrower brown end-bands, and vice versa. Unless, of course, the woolly bear is bald in the middle; and I never saw one so marked.

Whichever method one uses—and I have tried them both—one comes up against the fact that even the woolly bears cannot seem to agree among themselves. Only the other day I saw two of them humping along almost side by side, and one had a broad band of black, the other a narrow black band. Long ago I decided that they are like statistics—you pick your woolly bear, or your set of statistics, to prove what you want to prove.

The marvel to me, however, is not their supposed ability as prophets but their ability to withstand the frost. They freeze solid, and it doesn't seem to hurt them at all. One year I took one from the garage on a day when the temperature was down to zero, even inside the garage, and put it in a jelly glass and left it in the kitchen to thaw out. Or not thaw. In less than an hour it began to uncurl, and in two hours it was completely thawed and awake. It crawled around the bottom of the jelly glass, looking for a plantain leaf, no doubt. It was a normally alive woolly bear caterpillar. The deep freeze hadn't hurt it one perceptible bit. I watched it a little while, then took it back to the beam where I had found it. It curled up, settled down and apparently was all set to go into an icy coma again.

On a warm afternoon in September, the woolly bears hurry as though pursued by a deadly enemy. They are, of course; the enemy is cold, which immobilizes them, and they are driven by impulse to get to some safe place before this happens. But their speed always fascinates me. I once timed one of them as it made its hump-backed way across the lawn toward the garage. It had to detour around certain tall stems and it didn't go in a straight line, for reasons of its own, I suppose. Even so, it traveled fifteen feet in five minutes, a yard a minute or about 1/30 of a mile an hour, the way I figured it out. Then I estimated relative weights and decided that I weigh at least five thousand times as much as a woolly bear caterpillar. Armed with those figures, I then calculated that if I could walk or even run as fast as that particular caterpillar, ounce for ounce, I could travel under my own steam 170 miles an hour.

I don't vouch for the figures, which I never took the trouble to check, but when I was all through I decided that it proved one thing beyond a doubt. All such comparisons are sheer nonsense. It's like proving that if I were as strong as an ant I could lift an elephant, or that if I were as good a digger as a mole I could tunnel two miles in a night.

All I really know is that the woolly bears are now hunting places for their chilly hibernation. And that they don't know anything more about the coming winter than I do. Maybe not as much.

A COLD AIR MASS moved through night before last and brought frost that hopped and skipped through this area, whimsical as first frost so often is. Gardens in the village got nipped, and some of them got a real blighting. But here in the valley we got off easily. My registering thermometer showed the night's low was an even 32 degrees, but the frost seemed to flow down the hollows. The summer squash, at the low end of the garden, was right in its path. No more summer squash. But the tender pepper plants, not ten feet from the squash, escaped unscathed.

We had warning that frost might come, so we had covered most of the tomato plants. Those we had to leave uncovered, however, were unhurt. So were the late beans. And even the tender annual flowers showed no sign of damage, though they drooped unhappily all day afterward. Last night was just as cold, according to my thermometer, but we found no further damage.

One reason we got off so lightly was the mist from the river. When I got up yesterday, and again this morning, the valley was white with mist. It was like a blanket that held the ground's warmth down where it would do the most good. The fingers of frost had to reach in under that warm blanket. And the mist hung here, silvery and shimmering, until the sun was an hour high. The maples shimmered and dripped moisture from their leaves until midmorning, and the grass was as wet as though there had been a shower. That mist saved our garden, as it so often does in early autumn.

By this morning the cold crisis seems to have passed, though one can't be too certain about such things. Anyway, the whole valley glows, looking washed and polished. The elms are showing that September rust color, and a good many of the maples are in color. But only a few of the sumacs have turned. The real color, aside from those early maples, is in the woodbine, the Virginia creeper. As always, it is spectacular with its reds that range all the way from a clear mahogany, very dark and deep, right through to brilliant crimson.

Perhaps those who now say that the salt on the roads is responsible for the early color in the maples are right. Salt certainly doesn't do any good to the roadside trees and bushes. But I wonder how they explain the maples out in the middle of a pasture, or off on a hillside several hundred yards from the nearest road. Far be it from me to defend the salt, which despite its utility on the roads is ultimately poisonous to roadside plants; but those early maples remote from salty run-off do baffle me. I wonder how much real foot-work the researchers did, how often they got out of the cars and walked up the hillsides and into the woods.

Anyway, we now are having beautiful days with that

sense of excitement that comes with perfect early fall weather. You can see 40 miles, it seems, and the air has a tang. The sky has depth and the wind is invigorating. It is exactly the kind of weather I thought of Thursday night when I saw the flare of the northern lights for the first time this season. As aurora, it didn't amount to much, no more than a rather pale glow that flared in typical aurora fashion but lacked the vivid colors. But the northern lights always seem to me to be an accompaniment of brisk nights and crisp days. Or, later in the season, of brittle nights and downright sharp days.

It is the kind of weather when walking is a pleasure. So we walked a bit, and saw the milkweed ripening pods and still clinging to leaves that now are golden. We saw the flickers, flocks of them, and laughed at their white rump patches when they flew. They are the cottontails of birddom, it seems to me. We looked for hazel nuts, and found that the squirrels had been to all the bushes ahead of us, as always. In one small patch we found black-eyed Susans, lavender bergamot, purple asters, bouncing Bet, tawny hawkweed and burr marigold all blooming at the same time. We saw the fantastic tangle of ripe stamens on the wild clematis which gave it the autumn name Old Man's Beard—in midsummer it is Virgin's Bower, and properly so. We saw the blue berries on Solomon's seal 6 feet tall, the lacquer-red berries nestled in the grass where Jack-in-the-pulpit preached last May.

But we saw little evidence of frost. It came, no doubt of that, but it leaped right across our fortunate valley.

SOMETIMES it is the little things that point up the big mysteries and show how little we really know about the world around us. For instance, at an international conference on magnetic fields held at the Massachusetts Institute of

Technology, one of the most exciting reports, or at least the one that stirred up the most talk, was about worms and moonbeams. Certain worms and snails and paramecia, which are one-celled semi-microscopic animals, seem to be able to detect faint magnetic fields and react to phases of the moon. Dr. Frank A. Brown, Jr., professor of biology at Northwestern University, made the report. It was based on experiments and Dr. Brown said his results seem to apply to most living things. In other words, you and I and our dogs and cats and chickens and cows and the migrating robins all probably are sensitive to the moon and to terrestrial magnetism.

One of the first things that occurs to mind, with this report at hand, is that the migrating birds, just as some have suspected, probably are guided by a kind of built-in compass. Also that carrier pigeons, which are phenomenal in their homing ability, probably make some use of that magnetic sensitivity. Possibly dogs do, and cats, which would explain the way they make their way through strange territory, sometimes for long distances.

Then there is the matter of the moon and its phases. Man has thought for a long time that the moon had a profound effect on the mind, or at least the emotions. It used to be said that madhouses were in turmoil at the time of the full moon because the moon has some strange effect on the deranged mind. The term "lunacy," of course, comes directly from the moon and reflects the belief that the moon was in some degree responsible. Perhaps there was more than superstition in that belief.

There is also the old belief in the moon's effect on crops and planting. Some gardeners, and even some farmers, still hold to the old moon tables when they plan their planting dates. *The Old Farmer's Almanac* regularly carries, in its "outdoor Planting Table," a column indicating when the moon is most favorable for each crop. It labels this "superstitious." But perhaps its caution in this matter may yet be proved unjustified. If the moon's phases can make a snail or a worm turn a certain direction, it is possible, I would think, that the same moon effect might hurry or retard the growth of a seedling. Call it magnetism, or what you will, if it works on a snail, why couldn't it work on a bean or a squash?

Some fishermen have their own ideas about the moon's phases and the way fish bite. Even commercial fishermen sometimes drop hints of such belief. A few years back, talking to a shrimp fisherman in Florida, I mentioned this and the man gave me an odd look and said, "Well, last week at the time of the full moon we had full nets." Then he smiled and changed the subject. But another shrimper said he timed his trips by the moon's phases and explained it in terms of weather. After all, it is not quite so superstitious, I suppose, to say that the moon has something to do with the weather. And it isn't superstitious at all to connect the moon with the tides. That is a "scientific fact."

Not too many years ago a botanical researcher came up with an explanation of why vines twine and why they nearly always twine one way north of the equator and the other way south of it. It had to do with the sun, he said. Something in the sunlight made one side of a stem grow faster than the other, hence the twining. It seemed to add up. And yet, that didn't explain why smoke curls one way coming out of a chimney north of the equator and the opposite way down in the Southern Hemisphere. Or why water swirls counterclockwise going down a drain up here and clockwise in Argentina, say. All right, so the earth's rotation is involved in both those inanimate motions. But that doesn't explain the fact that the animate movement of a vine is in the same direction.

Obviously there are forces at work that we still don't understand, and they undoubtedly are at work on us as well as on bean vines and snails and worms and paramecia, plural for them. Call it magnetism, or lunar effect, or whatever you wish, there is some effect from the moon. Some of the things can be called coincidence, and some can be dismissed as superstition. But not all of them. The chairman of the conference at MIT tossed the matter of magnetism and the moon right back at the scientists with the request, "Either explain it or explain it away." And nobody has done either, yet.

THE AUTUMNAL EQUINOX occurred just before dark last evening, and today is the first day of fall, by the almanac. But this year we had our first fall days, in every sense except by date, back in August, so the season is pretty well mixed up. But the summer sounds are vanishing day by day, and when the Silence begins to move in there is no denying that we are verging on October, and November is just ahead.

The Silence comes so gradually that we are scarcely aware of it until we hear one lone katydid scratching at the evening, and not a tree cricket making a sound. It's a little like the way the bird songs taper away in midsummer. In May and June and mornings are loud with song, and even the afternoons have their quota. Most evenings are filled with the calls of wood thrushes, brown thrashers and whippoorwills, with an occasional robin or tanager singing well into the dusk. But by hot July there is little song except at dawn, though the doves and wood thrushes still sing at dusk. The music just tapers off, day by day, and one day in late July we remember that most of the birds haven't been singing for several weeks.

That's the way the insect sounds, so characteristic of

August, taper off. First the shrill buzz of the late harvest flies dies away and isn't repeated. Then the evening hum of the mosquitoes ebbs, and the millions of dead male mosquitoes, with their feathery antennae, are seen floating on the ponds and sluggish streams. By then the crickets have been rising to crescendo, and the katydids have begun. A few chill nights quiet them somewhat, but when a warm night comes again the fiddlers are louder than ever. Or so it seems. They apparently are trying to make up for lost time, with time actually so limited in their brief lives.

But by mid-September even the loudest and most insistent of them have begun to run down. You can hear individual katydids, though the crickets are still making a chorus. Some of them have lived their lives and died, some have worn out their sound makers. The ranks are thinning. Then comes a first frosty night, and we have the prelude to the Silence. We wake some time around 2 A.M. and listen, and there isn't an insect sound anywhere. At first it is uncanny, unreal; then we sense the temperature and know what happened. The oldest and the weakest of the cold-blooded pigmy hordes have been victims of the cold.

Another night of frost, and still more of them have been silenced. But not all, by any means. Crickets creep into shelter, in houses and barns and even into woodpiles. Katydids hide under leaves and in cracks in the bark of trees. Somehow a few of them survive. And the next mild evening sets them to scratching again. One year I heard the last katydid the second week in November, after three hard, killing frosts.

But at last the night comes when only two night sounds break the silence, the hoot of a barred owl and the bark of a red fox. And that is what I mean by the Silence, a night quiet broken only at long intervals by an owl or a fox, a day quiet broken only by the challenge of the jays and the cawing of the crows.

A few years ago a vicious midsummer hail storm swept over a small Colorado town. It was a town whose people had planted many trees and grown lawns and gardens in the midst of the high, dry plains. Birds lived there, even mockingbirds, and all the usual insects that gather in cultivated places. The hail came, tattering the trees, burying the lawns under 2 inches of ice, beating the gardens into the soil. When the storm had passed the people stood and looked and listened, and the quiet was almost unbearable. Virtually every bird had been killed and the insects had been stoned or chilled into silence. It was as though the town had been plunged, in an hour, into a vast vacuum. As one woman told me later, "It was so lonely it hurt. The damage was bad enough, but the silence was worse."

So I am always glad the silence of autumn comes as it does, by degrees. If it all came at once, if every cricket and katydid vanished with the first cold night, it would indeed be "so lonely it hurts." I am grateful for the few surviving katydids, and even for the crickets that get into the house and hide under the bookcase and chirp. November is early enough to have the Silence, and it is best to hear the foxes and owls even then. We shouldn't be able to hear the snowflakes nudging each other as they fall at least until December.

But the Silence is now advancing. I can even hear the crisp leaves rustling along the road, it is so quiet. By the next full moon, the Hunter's Moon, even the leaves will have ceased their whispering.

I DOUBT that anyone ever has done or ever will do justice in words to the autumn color in New England. Descriptions tend to fray out into clichés, not because the words themselves lack color but because the spectacle itself is so huge and so varied. Its colors cover the spectrum and even demand a spectrum of their own.

Who, for instance, can pin down that shade I think of as blue, which comes to the leaves of the white ash at a certain moment and in just the right light? It isn't blue but what is it? It gives me the impression of blue. Or the pink that I saw only yesterday in a certain maple. Almost a flesh-pink, and yet with some tinge of lavender in it. And when I come to the oaks, I run out of terms for their tans, browns, red and purples, mingled and overlapping. And the maples! Add half a dozen shades of pines, hemlocks, cedars and spruces, add the blue of sky, the white of cloud, the opalescence of mist—how capture the whole of it in words?

Then there is the matter of light. I have been watching my valley take on color, first leaf by leaf, then twig and branch at a time, then tree by tree. It is always exciting to watch, from the first flame in the sumac, which sometimes comes in late July but usually waits till August, to the flash of scarlet in the swamp maples. But we usually see it during full daylight, from midmorning till late afternoon. That, however, is only one phase of it.

I was up and out at dawn the other morning. The sun came up clear and dazzling, and suddenly it shot through all the trees along the riverbank. The maples hadn't yet turned more than a few leaves, here and there, but as that newly risen sun flashed through them those green leaves were like beaten antique gold. The scattering of elms, almost nondescript in their pale, creeping rust, were yellow as the sun itself, lemon yellow. The big popple's thick leaves quivered, twinkling like coins in firelight. And a sumac clump was scarlet, translucent scarlet like stained glass in a holy window.

I turned and looked up the mountainside, and in that long light of dawn every turning leaf up there was a dazzle of color, yellow-green, corn-yellow, lucent tan, berry-pink, wine-red, even a kind of amethystine purple. With the massed green of pines and hemlocks, and with the white boles of birches adding emphasis. And with a lower fringe of sumac, crimson and yellow and orange.

And that evening, when the sun was just above Tom's Mountain to the west, I looked again, and once more the color was different, with new emphasis, new shadings, even new tones. So there, within less than twelve hours, I had the color in three variations. And, with change coming as swiftly as it does now, all was different by another dawn, another sunset. If I could accurately describe even one tree in color today, my description would be outdated by tomorrow noon. In other years I have heard people say, "I went up last weekend and saw the color in the Berkshires." And always I have thought: You saw only last weekend's color. It's different today, and it will be still different tomorrow. Even we who live with it never see it all, for it changes year by year.

There are a few certainties. I know, for instance, that of the sugar maples in front of my house three will turn yellow and four will have their yellow touched with red. I know that a younger maple beside the big barn will be scarlet, and that it will be tinged with orange on its lower branches. I know that when I stand beneath the yellow maples at a certain stage, even a darkly clouded day will seem full of sunlight. And I know that a certain hickory tree comes, for two days and not one minute longer, to a magnificent gold of leaf, which turns sere and brown after those forty-eight hours. I know a particular clump of oaks that waits till the swamp maple leaves fall before they turn russet and wine and purple.

And I know that it isn't frost that makes the color. I had thought that this was so widely known by now that Jack Frost and his paint pots could be dismissed for the childish legend it is. But I repeatedly hear someone say that frost has brought the color. Actually, frost can ruin the color, if it comes early and hard.

The coloring is a chemical process, based on sugars and acids and pigments in the leaves, and it is a part of the tree's process of closing shop for the winter. This happens regardless of frost, normally, and its timing is governed by the earth's own timing, probably by the length of day. In some strange way, it parallels the rise of sap in the spring, for the process is at its best with warm days and chilly nights. A hot or rainy autumn washes out the color. An early, hard frost burns the leaves before the color comes.

Autumn color, of course, is not unique to New England. It is spectacular here because of the variety of hardwoods we have, and because our autumns are usually ideal color weather. Michigan has maple color, somewhat muted by the Great Lakes. The Ozarks have a spectacle of color in the native oaks. Colorado has vivid color in oaks and aspens, but the range is narrow. This is the real Color Country, right here. And this seems to be one of those spectacular years.

OUR HOST met us at the gate, and we drove half a mile or so through the woods and past the swamp, and there on the lakeshore we saw them. It was a brilliant day, and the gentians were at their prime. There were hundreds of them. Not quite the blue cloud on the grass that I have heard about, but more than I have ever seen before. I didn't even try to count, because it was hopeless.

There were both kinds, the fringed beauties and the darker, closed bottle gentians. They grew in all kinds of soil, leaf mold, almost pure sand, even in the gravel at the edge of the road, and they grew in shade as well as sun. Those in full sunlight were widest open, but it seemed to me that those in the shade, and especially those that grew in clumps at the foot of the big white birches, were the tallest of all.

The fringed gentians, we all agreed, were almost a perfect periwinkle color, as the artist knows and identifies color. The bottle gentians were very close to the artist's ultramarine. Most of them were, that is; there were a number of pure white ones, too, and in their way they were even more spectacular than the blue ones.

I was looking at one of the white bottle gentian plants, with a cluster of five blossoms, when a big bumblebee arrived. Remembering old discussions about how these blossoms are fertilized, I watched the bee with special interest. It climbed about one flower, looking for an opening, found none. It climbed on top, thrust a foot down between the tightly closed petals, got both front feet in, braced itself and pried. Slowly it forced the petals open, got its head inside. Squirming, pushing with the four hind legs, it thrust itself down and in. The petals closed tightly. The big bumbler was gone completely, encased in that gentian. The flower swayed as the bee moved around inside. I glanced at my watch. The bee was inside almost ten seconds. Then the petals parted slightly at the top, Mr. Bumble's head appeared, then his front legs, and he hauled himself out, seemed to catch his breath or at least rest for a moment, and flew away.

I watched the same thing happen at several blue bottles. Then I found another white one where a bumblebee had cut a slit near the flower's calyx. It forced its way through the slit, fed for a few seconds, and tried to back out. It couldn't make it that way, so it went on in again, turned around and came out head-first. That was the only bee I saw cut his own side entrance, though I have often seen bumblebees slit petunias near the base to get at the nectar sac.

Among the gentians were a good many of the creamy blossoms of Grass of Parnassus. Most of them were past their prime, but a few were freshly opened and small bees were very busy at those flowers.

Close by, in the edge of the thicker woods, we found a number of lesser gentians commonly called ague-weed, *Gentiana quinqueflora*. They were smaller than the fringed beauties, both in plant and flower, and instead of daintily fringed petals they had toothed margins. Their color was a trace lighter than that of the fringed gentians. These are not rare, but they are often misidentified and overlooked as true gentians.

How, we asked our host, did he happen to have this gentian garden? It wasn't a garden, of course, since it never has been cultivated and, as far as he goes, never will be. It was just a relatively wild place with natural growth that was kept somewhat in check. The gentians, he said, just came, to start with. There were a few of them, all three varieties. He cherished them, protected them, and forbade anyone to pick a flower. Then, when the fringed and bottle varieties came to seed, he gathered what seed he could and helped scatter it. Some of the seed grew. Gradually the original plants spread, with his help.

I have heard it said that fringed gentians don't bloom till after frost. I can vouch that that isn't true. Nor is it true that they open only in full sun. But as for their color, that has never been overrated.

IT WAS a remarkably good year for apples, at least on my own trees. They bloomed profusely, were a glory in May, and the "set" was heavy. By mid-July the boughs were taxed with the weight of fruit, and from then on I welcomed every wind because the winds somewhat lightened the burden and eased the strain on the limbs. When the first apples ripened and began to fall—the trees are too tall to pick, at least with my resources, so we use the windfalls—when the first fruit fell, I cut into a few and found them more free from worms and blight than in any other season since we came here. We do no spraying, for a variety of reasons, including the fact that we don't like sprays and we don't sell apples. But something about the season protected the apples; and I credit the birds for a good deal of this good fortune.

The trees were full of apples when we left on a brief trip, and when we returned the grass beneath them was covered with apples. I wished I owned a cider press, though I don't know what we would do with ten barrels of cider, which I am sure we could have had. So we used what apples we wanted for jelly and apple sauce, and we ate them raw and baked, and still we didn't make a dent in the supply.

They are old apples, the old varieties, for our trees are the remnants of an orchard planted here many years ago. The orchard was cut off a few years before we bought the place and we removed the stumps and made pastureland of the lot. But those who cut the orchard had the good sense to leave a row of trees along the backyard fence and a few of them standing in the home pasture. Some of them are 40 feet high and one old veteran beside the woodshed is a good 2 feet through at the butt. That one is the Snow apple tree, a particular pet of mine.

Orchardists keep telling me I should have the apple trees trimmed and that I should spray them. I still haven't heard one good reason for doing either. "Low trees are easier to pick." But I don't want to pick apples. "Proper spraying would insure wormfree apples." We get enough good apples, without spraying, to satisfy our need ten times over. "They would be healthier trees if the dead branches were taken out." The woodpeckers love those dead branches, nest in the knotholes. A pair of wood ducks once nested in one of those trees. I like them the way they are.

I do wish I knew more about their varieties, however. The Snow apple is my favorite, and I know another name for it is Fameuse. I know one of them is a Spitzenburg, a very old variety from which the Jonathan evolved. One in the back pasture is a Russet, and there was a Greening there until a few years ago when a big wind brought it down. But most of the others are beyond my knowledge. Oh, there is also one that I am sure is a Ben Davis, but it didn't bear very well even this year. I am particularly curious about the tree that bears huge, beautiful apples, some of them more than four inches in diameter, marked with a rich, deep red when they are ripe. They are as pretty an apple as I ever saw, but they aren't worth picking, punky in texture and insipid in taste. And nobody seems able to identify them.

Now I hear that the Worcester County Horticultural Society has planted an "Old Variety" apple orchard at North Grafton, Mass., to preserve some of these famous old apples. More than fifty varieties are said to be there, among them Northern Spy, Blue Pearmain, Duchess of Oldenburg, Esopus Spitzenburg, Maiden Blush, Ribstone, Yellow Bellflower, Grimes Golden, Red June, Smokehouse, Mother, Lady, and Fameuse—my wonderful Snow apple. I don't recognize many of those names, not being an apple man, really. I wonder if the list also includes yellow Pound Sweet, which Barbara remembers with special pleasure as the best apple grown when she was a girl. It, too, is probably there in the "Old Variety" orchard. Some day we shall go and see.

Meanwhile, most of our apples have fallen and been gathered and hauled away. But not very far, because that fragrance is something special. They lie in softening heaps, slowly browning as they rot, out where the wild folk can help themselves. And I wonder if I shall ever see another such season, so many wonderful apples on these old trees. I wish we could have stowed ten barrels of them to enjoy till apples ripen again, but it would have been fool's work to do it. Windfalls don't last, and I refuse to climb a tall ladder to pick apples for anyone, even myself.

I KEEP HEARING that Canada geese are already migrating through this area southward. Maybe so, but I have my doubts. Some of them may have moved down from the north, but that doesn't mean that the migration has begun. Besides, we always have a few geese that spend a good deal of the summer around here; so when someone reports seeing a migrating flock in early September I always discount it. One pair of Canadas has nested and raised a brood on Beaver Dam Pond, over in Taconic, for at least the past four summers, and I saw a pair of Canadas on the Housatonic River down near West Cornwall the last week in August. They certainly weren't migrating.

I won't believe the goose migration is on until I hear that high, distant, unmistakable gabble some morning—it could be tomorrow, but I doubt it—and go outside and look up and see that long, straggling line, like a wavery penciling on the autumn sky, and watch them out of sight, heading south. Then I will know that hard frost and imprisoning ice are threatening to close in the ponds somewhere up north, and that in due time frost and ice will reach me here.

The wild goose is a canny bird with more weather knowledge than all the woodchucks in New England, despite the Groundhog Day nonsense. That is as it should be, for the goose doesn't curl up and sleep all winter and thus know only a part of the year at first hand. The goose lives with the weather and the world is his home, the world of high winds and limitless horizons. When fall comes, a goose can sense a freeze-up or a sleety northeaster two days off. When he does, he simply says to his neighbors, "Let's get going. We've been here long enough." And off they go, the whole flock heading south. In the spring, when the first break occurs in the ice up here, some goose away down south goes upstairs, as human fliers say, takes a look around, senses that winter is retreating, and gets homesick. A few hours later the whole flock is on its way north.

And almost never does a Canada goose misread the signs. Robins, sometimes do, and so do warblers. But geese have built-in radar or barometers, or something even better. They don't need any morning weather man trying to outguess an isobar. They just know.

One fall, when most of the signs I could see said that a cold wave was about to hem us in, I was driving the back roads when I came upon a pond that looked as chill and forlorn as gray water under a gray sky can look. I would have bet that we would have snow and ice within another twelve hours. Then I rounded a neck of the pond and saw a Canada goose. He was standing on a tiny island, craning his neck and studying the sky. I stopped the car, got out my field glasses; but before I could focus them three more geese were there on the island. They seemed to be conferring with the first goose. All of them lifted their beaks and sniffed the wind, or seemed to.

By then I had them in the glasses. They didn't look worried or restless. As I watched, a whole line of geese appeared from behind the island. I counted twenty-six. They swam around and watched the four who were in conference, and at last they began quacking questions. The council on the island quacked a reply and the whole flock relaxed and began to feed. They obviously weren't going to pack up and go south that day.

I came on home, still skeptical, still watching for sleet or snow riding a northeaster. But it didn't storm that day or the next. The third night I heard the gabble of geese high overhead, heard it fade away to the south. And the next afternoon we got our first storm. Those geese knew, almost to the hour, when that storm was going to strike.

So I discount these reports of migrant geese. It's too early. I don't know when the freeze-up will come, and I won't forecast either an early or a late fall, at this moment. Maybe a little later I will hazard a guess, but it will be nothing more than a guess if I do. I am of a species that has become too civilized, if that is really the word, to know a great deal about these matters. I know ice when I see it, and I can read a thermometer, but I can't feel the weather the way a goose can. All I can feel is the occasional twinge in my old football knee. Sometimes that twinge seems to mean a cold snap is in the offing, sometimes it means a cold snap is here, and sometimes it means I'm just plain tired.

Man devised the calendar and he established arbitrary dates for the seasons. He charted the solstices and the equinoxes. He invented barometers and anemometers and hygrometers and all kinds of ometers, but he still has to make what he calls "informed guesses." And the weather goes right on ignoring man's "norms" and "averages." All man really does is sum up the past and hope that the future will conform to the charts. And that is nothing but wishful thinking. The geese do it much more easily. I sometimes wish I had as much sense as a goose.

IT WAS THOREAU who said, I think for the first time, that most people live lives of "quiet desperation." But those of Thoreau's day had no such pressures as we know today, with cities grown so huge and sprawling, traffic almost a nightmare, and the problems of mass society dinned at us every hour of the day. For many, life has now become a matter of noisy desperation, and escape from those pressures has become a persistent dream. Such escape is difficult, but now and then someone achieves it.

From time to time I receive letters from those who hope to escape, or plan to escape, or wonder if it is worth the effort. In the past few weeks I received letters from two who did escape, and they are so perceptive that I would like to share them here.

The first is from a woman who, with her husband, reasoned things out. For years they had lived in the city. The husband is a professional man, too young to retire. They wanted none of suburban life. So they went to the country, bought a place a hundred miles from the city. Life there is a compromise, since the husband must spend several days a week in the city. But it is their haven, the place where they really live and come alive. More and more often, the wife spends the whole week at the house in the country. She is a stranger to me, which is perhaps one reason she would write as she did, for she was obviously thinking out loud.

"What's the matter with me," she asked, "that I ignore all the delights that one of the world's great cities offers?

Why would I rather see the morning sun hit the asparagus ferns, dew-covered, turning the bed into a crystal forest, than see a great art exhibition?" Then she answered her own questions. "There is a time when one must take life directly, not someone else's interpretation. So I can miss the plays and the movies and the galleries (and the endless display of *Things*) and take what seems good to me." And what seems good is that house on its few remote country acres.

The other letter is from a woman in the Midwest, also a stranger to me, who came to much the same conclusion in a different way.

"For the past year," this woman wrote, "we have been cleaning up an old empty farmhouse on our farm. We've owned the farm for more than ten years, but live about 12 miles from it, in a small town, and only went there to see to things with our farmer, who lives in another house on the farm. Finally we started to fix up the empty farmhouse just for us to go to occasionally.

"We so thoroughly enjoy just being there that the work just sort of slips away. The results appear rough, I imagine, to my town friends, but we've made it livable, homelike. It still lacks most of the modern conveniences, but I've discovered how unimportant most of our 'musts' really are. I get a certain satisfaction out of going to the pump on the back porch to get water to do the dishes, the way my grandmother probably once did. I'd really hate to have things too easy out there. It would take something away from it.

"Our house sits on a little hill, more of a rise, with big old maple trees across the front, a butternut and more maples along the side, and a walnut and maples at the back. At the bottom of the backyard starts a meadow that rolls up the hill to the woods, close enough that I can walk in the woods every day. My favorite times are very early morning, just about sunrise, and again around dusk. This is the most peaceful spot I've ever known and I enjoy a special feeling I've never known before and can't even convey to others. It's enough just to sit and look and feel, a certain contentment that I don't imagine some people can ever know. Most of our friends can't understand why we want to spend most of our time out there 'away from everything,' and I don't even try to explain."

Two examples of escape from things that gall and hurt, from Thoreau's life of quiet desperation. And both of them seeking basically the same things—a kind of simplicity, a reality, a contact with something other than the man-made city and all its accompaniment. From a small town, in the one instance; but today's small towns are still in many ways harried by the same problems and equivalent pressures, probably because they are the modern way of life wherever people congregate.

And neither of these people can quite explain the inner need. The first one comes close when she says there is the need to "take life directly, not some one else's interpretation." Perhaps that is as close as anyone can come to explaining. Perhaps that is the deep, insoluble problem of today, how to take life directly in the midst of the crowd.

THE SQUIRRELS have harvested most of the nuts in my woodland. I had hoped to gather a peck or so of butternuts, maybe a few handfuls of hazel nuts, and at least a few hickory nuts, but the squirrels seem to have made off with most of them. With luck, we will get a few hazel nuts, and maybe a few butternuts, but that's all. Maybe it's just as well. The squirrels will eat their fill and hide the rest and forget where they hid most of them. And next spring or the spring after they will reappear as seedlings and I shall be a tree-planter by proxy. Besides, any nut harvest I had gathered would have been primarily a harvest of memories.

When I was a very small boy we gathered black walnuts in the groves down along Nemaha Creek. My father went along, and sometimes my mother went, and we made a Saturday afternoon outing of it. We took gunny sacks and we gathered the nuts, and we watched the cottontail rabbits scurry from the brush and lope along the paths beside the creek. We listened to the redbirds whistle, and we talked back to the red squirrels when they cried their insolent challenges at us. Skies were blue, air was balmy, the world was young and boundless. The nuts were only an excuse, not a prime purpose.

We took the nuts home and we let them ripen in the back yard, then hulled them by driving them through a plank with a proper sized knot hole in it. And my hands were dark-dyed for weeks. Later there were long winter evenings when we cracked walnuts between a hammer and a flatiron and picked out the meat and feasted.

Mother occasionally baked black walnut cookies or a cake, and friends came in and spent the evening making walnut fudge. And Grandmother always remembered her girlhood, when she helped card and spin wool clipped from their own sheep, helped dye it in a brew made of walnut hulls, and her mother knitted winter stockings for the family. A good, serviceable color, she always said. Like the black of the long cotton stockings of my own childhood.

Later there were piñon nuts, on the mesas of Nevada and Colorado. Piñon nuts grew on pine trees, squat, buxom trees that looked like the Paiute Indian squaws who were always there when the white folk went to gather piñon nuts. The Indians got the best ones, but we gathered the pitchy cones in bags and took them home and let them lie in the sun until they began to open. Then we shook them over a trap and got a shower of the small, shiny brown nuts which we cracked between our teeth to get the sweet, rich kernels.

Barbara and I gathered piñon nuts one fall, when we were there at exactly the right time. Nobody else was on the mesas we visited, and the nuts had fallen like a shower, more nuts than all the squirrels in Colorado could eat. We gathered them, on our knees in the deep mat of pine needles, and brought a peck or more of them home with us. The nuts and the memories of those amazing blue skies, that winy air, the black-and-white flashes of magpies, the lumbering lope of the jack rabbits, and the pitchy pine smell of the mesas.

The first year we came up here we went up the mountainside in October to gather nuts from the shagbark hickories there. To me they were hickory nuts, but to Barbara they were "walnuts." She had gathered them as a small girl, and everyone called them walnuts. A good many people still do, I find, though I still can't see the logic in saying you are going out to the hickory grove to gather some walnuts. Anyway, we went up the hill to the hickory trees and Barbara gathered "walnuts" and I gathered hickory nuts. We came home and cracked them, and as we munched Barbara told me about the Waterville Road when she was eight and I told her about the Nemaha valley when I was eight. Simply because nuts are more than nuts, to us at least. They are memories, too.

This year was a good nut year. There were more nuts on the hazel bushes than I have ever seen. I watched them jealously all through August and the first two weeks of September. Then I was busy with other things. When we went to look at them the other day they had begun to ripen. And the squirrels obviously had been watching those nuts too. They left us only a few handfuls, and I will bet even money that no more than half of those will be worth opening. The others have no kernels inside, and the squirrels knew it. That's why they left them.

How does a squirrel know such things? Don't ask me. A few falls ago I spent an hour under a hickory tree finding and opening the nuts the squirrels had left in the litter of hulls. I opened fifty or sixty nuts, and not one of them had an edible kernel in it. Moreover, not one of them had a tooth mark on it. The squirrels knew, just by looking, or listening, or maybe by hefting, that those nuts weren't worth opening. Even more baffling is the story told me by a man who planted a hundred black walnuts, hoping to get seedlings. He planted them in a row and 4 inches deep. Two days later he found that the squirrels had dug up ninety-two of those nuts. The other eight were just where he planted them, so he dug them up and cracked them, one by one. Not one had a kernel in it. The squirrels knew they weren't worth digging up. They knew, even though those nuts were 4 inches underground.

I don't begrudge one nut to animals that clever.

BARBARA sees the strangest things. There was the woodcock beside the woodshed. I was skeptical, till I looked; but it was a woodcock, sure enough. There was the wood duck in the apple tree, a sure-enough wood duck; a pair of them nested in another apple tree not a hundred yards from the house. There was the bald eagle flying down the river. There was the sandpiper that I insisted must be a killdeer—until I looked again.

So this morning when she called to me, "There's a fox playing in the pasture just beyond the garden!" I hurried downstairs and got my binocular. It was a fox, a big red fox, and it was in the tall grass and wild mint along the dry brook bed not 75 yards from the house. It was 8 in the morning, a frosty morning, and the white shadows still lay on the pasture grass where the sun had not yet reached. The binocular brought the fox so close I could almost count its whiskers.

It was hunting mice, or more likely meadow voles. But it wasn't making a chore of it. It was playing games, probably because it had eaten breakfast before full daylight. But there it was, playful as a kitten. It would nose the grass, lift its head, move a few steps, nose the grass again, then pounce. Then it would wait a moment, watching the grass, take a few more steps, and pounce again. Its long tail was wonderfully graceful, much darker than its body except for the frosty tip, and its ears were sharp and black. Its coat was chestnut along the back, shading almost to sand color on the sides and white on the belly. When it pounced it leaped 2 or 3 feet off the ground and came down with its nose between its forefeet.

It was several minutes before I realized what it was doing. It had caught a vole and now was toying with it, as a cat toys with a mouse, letting it run a few feet, then trapping it, only to let it go again. Cruel sport, from the human point of view, but something that happens, something as natural to a fox as breathing. A man does it with a trout, trains his dog to do it with a rabbit or a fox or a raccoon.

So we watched, reluctant to moralize.

Five minutes, ten minutes, and at last the fox lifted its head after a pounce and flung something into the air. It was a vole, short-tailed and grayish brown. It spun in the air, came down in the grass and the fox pounced at once, flung it into the air again. A third time, and the fox flung the vole 6 feet into the air, danced on its hind feet and tried to catch it as it came down, like a puppy playing with a ball. It missed, tried again and this time caught the vole in midair, paused a moment as though waiting for applause, then gulped and the vole was gone.

The fox eyed the grass again, nosed it once, then lifted its head, looked around, and bolted toward the far side of the pasture. It was like a puff of reddish-brown mist, so light and graceful, it seemed to float rather than run.

I looked for an approaching car on the road, some cause for alarm, but no car appeared. And the fox stopped after a 50-yard run. It had just been practicing its sprint, apparently. It posed there in the pasture, flirted its tail, then trotted toward the cross-fence and the old stone wall. Nothing there to interest it, it came back toward the brook, changed its mind, stopped to stare at a thistle stalk from which a breath of a breeze had drifted a few tufts of thistle down. It watched the tufts float away, then went to the wall again, lightly leaped over it and went up the other side toward the woods. All we could see was that dark, bushy tail, its white tip gleaming.

But it didn't go back to the woods. It crossed the middle pasture, whimsical as a boy chasing a butterfly, and followed the dry brookbed there into the lower pasture, a quarter of a mile away. Maybe it found another vole. I wouldn't know. The brookbed curves around a slight rise and the fox was soon out of sight.

We see foxes every year, usually in the fall, sometimes when there is snow on the ground. But never before has one so completely ignored the house in broad daylight, nor has one been so openly playful. We wondered if this was the one that walks the rails on the railroad track from time to time, and leaves its record in the snow. Or if it was the one that once barked a challenge to Pat in midafternoon and led him for an hour's noisy run on the mountainside, apparently just for the fun of it.

Whoever it was, when we were wakened that night by a fox barking nearby in the home pasture Barbara said, "There's my fox!" And I am willing to lay odds that it was.

THERE ARE two times in the year when any person with a grain of sense, or sensitivity, can't stay indoors. One is in the spring, usually late April, when the outdoor world is on tiptoe, ready to burst into spring. That is the time when one walking along a country road or taking his time across an open meadow and along the edge of a woodland is privileged to participate in a kind of annual genesis. The other time is right now, after the first hard frost.

The color hasn't yet vanished, but a good deal of it is down out of the treetops. Quite a few maples and most of the oaks on my own mountainside are still full of leaves, but when I walk there I am ankle-deep in crisp gold and crimson. The roadsides are scuffing, and every breeze is full of leaves, it seems. If I pause beside a clump of sumac I am sure to be showered with color, for the sumac leaves are so loose that even my own breath will bring a few floating down. And when I stand beneath a red oak I can't believe there are so many leaves still on the tree because the ground seems to be covered with them. Which proves only that even an oak, which hasn't as many leaves as a maple the same size, has more leaves than I could count in a week.

I come to a tangle of tall weeds, mostly goldenrod and milkweed. The goldenrod is all brown stems and shriveled leaves, but the gray fluff of its seed plumes is like mist, riding every breath of air. And the milkweeds are a golden beauty, the leaves startlingly yellow, yellower than willow leaves. The pods, still gray-green, are already spilling their silken contents, and when the breeze passes it takes on the shimmer of milkweed floss.

At the roadside stands a tree that I knew in boyhood as a box elder. There's not a leaf left on it, but its twigs are loaded with brown tassels of seed, keys like those of the sugar maples in front of my house. This tree, of course, is one of the maple family, the ash-leaved maple; the keys prove it, and if there were further doubt one could tap it in early spring and make syrup from its sap. Just beyond is a barberry bush, its leaves deep purple, its berries brilliant scarlet. It stands in a fencerow, obviously planted there by the birds, as are most of the barberries that grow at the roadside. And the birds busy at this bush right now will plant still more barberries along other fencerows. Just as they have planted that golden tuft of asparagus that shines in the sunlight. I never notice how much asparagus grows wild until autumn, when the fine-cut fern foliage turns that unmistakable golden yellow, twinkling with ripe red berries.

Wild grape leaves are a rich tan. I have to stop and pluck one and feel its texture, which is almost exactly like that of a paper napkin. And while I am standing there I wonder which birds ate all the berries from the big, red-stemmed pokeweed. There's not one berry left, nothing but the wine-red splay of empty stems where the purple-black berries hung in a loose panicle two weeks ago. Those berries are mildly poisonous to people, but apparently the birds have no trouble digesting them. Glancing at the wild grape vine again I look for bunches of fruit, see only the empty stems and remember the October evening when I found a possum in a tangle of wild grape vines, stained with their juice from black nose tip to his very paws. Possums like those little grapes. So do foxes, though I never caught a fox as red-handed as I did that possum.

The asters are looking rather sad, though here and there I find a few big purples that evidently opened after the night of hard frost. They are particularly gay looking, and their golden centers look almost orange. And here is a bunch of bouncing Bet, still blooming bravely though its leaves are rather forlorn. But when I look up the hillside I see a stand of Christmas fern, its fronds as lively and green as they were in July. This fern pays little heed to the weather, though its cousins are brown as oak leaves, crisp as corn flakes.

A small flock of flickers comes swooping across the pasture, and as they go past I see the white rump patches. They won't be here much longer. As I follow their flight I know that they, too, are seeing the distant horizon as neither they nor I have seen it since last April. There it is, in plain sight through the bare branches of the trees, and those few trees still in leaf only make the new openness more noticeable.

The world has new dimensions now. It has broadened beyond summer belief. It summons the flickers to migration, and it summons me to reach and travel at least with my mind and my imagination. Valleys broaden now, and hilltops are out in the open. This is a world complete for another season, and if I do not go out and see it I am without understanding of creation itself.

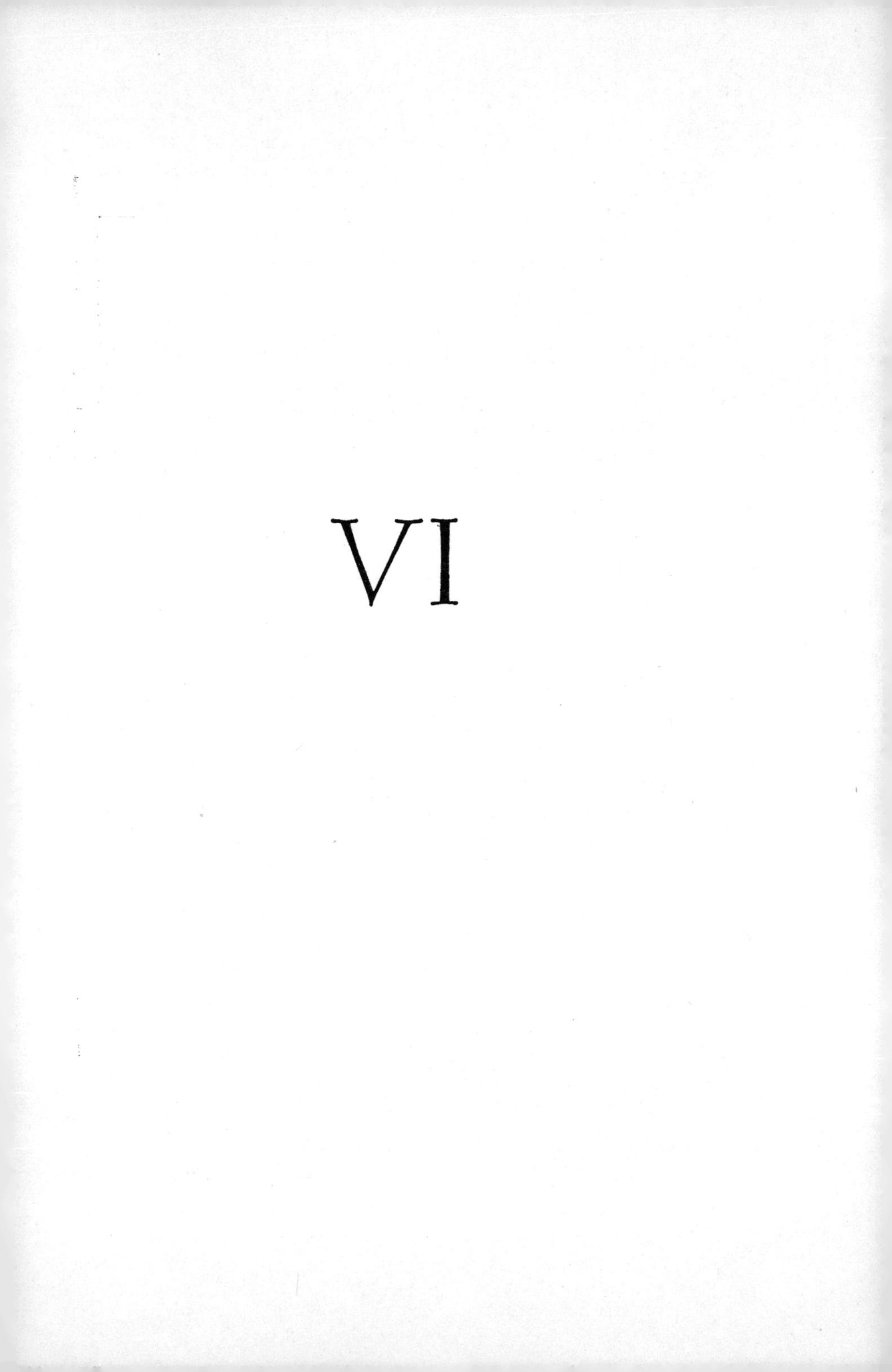

VI

IV

I have been going over the Farm Census form that came in the mail the other day. It is an elaborate questionnaire with sixteen sections and more than three hundred questions to be answered, and I am told that it is a part of a nationwide census of agriculture. It interests me as much by what it implies as by what it asks, because many of the questions would be so much Greek to the farmers I knew when I was growing up. They show how vast have been the changes in rural life in the past thirty or forty years.

As an example, one series of questions asks me to list the pieces of mechanical equipment on my farm. "Grain combines, corn pickers, field forage harvesters, motor trucks, wheel tractors, crawler tractors, garden tractors, automobiles." Also, "Home freezer, milking machine, electric milk cooler, crop drier, power-operated elevator, conveyor or blower." Except for automobiles, trucks and tractors, the equipment in the first list has all been developed since World War I, and almost every item in the second list was unknown in 1925.

Every piece of equipment on those lists is powered by either gasoline or electricity. And right there is an index to the change in times. Another is the fact that I am not even asked if I have electricity. It is taken for granted that I have. In other words, life on the farm today is no longer considered a life devoid of comfort and convenience. The

Bureau of the Census, at least, doesn't think that we who live on farms are outstandingly underprivileged. The questionnaire doesn't even ask if my house has running water or an inside toilet or a bathtub. That's progress. If the returns from this census get any kind of publicity, maybe my city friends will stop asking me if I really like to prime the pump every morning and use an outside privy and take a bath in a washtub. Maybe.

Farming isn't what it used to be, thank goodness. Every now and then I see some urban comment to the effect that we are facing starvation because there aren't as many farmers as there used to be. True, there aren't as many farmers. In the late 1930s there were about 31 million persons living on the farms of this country, and by 1960 the number was down to around 21 million. But during that time we piled up the biggest farm surpluses in history, despite all the government restrictions on planting. By now we have given most of those surpluses away, to hungry people elsewhere in this world, and now we are talking about shortages again, increasing the acreage planted, and all that. The pendulum has swung the other way—or has been made to swing. Farm population is still going down, however. But I haven't heard recently of a recommendation, made only a few years ago, that 2 million people be taken off the farms and put into industry, just to clear the land of what was called uneconomic distribution of the labor force. Once you get enmeshed in managing such matters—and we have been enmeshed in the management of farm problems for the past thirty years—the whole thing becomes almost hopelessly contradictory from one year to the next.

But I was about to say that the farm surpluses of only a few years ago are somewhat explained by the questionnaire here on my desk. Besides asking about mechanized farm machinery, which makes it possible for one man to do four times the work he did thirty years ago, it asks about the amount of chemical fertilizer used. Fertilizers and better seed have doubled and even tripled the crop yield per acre. When I was a youngster in the Corn Belt, corn that yielded more than 60 bushels to the acre was exceptional. Today, right here in Connecticut, some corn fields are yielding three times that much.

And if anyone thinks this doesn't mean much in dollars and cents, he is grossly mistaken. In 1960 the National Industrial Conference Board made a survey which showed that this country's total income from sale of farm products was more than 35 billion dollars. Billions, not millions. This was 265 per cent more than the farm income of twenty years earlier, and that figure is adjusted to take account of the change in the dollar's value.

The old legends die hard. I still meet people who talk as though the typical farmer was illiterate, underfed and too dumb to comb the hay out of his whiskers. Better informed people try to tell me that farming is a dying occupation, the individual farmer a vanishing species. Just the other day a man told me that there wouldn't be a small farmer left in another ten years, that corporation farms would cover the land. I came home and looked up a Department of Agriculture report on farm ownership in 1960. It covered only 47 per cent of the farm and ranch land in the United States, but it showed that less than 1 per cent of the farms and about 8 per cent of the total acreage were owned by corporations. Unless the other 53 per cent is totally owned by corporations, I can't get excited about such figures.

As I went over this current farm census questionnaire I thought about Pittsburgh and Akron and Detroit and Chicago and New York, and about my neighbors and the other farmers I know in various parts of the country. And I thought that if the old legends died and the truth about rural life today was generally known, we would be trampled underfoot in the rush to the country. So I won't say another word to scotch the legends. I quote, instead, from an interview with a New England farmer in *Travels in the Confederation, 1783.*

"I built these stalls and that shed," the farmer said. "I am barber, leech and doctor. I am a weaver, a shoemaker, a farrier, wheelwright, farmer, gardener and, when it can't be helped, a soldier."

I wonder what *that* farmer would have made of this Farm Census questionnaire.

THIS IS the time of year when we become house-folk again and the focus of life shifts back indoors. Particularly in the evening, now that we are back on standard time and the sun sets when it should. This means that we have an open fire.

This farmhouse of ours originally was an eight-room place with twin chimneys providing a stovepipe hole for each of the four rooms on each floor. There wasn't any fireplace, and there still isn't. When we bought it there was a Franklin stove in the living room, and I was just stubborn enough to say I wouldn't take the house without the stove, because I like an open fire. I got the stove, and my antique-wise friends say it's rather a rare stove, with big brass balls and a big smoke dome. Anyway, it provides a fine and friendly glow as well as a good deal of heat.

There's a furnace in the house, too, with a thermostat that kicks it on and off and makes the house comfortably warm and "modern." In practical terms, that furnace is Efficiency, and the Franklin stove is just one step advanced from the open fire in a cave man's dwelling. But sitting in front of the fire the other evening I decided that Efficiency is a false god. Efficiency has smothered more dreams, blighted more friendships, and warped more happy, human impulses than any other thing I know except possibly amateur psychiatry. And I am not sure about the need for that qualifying adjective.

I don't know what it is about an open fire that means so much to mankind, but it may be that it represents man's mastery over one important phase of the elements, fire itself. Speech was man's greatest invention, but the mastery of fire was his greatest conquest. It made him the only creature really independent of the weather, the only creature who could create his own climate and even take it with him from place to place. Fire also became the basis of modern industry, but I would rather not appraise that today. Let's leave that to the economists, this time around.

Anyway, man tamed fire and brought it home. When the smoke got too thick in the living room he built the first fireplace. Some bright fellow finally made an iron box and put the fire in that, with a pipe stuck through the roof to carry off the smoke. That made a hit with the women folks because they didn't like having the ashes dirtying up the curtains and the rugs. But some reactionary man wanted to see those dancing flames, so he knocked one side out of the iron box and made a Franklin stove. Ben Franklin gets the credit, but he wasn't the first to do it; he merely did it better.

But finicky folk kept putting the fire back in the box. Now and then someone put isinglass in the doors and made such things as base burners and other parlor stoves. To satisfy the cook, they made kitchen ranges, with ovens which the women thought were for baking and roasting but which the men knew were really made to put your feet in when January chores frostbit your toes. And finally someone moved the stove into the cellar and cut a hole in the floor to let the heat and ashes up through the house. That, they thought, was living. That was luxury.

But all along the line there were sensible, sentimental people who kept building fireplaces and making Franklin stoves. They knew Efficiency when they saw it, and they knew what it would do to them if they ever gave in all the way. Some of the fireplaces they built didn't draw. Some were so jim-cracked up they looked like marble wedding-cakes. Some were even equipped with gas logs, the ultimate in fraud. But tradition persists, and so does the open fire. We've taken away man's breech clout and his bear-skin robe, but we can't take away his fireplace, even if it is as outdated as the stone axe. Thank goodness. I've seen fireplaces in chrome-plated penthouses and glass-and-aluminum houses, and even in houses where people really live. Some of those fireplaces are used.

A few years ago I wrote a piece about the care and feeding of a fireplace, and I got a letter from a woman in Princeton, N. J., asking me, please, to tell her how to build a fireplace fire. Her husband was a professor, they were originally big city folk, and they had built a house with a fireplace. They couldn't build a fire in that fireplace that burned right and didn't smoke the place up, and their happy marriage, she said, was imperiled. I thought I was being ribbed, but I played along with the gag. I not only told her how to build a fire but suggested that they find the chimney damper and open it. They did, and the last I heard all was serene in Princeton. So if your fireplace smokes, open the damper. If you don't know how to build a fire, ask any neighbor who has a fireplace. If he doesn't know, maybe the two of you can find someone in the neighborhood who does.

Let's see. Where was I? Oh, yes, sitting in front of the fire, feeling grateful to Ben Franklin, or whoever it was who first knocked the front out of that iron firebox. Man just has to see the flames, because his whole progress from the caves is there in the firelight. Right there on the hearth, not down cellar in that impersonal, inanimate piece of machinery. I'm glad I've got a furnace, but without an open fire I would be just another victim of Efficiency, another robot caught up in a dreamless, friendless, uninspired round of mechanical living. I think I'll go out and shoot a hairy mammoth tomorrow, if the weather holds.

THIS MORNING I watched a blue jay in one of my old, gnarled apple trees for five minutes and could hardly keep from laughing. He was playing a game I've seen jays play a hundred times, but usually there are two or three in on it. This time there was only the one. The game is to pick the thickest area of untrimmed sprouts and twigs on an upper branch and fly through it without touching a wing to a twig. If you are really good you can even fly a figure 8 among those twigs, and if you are tops you can fly two consecutive figure 8s among them.

This particular jay was just pretty good. Maybe that was why he was practicing alone. He could make one circle with complete success, but he couldn't quite manage a figure 8. He tried at least ten times, and every time he ticked a wingtip and lost balance and had to stop and catch his breath. Finally he squawked in disgust and flew away.

I have a good many jays. They live here because there is a free lunch counter out at the corn crib. They have to compete with the family of gray squirrels that lives in the big barn, but they make out pretty well. And I have an idea that the squirrels are unwilling helpers of the jays. The jays can reach through the wire mesh of the crib and steal the corn, kernel by kernel, but once they have cleaned all the kernels from the near side of an ear they are through with that ear. The squirrels somehow manage to turn the ears so that a fresh side is available. I don't know how they do it. I've watched and never caught one at it, but I know they do. And of course the jays benefit. The squirrels don't like the situation, and they are constantly squabbling with the jays, but the jays just fly off a little way and laugh.

A blue jay can manage the most jeering laugh of any bird alive. Not even the catbird can really compete, and the catbird has quite a capacity for the jeering remark. A jay can even sneer without making a sound. He just sits and looks, and rolls an eye and lifts or lowers his crest.

If a jay hasn't a sense of humor, I don't know what to call it. It's often a distorted sense, but it's there. I have seen a jay sit and watch a squirrel at the corn crib for five minutes, not making a sound. Then he will squawk the alarm signal. Jays are the most ardent alarmists in the woods, by the way. Anyway, he squawks the alarm, the squirrel drops from the crib to the ground and dashes for safety. And the jay, watching every move, begins to laugh, "yak, yak, yak!" The squirrel, halfway up the side of the barn by then, looks at the jay in disgust, then slowly comes back down, looks around, and returns to the crib. I've seen this happen four or five times in a row. The squirrel never learns that he is being the victim of the jay's practical joke. Maybe squirrels can't afford to take any alarm as a joke.

I've seen jays sulk in an apple tree while the lesser birds make a feast at my feeders, two of which I hang in that tree. The jays sit there, watching and sulking, and suddenly one of them looks around at his fellow jays and utters the alarm cry. Not a jay moves, but every chickadee and sparrow and nuthatch at the feeders takes off in a flutter of desperate wings. The instant they are gone, down come the jays, all of them. They try to perch on the feeders, flip them sideways, dump out the grain, then gather on the ground to eat. And to laugh. It's all a huge joke. Sometimes a jay laughs so hard he can't eat and another jay grabs a choice bit from right under his nose. Then a fight starts. The two of them go at it, wing and beak, and the others stand aside and watch and chuckle.

Jays are clever, but I don't think they are very bright. They collect acorns and other nuts, hide them, and seldom remember where they hid them. I would guess that jays plant as many oaks as the squirrels do. And at my corn crib they don't seem to be bright enough to eat from an occasional ear that was left on the ground when corn was taken from the crib. The squirrels never miss such an ear, but I have seen a whole flock of jays ignore several ears on the ground and perch on the side of the crib and worry kernels from the ears inside. Maybe they just have to do things the hard way, but it seems rather stupid to me.

One thing I will say for the blue jay. As I have noted earlier, he can sing. He does it mostly in secret, but from time to time, especially in the spring or early summer, I catch one who thinks there's nobody around and is singing a surprisingly sweet little song, a kind of whisper song. It can't be heard more than 15 feet away, and I have never heard a jay sing this song when another jay is nearby. If another jay comes along or if I move and the jay sees me, he stops the song in midphrase and squawks. He practically yells, "Snooper! Scum! Sneak!" And he gets really profane. That's one time when a jay doesn't seem able to laugh. Maybe, like most practical jokers, jays can't laugh at themselves.

ONE OF THE ELMS on the riverbank showed signs of sickness two years ago, leafed out late last spring and began to die in midsummer. It cast most of its leaves in August and is now dead, another victim of the insidious elm disease. We were sorry to see it go, but it has been most interesting to watch the woodpeckers go to work on it. Almost a month ago the little downies began tapping its upper limbs, obviously finding enough borers to be worth their work. Then their bigger cousins, the hairies, appeared and attacked the bark on the main trunk. Three or four of them would be working on it at the same time, making quite a chorus with their rattling excavations. Within a week they had taken off the dark outer bark in big patches, leaving the light tan underbark, which was marked with countless punctures.

Then, just the other morning, I heard the hammer-blows of a pileated woodpecker, the rolling, echoing *Brr-rrrr* that means the big, colorful Cock of the Woods is at work. And when I went to look a little later, there he was, halfway up the trunk, cutting the dead bark into shreds, chiseling into the dead wood beneath.

Few of our birds are more spectacular than the pileated woodpecker. Almost as big as a crow, he is glistening black on the back, immaculate white under the wings, and has a vivid red cockade on his imperious head marked with a white line down each side from his beak all the way to his shoulder. His beak is long and heavy, with a chisel tip, and when he is at work his head can be almost a blur, he works so fast. Yet when he wants to deliver a particular hard blow he can swing that head through an arc of 6 inches or more.

It is incredible to see a pileated seriously at work. He can rip out a strip 6 or 8 inches long. I have examined the chips under a tree a pileated woodpecker has excavated and they are as cleanly cut as though a carpenter had used a chisel and hammer. Not all of them, but a good many. Last spring a pair of flickers I watched here in the yard opened a knothole in a big apple tree, and before they had finished they took out a good peck of chips; but those chips were of rotting wood and looked like coarsely ground cork.

In contrast, the ground beneath a tree on which a pileated woodpecker is working looks as though a woodchopper had been cutting firewood with a sharp hatchet. This awesome method of work, along with the big woodpecker's whole appearance, undoubtedly accounts for the common name sometimes used for him, Lord-God. One is tempted to exclaim in just that term when one has seen what the pileated woodpecker can do to a tree.

A few years ago I watched one of those big fellows at work on a rather large gray birch over at Twin Lakes. The birch was about 10 inches in diameter and seemed to be thriving. But this big woodpecker acted as though he had a grudge against it. The first day he cut a hole halfway through it 10 feet from the ground, a typical pileated woodpecker hole about 4 inches wide and 8 inches high. The next day he cut another hole a foot above the first one. The third day he cut still a third hole from the other side of the tree, this one almost all the way through. Then he began chipping out the wood between the holes. Before the week was out he had so weakened the tree that a light wind snapped it right off. I never saw him at that tree again.

For years the pileated woodpecker was a rather rare bird, but for at least the past ten years it has been increasing here in this area, where it nests and stays the year around. I can hear these big fellows almost any week, either drumming on a dead limb or uttering their calls, which are much like the *wick-wick-wick* of a flicker but louder and lower in pitch. And from time to time I see one, either at work or on the wing; and always the sight makes me catch my breath. Incidentally, both sexes are marked alike, though the female's crimson crest is somewhat smaller than the male's. Thus they differ from the little downy and hairy woodpeckers, among which only the males wear the red cap.

I haven't seen that pileated dandy at the dead elm since that one day, but I have heard him twice hammering away at it, and I heard his loud, clear call three times. He hasn't opened much of a hole in the trunk yet. Maybe he is waiting for colder weather. Meanwhile, the little woodpeckers are using that tree as an all-day cafeteria, and I am cheering them on.

NOT LONG AGO I wrote about a certain group of city hunters who demanded that they be allowed to shoot on my land, even though it is posted, because they had hunting licenses. I refused them permission, in the face of some rather strong abuse, and in writing about it I said that as a landowner and taxpayer I thought I had the right to forbid such trespass.

A few days ago a writer in the *Waterbury Republican* took me somewhat to task for this attitude and pointed out that my unwelcome visitors "should at least have been credited with an important assist" when they mentioned taxes. And he went on to say that our local schools, roads and state police protection are largely paid for by funds that come from Hartford.

I have heard this argument a good many times, and

repetition fails to add logic to it. For the life of me, I can't see how anyone can say that the rural landowner is a preferred person or specially privileged when it comes to taxes or what the taxes pay for. To the best of my knowledge, we folk in the country pay the same state taxes as do the city folks. In the case of Connecticut, we pay the same rate of sales tax, the same gasoline tax, and all the other taxes levied. There certainly isn't any special discount at the tax office for the rural landowner.

And, of course, we all pay the local taxes and the federal taxes. Even in the matter of hunting and fishing licenses, we pay the same fees as anyone else. There just isn't any out, no matter where you live.

And the assumption by some hunters, as well as fishermen, that purchase of a license should give one the right to go anywhere just doesn't hold water. If it did, the laws governing trespass would have to be repealed; and that hasn't yet happened. As far as I understand the law, the possession of a license to hunt or fish entitles one to hunt or fish on state-owned land not forbidden to entry and on privately-owned land where the owners are willing to allow access. The determining factor in the case of private land is the decision of the owner.

I have often used the example of a city man's house and dooryard. If I were to drive up and announce that, as a taxpayer, I intended to build a campfire and roast hot dogs in the city man's front yard, I am sure that it would create quite a rumpus. It should. But in effect that is what happens from time to time in the country, and when the countryman resents it he is abused for his lack of hospitality. The farmer's fields and woodlands are, to my mind, his own dooryard, just as much so as the patch of grass in front of a side-street house in the city. Size hasn't anything to do with it. And if I were not only to cook my hot dogs in the yard but to invade the man's house, leave his doors and windows open, kick his cat, use his bathroom, break his dishes and burn holes in his rug, I am sure the constabulary would soon be upon me. And quite properly.

Yet that is what, on a somewhat different scale, happens in the country. Gates and barways are left down, beer cans and papers are strewn, dogs and cows are shot or chased, crops are trampled, fires are sometimes set. Not by every picknicker or hunter, but by the stupid, arrogant, insolent few. And when the landowner orders such people off his land he is abused as a selfish so-and-so and told that "people have rights" and that the invaders are taxpayers, as though that made them a privileged class somehow.

I must say that such problems are infrequent around here, which may be what makes them even more painful when they do arise. People from the area have good manners, which is really at the heart of the matter. They abide by signs, knowing that the man who posted them had good reason to do so. They know a partridge from a chicken, a deer from a calf, a fox from a dog. They close gates and barways. They ask a man, even if his land isn't posted, if they may hunt or picnic there, or if they may fish.

If urban folk would like an equal welcome they should learn equally good manners.

Fishermen, for the most part, are good mannered no matter where they come from. They are quiet folk, considerate, friendly, careful. They are neither argumentative nor arrogant. I have yet to be threatened by a man with a fish pole.

But every year outlanders appear and want to picnic, literally, in my dooryard. I don't know why. And about twice a year I have a set-to with a group of tough-talking, gun-toting hunters from some distant community who try to scare me into saying they can hunt on my land. I resent them. I shall continue to throw them off my land as long as I live here. As I said before, I own this land. I am the boss here.

EVERY FALL I find another clump of larches along a road or in a woodland where I thought I knew almost every tree. They were there all the time, of course, but I had just looked past them. Then the leaves fall from maples and birches and most of the other deciduous trees, and there stand the larches, like golden-tan tongues of candle flame, almost exactly the same color as the leaves of the weeping willows. Once you know them, you can't miss them. They are conifers but not evergreens. They shed their needles every fall and grow new ones every spring. Before the needles fall they turn color, to that unmistakable golden-tan; and they hold those needles till well into November.

The larch is also called the tamarack, sometimes known as hackmatack, and in the mountain West it is often called the buckskin tree. Though it sometimes grows as far south as Northern New Jersey, it really flourishes in Maine, New Hampshire, Vermont and Canada. And it is the only real tree in some parts of the Arctic Circle. In Northern Idaho I have seen stands of the western species so thick you couldn't ride a horse through them. The western species is taller and slimmer than the eastern larch, often well over 100 feet high.

The tamarack and the white birch often grow in the same valley, reminding one that the Indians used the two trees in building canoes. The white birch provided the bark and the tamarack provided the tough, durable roots that were used to sew the bark together. The white man hasn't much use for the roots, but he makes fence posts of the slim, tapering trunks; the heavy, resinous wood is slow to rot. It also makes a hot but smoky fire.

The trees also make quite a showing in the spring, when the new needles appear. They are one of the brightest, yellowest greens in the woodland. And when the pale yellow staminate blossoms appear at about the same time the needles come out, you can see a tamarack—or larch—a quarter of a mile away. Soon after, the tiny pistillate flowers open and give the trees a faint rosy glow. From those pistillate blooms come the cones, only about half an inch long, which ripen in early autumn to a light chestnut brown. With cold weather the cones open, about the time the needles begin to fall, and the seeds are scattered. The empty cones remain on the branches till the following spring.

There is a European larch that has been planted and cultivated as an ornamental tree in parks and gardens throughout the Northeast. It has heavier branches and longer needles and looks more fully feathered, as it were. It is easily recognized because the limbs are more pendulous than those of the native larch, and the cones are fully twice as long. In late autumn, though, it has the same luminous tan color, and in the spring it is vivid light green with its new dress of needles.

As a general rule, the larches prefer damp soil; they are often found on the borders of swamps and at the edges of marshy lowlands. But the rule has many exceptions. In Maine the larches are common on the upper slopes of Mt. Katahdin, at altitudes of around 4,000 feet. In the White Mountains, on the other hand, they are seldom seen on high ground, usually grow in the valleys and along the swamps and ponds. Here in the Berkshires I find larches growing on high ground and low, in wet places and dry. There is a surprising number of larches within a hundred yards of U. S. Route 7 between Stockbridge and Lenox, which is by no means a low or marshy area. There are scattered clumps of them in the valleys just to the west of the highway and other clumps all up the hillsides beyond.

The name tamarack seems to be of Indian origin and is said by some to come from hackmatack, though I don't see much resemblance. Hackmatack is from an Algonquin term, *akemantak,* meaning "snowshoe wood" and apparently was the original Indian name for some tree, possibly the larch. But larch isn't the kind of wood one would use to make snowshoe frames. Possibly one could make the web from a mesh of larch roots; but that seems to be doing it the hard way. When the whites took over Indian names for things, however, they often missed the mark.

No matter what the name or origin, the larch, the tamarack or the hackmatack is a beautiful tree and I'm always glad to identify one where I thought none grew.

WE WERE TALKING about colds, which none of us had so it was a purely academic discussion, and Clyde said, "When I was a boy and got a cold on the chest my father took a small cloth bag and filled it with salt. Then he poured coal oil on the salt, and he hung the bag around my neck."

Barbara said, "Did you say, 'a cold *on* my chest'?"

"A cold on my chest," Clyde said again. Clyde was born in the Midwest. "How would you say it?"

"A cold in my chest," Barbara said.

"Or," Lois spoke up, "a chest cold." Lois is New England, as is Barbara, all the way back.

"I don't care what you call it," Clyde said. "It was a cold. And that bag of salt and coal oil—"

"Kerosene," Barbara broke in.

"Coal oil," Clyde persisted. "That bag of salt and coal oil blistered my chest. It even crept up the string around my neck and made a regular necklace of blisters. But it cured the cold."

"I never heard of a salt and coal oil poultice," I said. "My mother preferred a hot bread and milk poultice. But not for colds. That was to bring an infection to a head. She used it once for an abcess on my neck. For colds she usually made me a baked onion, and then gave me the juice."

"What did she use besides the onion?" Lois asked.

"Just the onion, as I remember. Maybe some butter, to keep it from sticking."

"My husband's grandfather had an onion recipe," Lois said, "and when the children were young my husband made it for them. He sliced several onions, put them in a pan, covered them with brown sugar, and baked them until the juice came out. The onion juice and brown sugar made a thick, brown syrup, and we saved it and gave it to the children. It stopped the coughing and it cured the cold. And it really tasted pretty good, with all that brown sugar."

Then I remembered that my mother also used brown sugar on the baked onion. So Nebraska and New England were not really so far apart, in those days.

"Some people also used New Jersey tea," Lois went on. "You know, that wild plant with the little fluffy balls of white blossom. They picked the leaves and steeped a tea from them. They also dried the leaves to make it in the winter. It was more of a tonic, though. And of course it was a physic. Most wild teas were."

"And it tasted rather bitter," I suggested. "I had some, long ago. I didn't care for it. At that, it was better than some of the herb remedies. My grandmother used to feed me what she called seeney tea. Made from the dried leaves of wild senna, *Cassia Marilandica.* She probably gathered the leaves herself."

"How about slippery elm tea?" Clyde asked. "We used it for colds and coughs. It wasn't too bad, and it did help the cough."

I remembered slippery elm. When I was a small boy we used to peel a strip of bark off a slippery elm, take the inner bark and chew it. It was just what the name says, slippery. And mucilaginous. But not bad tasting. Some folks made a paste of it and used it for poultices. You can still get slippery elm in most drugstores.

"Anybody still make sassafras tea?" Lois asked.

"Probably," I said, "though I haven't tasted it in years. A man in Indiana once sent me a recipe for a sassafras beer that still fascinates me. As I remember, it went like this: Take three barrels of sugar-water (maple sap, to you) and boil it down to one. Pour in a crock or two of yeast, beat it up, and add a few cups of strong essence of sassafras roots, cooked down till it is red and puckery. Let the barrel sit in a warm place for a few days and it will begin to bubble. 'Bubble with joy,' the man said. Apparently the sugar begins to ferment, and you know what that does to its alcoholic content. Then, he said, at just the right time you draw off a big pitcherful and chill it. And pour yourself a glassful."

"How much sap?" Clyde asked.

"Three barrels, boiled down to one."

"And how much sassafras essence?"

"Two or three cupfuls. And yeast, a crock or two."

"Let's see," Clyde said. "Sap will be running in March. Where can we get three barrels? And who is going to dig the sassafras roots? I guess we can get the yeast. But how much is a crock?"

As I said, none of us had a cold, so the whole discussion was purely theoretical. But, even in theory, I have no doubt that a few tumblerfuls of sassafras beer would make a cold better. Or make a person better able to put up with a cold. It should be better than a salt and coal oil poultice, anyway.

THE CRISP DAYS have come, and to me they are among the best of the year. New England really hasn't much of a spring, and what it has usually is packed into a few short weeks. But fall is a special glory here, whether hard frost comes early or late. The one thing we lack is rain. I never saw the river as low at this time of year as it is now. And the ground water is much too low, as all who have springs or shallow wells are well aware. If the forecasters are right and this turns out to be a cold winter with less snow than usual, we are going to have a considerable winter kill among the threes and shrubs.

I don't know whether it is the drouth or not, but I never saw such an autumn fall of pine needles as this year. I was up on the mountain the other day and it seemed to me that the fallen needles were twice as deep under the white pines as usual. Yet there are plenty of needles still on the branches. Probably just the typical economy of the trees, reducing the area of leafspan to check evaporation. Broadleaf trees do the same thing even in midsummer under drouth conditions.

The dry weather has made the partridges wilder than usual. Or maybe it just has made the hunters more noisy, with crisper leaves underfoot. Anyway, the bird hunters haven't had as much luck as they did last year. The week before the season opened, one hen grouse came down to the house and tried to come in through a closed window. Barbara was in the room at the time and got quite a start.

The careless bird must have been half-stunned, because it sat on the porch rail, shaking its head, for several minutes while Barbara watched from close up. She called me, but the dizzy bird took off when I appeared, probably associating man with gun, and went back up the mountain.

The next morning, though, it was back, apparently the same grouse. It didn't try the window again. It wandered about the yard for a time, then abided by tradition and perched in the pear tree for ten minutes. It came back twice more. Then bird season opened and it hasn't appeared since. Don't tell me that grouse can't read the calendar and the game laws!

Speaking of grouse, Morris tells me that when he opened the crop of one the other day he found it packed with bittersweet berries. I didn't know bittersweet was on the grouse diet. I know they love barberry berries. And they are fond of the leaves of an insignificant weed called ditch stonecrop, which has small green leaves well into winter. It seems to provide their late fall salad.

We have had pine grosbeaks around in greater numbers than usual the past two weeks. A month or so ago I saw a large flock of evening grosbeaks in Canaan, having a royal time of it in a box elder tree. They were squabbling over the seeds, which they ate like peanuts and which were in good supply. The pine grosbeaks have been busy in my big Norway spruce, apparently finding what they want because they keep coming back, day after day. There are half a dozen of them out there right now, as I write this, not more than 10 feet from me, two males and four females.

I always know when the turn has come by the way the grass looks. It is still green here in the yard, but it was well frosted this morning, and when I walked across it I left my footprints, of course. Two hours later, when the sun got well up and the day had warmed a bit, the frost was all gone, but my footprints were still there, almost black. Everywhere I walked I had crushed that crisp, frost-covered grass, and it didn't recover. The frost apparently did little damage, but my footsteps did. I can still see where I walked a week ago on such a frosty morning.

The days are much shorter now, and seem even shorter than they are since the time changed. If I want to have a sunny walk in the afternoon I must get out by three o'clock. Dusk comes early, and that long light of evening which we had a month ago has vanished. Day doesn't linger. But the nights are brilliant, if the sky is clear. The stars always seem to come several degrees closer after the first of November. Probably this is because the air actually is cleaner and clearer than it was, say, in July. These are nights to study the stars, if you don't mind getting chilled. Besides, the winter sky is a more interesting sky in terms of constellations than is the summer sky. Maybe that is a kind of compensation. With no flowers now, maybe we are supposed to look up and get acquainted with the world out there.

In any case, autumn nights are good, too, here in the Berkshires. I have yet to see a really vivid display of the Northern Lights, but we will have them, too. Then the nights will be spectacular.

WE LOST a big maple the other day, one of the old sugar maples in front of the house on the riverbank. It was a victim of electricity, both natural and man-made. Years ago, nobody knows how far back, maybe fifty years, it must have been struck by lightning which opened a deep scar down one side of the big trunk. The tree healed itself as best it could and went on growing, but it never healed itself completely. Age and decay weakened it at the main crotch 15 feet from the ground and the big limbs that overhung the road were declared a menace to the power line.

We debated it for a week, whether to hold out for the tree or give in to the power line. Electricity, which maimed it to begin with, finally won. "Take it down," we said. So they came with their grasshopper-leg bucket crane, their ropes, their chain saws, and took the old tree down. It came down peacefully, but when the big limbs fell they shook the ground and when the trunk came down it shook the house and rattled the windows.

We tried to cut a section of that big trunk, more than 4 feet through, to put in the garden as a seat on which to rest from summer weeding, and almost succeeded. But three-fourths of the way through the chain saw began throwing sparks. A stone embedded, one man said. Metal, another said, remembering the old-style wrench he struck deep in the trunk of a venerable elm he had sawed up a few days before. So we gave up on the cut, split sections out to see what it really was, and never did get to it, but decided it must be a metal spile left there long ago by some sap collector. We found half a dozen old spile holes 6 inches in from the surface, wet black pockets still showing the old auger marks. I had thought spile holes healed and filled, but these never did. New wood grew over them, but they never really healed.

We also found spile holes I drilled twelve years ago, when I first tapped those maples. I could date them by the growth rings and they still had the soft pine plugs, now rotted to wet pulp, that I drove in when I pulled the spiles. We used the last cake of sugar from that run only a year ago. I still remember that that tree had the lightest sap run of all those we tapped. But when we took it down that big trunk oozed all day, making the sawdust wet and dark, and the stump was still oozing three days later.

We cut it up, all but that big butt with its embedded spile, or whatever it was that wouldn't yield to the saw. The butt was hauled away. I stacked the wood I could handle to season and will have many hours of work with axe and wedge splitting the rest of it where it lies. There will be enough hard maple to feed our open fire for years, at least a couple of cords of it, maybe three.

But an open fire is small recompense for a majestic old maple. We will appreciate it, I suppose, on a bitter winter evening, but when we watch the flames we will be seeing spring come to that tree, with its yellow tassel-blossoms and its pale green leaves. We will hear the bees, busy and loud among its blossoms. We will remember the shade at midday and the soft whisper of the leaves at dusk, when the breeze creeps up the river. We will see the color come, the warm golden color that always came late to that tree. We will see the leaves fall, a golden shower in midmorning after a frosty night, and we will feel the crispness underfoot as we walked there, knee-deep in late October.

It is easier to lose a tree in winter than in spring or summer. It hurts less because you don't see the green of life wilt and die. In a sense, a tree lost in winter dies in its sleep. But still it hurts. There is a gap where it stood. The morning sun strikes the front windows more directly. It will be still more of a gap next May when sun will blaze across the grass where there has been shade ever since we have lived here. And when we go down to the river we will, out of long habit, walk around the tree that is no longer there, our feet still not knowing it is gone.

The squirrels will miss it, and the birds. I wonder how the squirrels will travel their skyways next summer, with a chasm where they have always known a fragile bridge.

And I wonder if the orioles that sang from its topmost branches will know what happened. No oriole has nested in that tree these past five years, but they always came there to sing. I wonder if they knew it wasn't a safe nesting place. Well, it is gone now, reduced to chips and firewood. And we are living in a strange, unfamiliar place though we haven't moved an inch.

THIS IS A STORY about Ethan Allen, and it concerns Thanksgiving Day in Salisbury a good many years ago. You can believe it or not, as you wish. I set it down as it came to me.

It was the late fall of 1769. The weather was cold, so frosty that there was a fringe of ice on Lake Wononscopomuc. The warmest place anywhere around the lake was the furnace at the lake's outlet, where they were running a charge of limestone, charcoal and ore from Ore Hill. One of the men at the furnace looked out and saw a spit of snow in the air and turned to another workman and said, "Old Ethan'll be along, if I know Ethan. Mark my word, he'll be along, to get one of those geese out there on the lake for his Thanksgiving dinner." And the other man, who was too young to remember when Ethan Allen was a partner in the furnace, along with the Forbes brothers, Samuel and Elisha, and Mr. Hazeltine, said, "It's too cold to get a goose." And the first man laughed. "You don't know Ethan. He's tough as rawhide and hard as pig-iron, and this is weather just to suit him. Besides, Ethan likes roast goose."

The man was right. Soon after noon Ethan Allen appeared, riding a big bay horse and carrying his long-barreled Pennsylvania rifle. He had ridden down from North Canaan, where he and Samuel Forbes were partners in a furnace and forge on the Blackberry River. He rode down to the forge there on Wononscopomuc and tied his mount to the hitching post and came in under shelter beside the furnace long enough to warm his hands. The man who had predicted his coming greeted him and asked, "You come to get a goose, Mr. Allen?" And Ethan nodded. He looked at the man shrewdly and he asked, "How'd you like to take a jaunt to the New Hampshire Grants? You look like a stout enough man to be welcome up there."

"The New Hampshire Grants!" the man exclaimed. "You going up there, Mr. Allen?"

"I asked," Ethan said, "how you'd like to go?"

"And what if I got killed up there, by the York Staters, or the Indians?"

"You'd go to glory," Ethan said. "You'd like as not turn up, as soon as your soul got free, as a panther, or maybe an eagle."

"I'd rather be a man," the furnace worker said.

Ethan spat in disgust and turned away. He walked along the shore, watching a flock of geese, and at last he lifted his long rifle and fired his shot. The geese took wing, all but the biggest goose of all, which fluttered once and floated, dead. And the men at the furnace watched as Ethan Allen stripped off his clothes and swam out and got his goose and swam back to shore and shook himself like a huge dog and put on his clothes again.

The men at the furnace were still staring, unbelieving, when Ethan returned, the goose over his shoulder. He didn't even come to the furnace to warm his hands. He tied the goose behind his saddle and was about to mount when the men at the fire walked out to him, and the older of the two touched his sleeve, just to be sure, and said, "Mr. Allen, when are you going to the Grants? I'd admire to go along. Mr. Allen, I'd even admire to die, if it happens, and be a panther, maybe, or an eagle. When are you going, tomorrow?"

"Tomorrow," Ethan said, "is Thanksgiving. I've got me a goose to eat tomorrow, and I intend to eat it." He got on his horse. "Come along," he said, "if you'd like to. You'll likely starve and freeze and die, up in the northern hills, but you'll die in glory." And he rode off, back toward North Canaan.

The two furnace workers watched him go, then went back and laid down their tools and followed him. And at every turn of the road they were joined by other men who had talked to Ethan.

They caught up with Ethan at a tavern along the way. Ethan had stopped to warm himself with a drink or two. They joined him there, and one drink called for another. Day thinned to dusk and dusk became night, and bully-boys from all the furnaces and forges came to the tavern, hearing that Ethan was there.

That was a night, as they say. When the sun came up on Thanksgiving Day Ethan Allen was still on his feet, though few could still stand with him. He went out and brought in the goose and gave it to the cook, and the cook roasted it while Ethan got all his recruits on their feet and led them in a prayer of thanks for life and country and the cause of freedom. Then they ate. They ate roast goose till they could eat no more.

And the next day Ethan Allen started north, leaving a deserted tavern behind him there at the foot of Smith Hill. Fifty men went with him, fifty of the toughest men in all Connecticut, but only the first of well over two hundred Connecticut Yankees Ethan rallied to fight the British. They were the Green Mountain Boys, of course, but don't forget that they came out of these Connecticut hills. Ethan Allen recruited them here, on Thanksgiving Day of 1769. Or so I have been told.

I SOMETIMES WONDER what it would be like to have a cumulative memory, to be able to reach back and remember things that happened long before we were born. I'd like to remember the first Thanksgiving. In theory, at least. Actually, it must have been a pretty bleak day, and the turkey probably was tough. But something must have happened to relieve the solemnity and the bleakness. Something always did happen on the Thanksgivings I can remember.

As far as Thanksgiving goes, my memory actually reaches back only to the age of eight, and it is first centered around a song:

> Over the river and through the wood,
> To Grandfather's house we go;
> The horse knows the way
> To carry the sleigh,
> Through the white and drifted snow.

Lydia Marie Child wrote that song a hundred years or so ago, and it used to be school favorite. It ended, "Hurray for Thanksgiving Day!" I can still hear a roomful of third-graders singing it in their barnyard-hen voices, and I remember wondering how come, and where, there was enough white and drifted snow for a sleigh ride. We never had enough snow on Thanksgiving for a good snowball fight.

But, snow or not, we went to Grandfather's house for Thanksgiving dinner. Several dozen aunts, uncles and cousins were there and the house was full of the fragrance of turkey, stuffing, cranberry sauce, mince pie and pumpkin pie. It wasn't just Thanksgiving, it was a family reunion.

Thanksgiving may have been a kind of religious holiday in New England, but where I grew up it was as secular as any other Thursday in the month. When the food finally got to the table, Grandfather shushed everybody but the small babies and told God he was thankful everybody was there and that there seemed to be enough to eat, which was a major understatement. Then he said, "Amen," and reached for the carving knife.

Thanksgiving was almost as much fun as a family wedding, and even more confused. The big farm kitchen was always full of women, who kept getting in each other's way and swapping family gossip and chasing hungry kids outside. One year someone hid a couple of cakes under the bed in Grandmother's bedroom. I still don't know why, but I know that some little sneak found them there and I helped make a shambles of them. Boy, did we eat cake! And did we get walloped! I was too sore to sit down at the table, so I ate standing up, as did two others; and we were sick as dogs afterward and got no sympathy at all. But an hour later Aunt Evy took me into the kitchen and gave me a big piece of mince pie, and that cured me. What a wonderful thing is the juvenile stomach. I wish I still had one.

Another year Uncle Art saved the tail feathers of the turkey and gave them to us when we arrived on Thanksgiving morning. We immediately became a tribe of Apaches, with feathers in our hair and warclubs in our hands. We prowled the place with whoops and general uproar, got chased out into the open, cut limbs from the box elder tree beside the back door, equipped ourselves with bows and made arrows from old shingles we found in the woodshed. The air was soon full of arrows and cries of the wounded. A six-year-old non-combatant cousin caught one blunt arrow full in the mouth, lost two teeth that needed pulling anyway, and bled like a stuck pig. The wrong aunt spanked the wrong cousin and for a while it looked as though the whole tribe, big and little, was in for a civil war. Then Grandmother came to the door and shouted, "Dinner's on the table!" and a truce was called. But Grandfather was so upset the best he could do was say, "Thank God, nobody got killed. Pass your plates. Amen."

There was also the Thanksgiving when Towser got into the act. Towser was the farm dog, a very woolly sheep dog who never learned to leave skunks alone. It rained that Thanksgiving and along about noon, just when Aunt Vera was mashing the potatoes, one small cousin let Towser in the back door. Towser, wet as a muskrat, crept unnoticed to a spot back of the coal range, hoping to get warm and dry. Nobody even thought of him for half an hour. Then his thick, wet fur began to warm up and release its rich store of odors. Aunt Vera sniffed and said, "Something's burning!" Aunt Ida exclaimed, "It smells like onion!" And then Grandmother said, "It's a skunk."

A posse of youngsters was sent outside to investigate. Their report, no skunk, sent an older posse outside. Still no skunk. By then Aunt Evy's eyes were tearing and Aunt Mable said her stomach was turning over. And finally Grandmother found Towser behind the stove. By then the cranberries had boiled over, the pumpkin pie had scorched and the gravy was full of lumps. Grandmother dumped half a can of pepper on the stove to get rid of the smell, and everybody began to sneeze. Oh, that was a Thanksgiving!

There must have been quiet, orderly, decorous Thanksgivings too, but I don't seem to remember them. Maybe I should have grown up in New England.

THIS STORY is no doubt apocryphal, and though I have heard it attributed to Benjamin Franklin I have never struck it in his writing. Whatever its source, it seems worth recounting.

Back in the early days of New England settlements, the people in one community came to November with a modest stock of provisions for the winter. Considering the way they planted and cultivated, their corn had given a fair yield. So had their beans and pumpkins. They hadn't ventured into the woods to make much venison, but they had caught and dried quite a stock of cod. Their cabins were nothing to boast about, but they had stout walls and reasonably tight roofs. There was plenty of firewood and the Indians were friendly.

But the people were dubious about the coming winter. Man's estate was precarious, and it was good for the soul to purge itself from time to time. So the leaders of the community called for a day of prayer and fasting.

The people gathered, most of them rather dour because they had gone without breakfast and looked forward to a foodless noontime. They assembled in the biggest cabin in the village and heard a long opening prayer full of apology for the manifold human weaknesses and shortcomings. The prayer finally ended on a note of what miserable worms they all were but with a plea for forgiveness and chance for penitence. And one of the elders, a man at least forty years old, got to his feet and began a long confession, not only for himself but for all the others. He was by no means proud of the human race, and he ended by saying that unless they mended their ways they would all die of disease or starvation.

Another man got up and spoke at length about the heavy burden of life. And still another talked at great length about the fact that they deserved all the misfortunes that lay ahead.

So it went, right through the noon hour, without even a break for a drink of water. Meanwhile, a good many of those miserable sinners looked at the bags of beans, the strips of dried pumpkin and the bundles of dried cod hanging from the rafters and were almost ashamed. They didn't deserve even that much; all the speakers had made that very plain. But down in their hearts they wished the day would pass and tomorrow would come, when they could eat again, sinners though they were.

And all this time a little man at the back of the room was getting more and more restless. Finally he could no longer contain himself. He stalked to the front of the room and said, "My friends, I must dissent. I have heard enough of sin and damnation."

The room was filled with gasps, but nobody moved to silence him.

"I must dissent," he repeated. "I have fasted till my belly griped. I have meditated my own sins till my mind festered. I have besought Almighty God for forgiveness till I was ashamed of myself for even asking. And now . . ." He paused. "Now I must lift my eyes in thanks, or lift them not at all."

A startled gasp went through the room, then a slight sense of relief.

"We have had privations," the little man went on. "Some of us died. We froze and we burned with fevers. We went hungry. But that was last year, and the year before. Now we have made a harvest consequent with our labor, and I see no dying people here. Every day I look about me I see water filled with fish, ours for the taking, wood for the cutting, deer and turkeys for the hunting. In this very cabin I see the harvest of our labors. We have done well. What is it, I ask, that we implore? What prompts our insistent abasement of ourselves? What are our sins, beyond the fact of being alive?" He lifted his head proudly. "Let us be done with whimpers and complaints! Let us be done with needless fasting! Let us, rather, lift our hearts and give thanks to the good Lord for the things we have."

And a sigh seemed to fill the room, a sigh and a sense of relief. Neighbor turned to neighbor and for the first time that day there were smiles. The most eloquent confessors looked abashed. Somehow the whole complexion of life had changed. Within an hour the fire on the hearth had been fed, the spits had been provisioned, the pots set simmering. The women cooked, the children got underfoot, the men brought planks for benches and tables. And before sundown there was a feast of thanksgiving for every soul in the whole community.

ONE AUTUMN DAY Pat brought in a muskrat. I don't know why unless he was keeping trim for woodchucks, which were safely hibernating by then and which were on Pat's own list of top priority public enemies. It was the first muskrat I ever knew him to catch, and he brought it in as a trophy, not as a supplement to his regular diet.

There have always been quite a few muskrats along the river, here in this valley. I see them from time to time in the summer, and one afternoon when I was out in the boat, fishing and sitting quietly, I saw one come down to the bank with a huge load of green stuff, leaves and grass, and swim across the river with it. It was one of the biggest green salads I ever saw, and that muskrat looked like a chunky little tug pushing a stack of green alfalfa.

And one evening when I was sitting on the bank of a small bog, watching a big water snake stalk an unsuspecting frog, a muskrat came swimming toward me through the maze of cattails. I thought he was going to come ashore right at my feet, but at the last minute he either saw and recognized me as a man or got a whiff of my scent. I never saw such a surprised creature in my life. He stared at me for an instant, then upended himself in a panicky dive. But the water was only about 6 inches deep, and there he was, nose in the mud, hind feet kicking frantically in the air. Finally he kicked himself into a complete somersault and scurried back into deep water, leaving a trail of muddy roil. What an adventure he had to tell the grandchildren on a cold winter night! Except that, to tell the truth, muskrat generations aren't really on speaking terms. They tend to be a quarrelsome lot.

The muskrat actually and biologically is just an overgrown meadow mouse adapted to life in the water. Its hind feet are partly webbed and its long, naked tail is vertically flattened and is used as a rudder. Its thick, soft, waterproof pelt attracts the trapper; 18 or 20 million muskrats are trapped every year for their marketable fur. Louisiana swamp people, and others here and there, I understand, think muskrat meat is good fare. Louisiana makes it somewhat more palatable by calling muskrats "marsh hares."

The Indians had a legend to explain the muskrat and its preference for marshes. According to that tale, the muskrat helped Nanabozho, one of the major gods, to control a great flood. How they did it, I have never heard, since it is beavers that build dams and muskrats that undermine dams and dikes; but somehow the muskrat put Nanabozho in his debt during the flood, and Nanabozho told the muskrat that as a reward he could live anywhere he chose. The muskrat picked the deep blue lakes as the ideal homeland. But after a little while Mr. Muskrat went back to Nanabozho and said he'd like to move. Nanabozho asked why, and Mr. Muskrat said that the lake was awfully wet and somewhat short of green vegetables. So Nanabozho said, "Well, how about moving ashore, then, and living in clover on the green bank?" Mr. Muskrat said, "Thanks, Nanabozho," and moved, bag and baggage, out onto dry land.

It wasn't long, however, before the muskrat was back once more. Nanabozho asked, "What now?" a little impatient by then. And the muskrat said he'd like to move back to the lake. His wife, it seemed, had been watching a bevy of mink gals showing off in the water, and she thought she had a pretty good figure too; and, said Mr. Muskrat, he liked a swim now and then himself. "How about it, 'Bozho?" he asked. "Just one more move."

Nanabozho's patience was fraying out. "Since you can't make up your own mind," he said, "I'll make it up for you. You will no longer live on land *or* water. The swamp for you, my indecisive friend! Go stick your head in the mud. And don't come back here again unless I call you!" And Nanabozho never called. So Mr. Muskrat still lives in the swamps. According to the legend, at least.

There are compensations, of course. There's plenty to eat in the swampy places, including flag and cattail roots and, now and then, wild ducklings. And on the dry banks there is clover, quite often, and now and then corn stalks and garden carrots and apples. The muskrat makes out. He does pretty well for himself, in fact. And his wife does her share in keeping the swamp and the riverbank populated, bearing at least three litters of five or six young a year. Which proves that the muskrat is first cousin to the meadow mouse, another prolific rodent.

Muskrats don't hibernate. Besides dens in the bank of a marsh or stream, they build stacks of aquatic plants at convenient places and use them for both pantries and bedrooms. I doubt that even Pat could have made much of a dent in the local muskrat population.

WHEN I ran across the word "leveret" the other day I wondered why we so seldom use the precise terms any more, particularly the terms of the field and hunt. Leveret, of course, means a young hare. But how often do you hear it, or even see it in print? We use the terms colt and calf and lamb and fawn and kitten and pup, but beyond that we tend to forget that there are distinctive names for both young and mature animals and birds of many species. Only the other day a man was talking to me about a family of Canada geese and spoke of their "chicks." He had simply forgotten the word "gosling." And how many of us remember that a juvenile swan is a cygnet?

The young of the muskrat are called "mice," quite possibly because the muskrat is closely related to the meadow mouse, or vole. Young coyotes and wolves are casually spoken of as pups, but they really should be called whelps, a word that goes all the way back to the Anglo-Saxon. Young foxes are sometimes called pups, too, though the proper term is kit, apparently an abbreviation of the work "kitten." Kit and whelp are also used as verbs, meaning to bring forth young. The young of the raccoon are also sometimes called kits or kittens. The young of mink are often spoken of as mink kits. And baby skunks are kits.

There probably is a special name for a young badger, since badger hunting and badger baiting go all the way back to medieval times, but I have never run across it. The badger itself was known, and in some places still is, as a "brock," from an old Saxon word for gray. The young of the otter are cubs, but the young of the sea otter are pups, just as are young seals.

The young of all three of our wild cats, the puma, the lynx and the bobcat, are kits or kittens, as might be expected.

Young deer are fawns, but young moose and young bison are calves. The young of pronghorned antelope are, on the other hand, called kids, possibly because the pronghorns once were thought to be a species of goat. They aren't goats. They belong to a distinct family whose ancestry reaches all the way back to the Pleistocene era. Mountain goats, as might be expected, have kids. Bighorn sheep have lambs, though they are quite different from any rocky-pasture New England lambs that ever went to market.

Turtles and tortoises seem to have such names from the time they are hatched, but when a female turtle deposits her eggs she lays a "clutch," just as a pheasant does, or almost any other fowl. I've never heard anyone say that a snake lays a clutch of eggs, but it would be just as logical. Granted, of course, that it is an oviparous snake, not a viviparous one.

Young frogs are tadpoles, and so are young toads. But young salamanders and newts are larvae. Young eels are elvers, which comes from "eelfare" meaning the migration of young eels up a stream. Young fish, newly hatched, are fry. Fry once also meant newly hatched bees, though I have never heard it used that way. Very young oysters once were called fry, but the more common term today is "spat," which is also used for the young of most bivalves. Whales, of course, bear calves; but whales are mammals, not fish. And adult whales are bulls or cows.

Adult deer are does and bucks. But moose and elk are bulls and cows. A male coon is a buck, for some reason. A male hog is a boar, the female a sow, and a partly grown hog of either sex is a shoat. A very young hog is a pig, though a hog of almost any age is loosely called a pig. An immature female hog is a gilt.

In most birds the male is a cock, the female a hen; there are cock pheasants, cock partridges, cock robins. But when you come to ducks the male is a drake and the young are ducklings. A fledgling is a bird newly feathered out; the word comes from the old Norman term for feather, and a fletcher used to be a craftsman who put feathers on arrows. A closely related word, "flitch," means to cut, has the same root as "flesh," and was used by the old Normans when referring to pork. We still speak of a flitch of bacon, meaning an uncut bacon slab. Feather, bacon, a young bird—an odd combination from the same lingual root.

Adult bears are called boars or sows, depending on the sex, but I have never heard a young bear called a pig or a shoat. It is always a cub. A female lobster is a hen. A male shad is a buck. Male hares, rabbits and rats are also bucks. Female hares and rabbits are does, but I never heard a female rat called a doe. A dollar of either sex is a buck, of course, and hundred-dollar bills are dough, for sure.

HE LOOKS LIKE a black panther, junior grade, and I'll bet that ounce for ounce he is as tough a fighter as any panther that ever lived. The only time I saw him even hint at what he might do was back in September when he came down out of the woods to make a meal on a woodchuck I had shot the day before. It was at the far edge of the home pasture, and soon after he began eating, two big, hungry crows arrived. They strutted around, trying to bully him away, and finally one of them made a pass at him. He sat back on his haunches and made a lightning swipe with one paw that barely missed. He got a few black feathers, though, and the crow squawked and got away from there in a hurry. So did its partner. They wanted none of this junior grade panther.

I wasn't sure I wanted any of him either, but there he was, and here he still is. We have been watching him since June, and he has been watching us, and though we haven't formed any real friendship we do seem to have reached a kind of tacit agreement. He can go on living somewhere back in the woods and coming down here to scavenge the compost heap and we won't bother him as long as he doesn't spend his days stalking the birds at the feeders in the big apple tree. Actually, he does little scavenging. He is a thoroughly feral cat. I am sure he would turn up his black nose at any handouts I might offer. Since I am not a cat person, I won't even try to tempt him.

My guess is that he is the one surviving kitten of Gimpy. Three years ago somebody dumped a black and white kitten at the roadside. The kitten took to the woods, somehow survived the first winter on her own, and the next summer had an accident, maybe was hit by a car. We didn't see her for weeks, and when she did show herself she walked with a limp and ran in an awkward gallop. Last spring she came down here, heavy with kittens but still wild as a deer. Then she disappeared for a time, and when I saw her last, in June, she looked sick and almost starving. A few weeks later this all-black fellow showed up, lean, long-legged and fugitive.

A fox may have killed Gimpy. She must have had a rough life, crippled as she was. But she wanted none of people, and neither does this black cat. If he is anywhere around and I step outside the house, off he goes like a streak. So I have been watching him through the binoculars.

As I say, he was a skinny, long-legged kitten when we first saw him. Over the summer he filled out and now he is sleek as an otter, with muscles that ripple under that black hide. And he is immaculate, nothing like the scruffy kitten he was. He usually comes down toward the house in the early morning, taking his time, working from grass clump to weed patch, hunting as he goes. He is light-footed as a fox, constantly on the prowl. I have seen him catch voles or field mice from time to time. Now and then he comes in late afternoon, but at that time of the day he is doubly wary of the house; and if I so much as open the door he vanishes, into the fencerow brush, into a culvert, into the grass clumps—he knows all the havens.

He is a handsome cat, as near cat-perfection as I ever saw. And I am not one to praise cats, though I do respect those that refuse to soften into fireside loafers. This cat is at his prime and undoubtedly will survive the winter. There is plenty of native food, mice, voles, rabbits, even a few muskrats. And he probably gets a grouse now and then. I don't begrudge him a decent diet any more than I do a fox.

His only natural enemies are foxes and great horned owls. By now he must have learned about owls or he wouldn't be alive today. His black pelt makes him invisible at night. On the snow he will stand out like a beacon, but he'll have to take his chances. And as far as foxes go, I doubt that any fox will do him in except by accident. He is big enough to put up a whale of a fight, even with a fox. And of course he can climb trees. The other morning I saw him leap, from a standing start, to a limb 5 feet from the ground. If pressed, I'll bet he could make that 8 feet easily. He is all muscle and sinew, and claws and teeth.

I don't know where he lives, maybe in an old woodchuck den or an abandoned fox burrow. He has found some place that suits him, maybe several. He is not a traveler, hasn't haunted any of the other farms up and down the valley. This is his place, these acres of mountainside and valley. I sometimes get the feeling that we are only squatters here, to his way of thinking. Anyway, here he is, and here he probably will be for some time to come. Just as long as he keeps the truce, I intend to. I rather admire him, to tell the truth.

THE OWLS have been hooting, and if I subscribed to the old superstitions I would expect dire events. But I hear them every year about now, and nothing worse than ordinary seems to happen. The moon is about half full and will be full a week from tonight, and the owls seem more vocal on moonlit nights, though some of the most eerie owl nights I can remember have been in the dark of the moon. But maybe they were eerie as much for the darkness as for the owls. We have a friend who insists that hooting owls always foretell something awful, and she shivers and looks for a black veil every time she hears one. But my memories are different. One of the most poignant funerals in my memory was accompanied by the whistling of two cardinals in the treetops near the cemetery. So I can't take a hooting owl too seriously.

We regularly have three kinds of owls here in the valley, the barred owls, the great horned owls, and the screech owls. Once in a while we have a snowy owl, though I almost never see them. But the other three are heard here in late fall and early winter every year, and I hear them in the spring at mating time. Some say they do most of their hooting in the spring, but that isn't my experience.

I like to hear the screech owl. When I say this, people

often look at me as though I were a zombie, but I suspect that such people know the little screech owl only by hearsay and in old-wives' tales. The screech owl doesn't really screech. It whimpers and wails, but it can also trill, a melancholy note but by no means frightening. Maybe my reaction is in part because I know it is a small owl, not much bigger than a robin. And it is a good neighbor, catching many mice and voles. Anyway, I like to hear the screech owls and find no note of doom in their calls.

The barred owls are something else again, but even they do not portend trouble. They seem to hoot mostly to hear their own echoes. Two or three of them, calling in the night, can sound like a whole flock, and they have individual voices. Some are baritones, some second tenors. After a few nights, one can recognize individual owls by their voices. I can recognize two that have been here in the valley the past four years.

The barred owl's call usually is a nine-note series of hoots that has been aptly put into the words, "Who cooks for you? Who cooks for you-all?" But the series may be abbreviated to seven notes, or even five, and I have heard one, obviously excited, practically stammer: "Who, who, who cooks, who cooks for you, you-all, you-all?" I have even heard one in a kind of cackling laughter with hardly one real hoot.

Barred owls are big birds, up to 2 feet long and with a 4-foot wingspread. Occasionally I see one at late dusk, winging silently up or down the valley, and it looks as big as an eagle.

Actually, the barred owl is as big as the great horned owl. But the great horned owl is more ferocious. On occasion the great horned owl will attack and kill a barred owl, and it has been known to kill and carry away a Canada goose or a domestic turkey. Normally it lives on lesser game, mice, rabbits and skunks. It probably kills more skunks than any other predator, as anyone who has investigated a great horned owl's nest can testify. It also kills rats and domestic cats.

The great horned owl has a gruff voice, definitely bass. Its customary call is four notes, "Woof-hoo, hoo-hoo," but it may repeat those last two notes several times. I have heard one sound almost exactly like the sound one can make blowing across the top of an empty gallon jug. This call in the night can be almost eerie, but mostly because of the gruff, deep notes. I never heard a great horned owl that didn't sound out of sorts.

Contrary to old lore, both the barred owl and the great horned owl have good daylight vision. Both of them do a good deal of daytime hunting, and on a dark day the great horned owl may be out and on the prowl by midafternoon. On a bright day the big owls prefer to roost and sleep in a big pine or hemlock. Now and then a crow finds one there and begins to scream. This rallies all the crows in the neighborhood, and they can drive the owl out of its tree. It seldom fights back in full sunlight. But if it is an overcast day, only a very stupid crow will start such trouble. There is no truce between owls and crows.

The night chorus of the owls cannot compare to the dawn chorus of robins, orioles and tanagers in May, but in December, or even in late November, they are worth listening to, if one doesn't take them too seriously.

IT IS HEARTENING, and at the same time vaguely disturbing, to learn that the "in" subject among the planners now is "environment." Nearly every conference on "problems in American life"—and conferences seem to sprout like mushrooms after a rain in May—seems to have "environment" somewhere on its agenda. And the Presidential

Task Force on Preservation of Natural Beauty had a good deal to say about "environment" in its report. It sometimes seems that there are at least a dozen special groups digging into the subject—the problem of living in the "environment" we have in this country, or adapting it to what we think we need, or what some special group thinks we need.

Two things are heartening about this trend. One is the fact that it apparently now is all right to talk about beauty—the beauty of a tree, or a lake, or a river, or even of a flower or a bird. For quite a while beauty was gauche, sissy and sentimental at the very least. The other is that "environment" now means more than air conditioning, wall-to-wall carpeting and Scandinavian furniture. Somebody has been looking out the window, maybe even taking a walk, feeling the grass and gravel underfoot and seeing the sky overhead. "Environment" has recovered some of its real meaning.

But, as I say, there is a disturbing factor here too. The reason seems to be that the planners are almost congenitally committed to building things and organizing things. And the environment, the land and air and water, achieves its own beauty and even its hospitality for the human race, by being left to organize itself and build its own special satisfactions. All it really needs is to be protected from man's vandal tendencies, his passion for tearing things down and putting things up, his slovenly habit of making sewers of rivers and fouling the air he breathes and the water he drinks, poisoning the soil which grows the food he eats.

Maybe these planners, who aren't afraid of the word "beauty," will do better. But again, how are they going to define beauty? There is one type of mind that insists a nonobjective piece of sculpture is more beautiful than a tree, an airplane more beautiful than a bird, a marble-rimmed reflecting pool more beautiful than a cattail-fringed pond. There are those who think a chair lift or a funicular railroad adds beauty to a mountain, and that no mountain is complete without a restaurant and a flagpole on its crest, to prove that man owns it and is its master.

And the worst of it is that esthetic fashions change, even when applied to man's own creations, even those we think of as classic. When those creations are limited to the usual arts, no lasting damage is done. Grotesque sculpture, nonsense painting and fad architecture can be discarded and forgotten. But once a woodland is cut, it takes years to restore itself. Once a hill is leveled, a valley filled or a swamp or pond is drained, only time and the elements can repair the damage. Once a river is polluted, it takes an act of Congress, a presidential proclamation, twenty years and millions of dollars to clean its waters again. Conservationists have been saying for a long time that natural beauty is a precious thing; but it wasn't the fashionable thing to say. Nature was, according to the prevailing fashion, to be used, to be blasted and cut and exploited for profit.

Well, maybe the fashion is changing. Maybe, now that we have lost so much, we will begin to value what we have left. If so, I expect to see among the planners' recommendations:

Some means of persuading highway builders to go around, not always through, priceless groves of old trees; and around, not always through, beautiful hills and mountains.

Some way to force cities and towns to stop dumping their sewage and poisonous industrial wastes into the rivers. And some way to clear riverbanks of their rotting slums and human debris.

Some effective control of air pollution by industrial fumes, aerial spraying and atomic, radioactive dust.

Some curb on the developers who would line the seashore, the lakes, even the rural highways, with catchpenny joints and dives and ramshackle shanties.

Some belief in the beauty of the natural landscape, just as it shapes itself when man keeps his eager hands off.

THE OTHER MORNING Byron, my neighbor up the road, phoned and said he had a visitation of crows . . . hundreds of crows, maybe thousands. "They're in the trees just beyond the pasture, at the foot of the ridge. They've been coming down the valley, from Massachusetts, for the past hour, and they all seem to be right here, making so much noise you can't hear yourself think."

I went up to have a look. By the time I got there some of them had gone, but there were still enough to blacken the treetops and make the top of the ridge look almost maggoty with their constant motion. Through the binoculars I could see them constantly moving from tree to tree, and though I tried to count it was a hopeless task. I did count up to two hundred with fair accuracy, and there must have been at least twice that many. Little flocks of twenty or thirty were still coming down from the north, and as they settled in the treetops other small flocks moved on down the valley. Just how many there were I don't know, but there were several hundred of them.

Byron and I watched them for ten minutes or so, and speculated on their purpose. I have known a flock of crows to gather and make a great to-do over a deer carcass in the woods, but that couldn't explain this tribal gathering. As far as we could see, none of them were down on the ground. They were all in the treetops, and through the glasses I could see how the birches, especially, bowed under the weight of fifty or sixty crows perched in a single tree. And they weren't fleeing from hunters. If anyone shoots into a flock of crows they don't wait around to see what happens next. They get away from there fast, and keep on going. These crows were almost casual. Even their clamor was crowd-clamor, not an expression of either indignation or defiance, as nearly as I could interpret it.

The best guess I could make was that this was a convention of several flocks such as I have seen most winters here in the valley. The flock I have known best has numbered between two and three hundred and often is seen down near Dutcher's Bridge. One morning two years ago, after manure had been spread on a field down there, the flock practically covered the ground over an area of 5 or 6 acres. I was driving past, and when I stopped to watch them they took off in a veritable cloud and flew to the trees along the river, where they acted almost exactly like this outsize flock we saw the other morning.

Now and then I have seen this winter flock going up or down the valley, and they always seem to fly in bunches, twenty or thirty to a bunch, but definitely in a pattern, as though they were platoons.

These winter flocks are not really unusual, though they seldom are as large as the one was the other morning. They seldom gather in such numbers in the summer, probably because they are busy with domestic matters. I have seen thirty or forty in a summer flock, but not often. And when they gather in such numbers it is usually a temporary gathering. They make a clamor, often in the early morning, and appear to be discussing the state of their world, even to be arguing about it; then they scatter for the day. When the nestlings are up to a size where they demand food vocally there may be temporary assemblages in or near a nest tree, but it seems to be a matter of curiosity rather than social instinct. A nestful of loud-mouthed young ones can summon half the crows in the neighborhood, for a few minutes, seldom much longer.

But after the young are on their own, when fall weather comes and family chores are done, the crows become gregarious. Why they should gather by the hundreds, I can't imagine unless it is for company. Such flocking actually increases the competition for food.

Crows, of course, will eat almost anything, from fruit to berries, from worms to eggs, from live frogs to roadside carrion. I have even seen them pecking at a dead skunk on the highway. Oddly enough, considering their liking for sprouted corn, they seldom eat dry corn. I've seen them pass up ear corn that blue jays and squirrels consider priceless. If the corn is moldy or water-soaked they eat it eagerly, however. It may be that they have a sweet tooth, for in sprouting corn and moldy corn a part of the starch has turned to sugar.

I don't know what happened to that big flock of the other morning. It was beginning to break up when I saw it. If I were romantic I might say it was a thieves' convention to apportion territory. But I'm sure it wasn't that. It was just a big flock of crows acting like crows, not human beings.

IF ANYONE has a kind word for snow it should be said before Christmas and New Year's. After that the speaker can't really put his heart into it and the listener just isn't listening. By February, snow is an abiding nuisance, by March it is a plague, and by April it is nothing less than an abomination. Some years I think that the first snow of the season should also be the last, and I begin to growl like an ill-tempered bear by the second day of January.

But just now I can say, and believe, that snow is wonderful, and beautiful, and magnificently mysterious. If I were exiled to a land whose winters never knew the wonder of a snowflake I should feel forever alien and deprived. And the landscape, whether it was the stark beauty of the desert or the lushness of the semi-tropics, would seem dull.

When the first snow begins to fall I have to get out in it, to feel the flakes as they fall and catch a few flakes on a dark sleeve and wonder at their symmetry. I have never seen two flakes alike, and in my heart I know that I never shall; but I must look each year to assure myself again. I suppose I could get the equivalent feeling by matching maple leaves, say, in June, and finding—as I certainly would—that no two of them are exactly alike. But there is something about the delicacy of a snowflake, the fineness of filigree beyond the craft of the best human artisan, that catches and holds my wonder. Besides, a snowflake is both fragile and ephemoral. If I so much as put my finger on it, it begins to vanish. One breath from my warm lungs can turn this incredibly intricate crystal into a prosaic droplet of water. Standing in a snowfall, looking at one flake, I am somehow privileged to look briefly and with vision blurred by my own limitations into one magnificent phase of the mysteries of the whole universe. I can there sense, but never quite capture, the abiding Answer.

The flakes grizzle the grass. They whiten the ground. I watch, and in their swirling fall I can begin to see the way the air swirls and moves, the invisible little eddies and currents. I look at the crystal curtain over the dark waters of the river and I see how the breeze flows above the quiet stream, how it comes and goes, in puffs as strange as my own breath, and how the snow curtain opens and closes and waves and wavers. The snow gives me sight, for a little while, with which to see the invisible.

The breeze rises and the fall increases. The flakes begin to drift. I can follow the course of the wind in the way the snow flows along the road, still dark with its own persistent warmth. But in the grass there is another kind of record. Small fans of snow begin to form behind each tussock, and each goldenrod stem has its minute drift to leeward. The wind again marks its own path, how it eddies and how it curves around an obstacle, even such a minor one as a goldenrod stem. And if I watch for ten minutes I can see the way that nature shapes her curves. A snowdrift, even one no more than an inch deep, is the sculpture of the wind, the wind's own shape made manifest, frozen motion as beautiful as the flight of a barn swallow in June.

I make my way across the pasture to the hillside, where the white pines and the hemlocks stand. Already they are twice as green as they were when November's grays and browns possessed the land. Of all colors, green most needs the contrast of white to assert its character. The hemlocks, with their feather-branches, are gathering snow. They are frosty, and when the gusting wind strikes them they create their own small blizzards.

I turn and look back across the pasture. The thistle stems still stand stiff, and the brown stalks of giant mullein. But they are wearing white caps with ear-laps. The snowfall is slackening, but the grass is nearly all covered, the benevolence of the snow, the blanket that can ease the bite of coming cold. And I wonder how many snowflakes it takes to cover 1 square foot of ground to a depth of 2 inches. I am sure nobody ever made such a calculation, not only because snowflakes can't be counted but because there are no numbers with which to count them. The astronomers and the physicists deal in numbers of staggering magnitude, but he who would count snowflakes would have to invent some system as incredible as light years or microseconds. Looking at that lightly snowed pasture and thinking of measurement, I face not only the impossible but the incredible. Yet there it is, snow, the currency of any winter, the wonder and the magnificence—and, by March, the plague of anyone who lives in New England's Berkshires.

I WAS on my way out to my garage this morning, to go to Canaan, when I looked up the mountain and saw a thread of smoke just below the big pines. Nothing to do but go up and see what fool was up there in the woods playing with fire, so I went. And just this side of the springhouse I found him, a funny little old man with white whiskers, a fat belly and a ratty-looking old canvas coat and scuffed, run-over boots. He was sitting beside a fire, warming his hands.

I said, "What's the idea? You're on posted land and I ought to call the troopers. I will, if you don't put out that fire and scram."

He gave me a tired smile and wrinkled his cherry-like nose and slowly shook his head. "I didn't see your signs," he said. Then he said, "I had a breakdown and had to stop here. Lucky I had a spare runner, but I almost froze my fingers getting it on."

"What do you mean, a breakdown?"

"Cracked a runner. Team was tired and couldn't pull up over a big pine. Don't you ever have a flat tire?"

"Not often. When I do, I go to a garage to get it fixed."

"No use going to a garage with a sleigh. Not that one, anyway," and he jerked his head toward the pines. Then I saw, for the first time, a beat-up old cutter with most of the red paint worn off. But it had one bright, new, red runner. The only thing in the sleigh was a moth-eaten old buffalo robe, as far as I could see.

"Traveling light, aren't you?" I asked.

"This time around, yes. This is just a dry run, checking the route and the schedule." Then he asked, "What time is it, anyway?"

"Ten-thirty."

"Eastern Standard? Gets kind of confusing, crossing all these time zones. That's why I don't carry a watch. Be resetting it all the time."

"Eastern Standard," I said. "And the date is December 19th."

"I know the date!" he chuckled. "Just six more days. To get home, catch a few winks, put on the red uniform, pack the sleigh and get going again. Keeps a man hopping, I tell you! Especially with a crippled team. Dancer bowed a tendon up near Pittsfield this morning, and Prancer always gets the heaves from the smog around Albany." He put another stick on the fire. "You don't mind? I've got chilblains in this right foot." And he pulled off a cracked boot and thrust the foot close to the flames. I was tempted to offer him an old pair of my boots, but his feet were at least three sizes smaller than mine.

"Why the dry run, as you call it?" I asked. "If you're the fellow I think you are, you know your way around."

He nodded. "I've got my landmarks, but they keep changing things. New highways and all that. And new TV antenna towers—I haven't got radar, you know!"

"Why not?"

"You know what a radar system would cost? I'm not *made* of money. And I've got a payroll to meet, too. Know what a good toymaker gets today, counting fringe benefits, pension and all? And Society Security on top of that. I do good just to keep going, *without* radar!" His foot was warm. He pulled on his boot, got to his feet, and asked, "What time is it now?"

"Quarter to eleven."

"Time's a-wasting." He thrust two fingers into his mouth and shrilled a whistle that made my ears ring, then walked over to the weather-beaten old sleigh. From up on the mountain came a clatter of hoofs. Two buck deer appeared, then two more, and after them another pair. The one in the lead limped and the third in line began to cough. He watched them come, counting to himself. Then he thrust his fingers into his mouth and whistled again, even louder than before. Finally two more deer came clattering down the path. He rubbed their noses, patted their necks, buckled the harness on them and lined them up, hitched the traces to the sleigh.

"No bells?" I asked.

"No bells. Not till next Thursday night." Then he laughed. "What do you expect for nothing? The complete show? This isn't even dress rehearsal. This is just the dry run." He settled himself, pulled the old buffalo robe up over his lap and buttoned his old canvas coat. He gathered the reins in one hand, lifted the other in a half salute.

"Be seeing you!" he said. "Hup! Hup!" and he slapped the reins. The sleigh went out of the little opening like a puff of snow, up over the birches and away. And I put out the fire and came back down the mountain and went to Canaan.

HALF A DOZEN evening grosbeaks came over to see us the other day. They sat in the pear tree for a time, then investigated the various feeding stations and apparently decided that we were not particularly generous with sunflower seeds. Then they took off, and the last I saw of them they were headed back toward Canaan. I hear that a flock of fifty or a hundred have been making Canaan their headquarters for several weeks, and probably these were a scouting party.

We have a few evening grosbeaks here every winter, sometimes as many as twenty-five or thirty at a time, but they never become regular patrons at the feeders. If we filled one feeder with sunflower seeds and nothing else we might have them regularly, but if we did that the chickadees would pass the word, too, and I would be refilling that feeder ten times a day. A friend in Canaan told me that she fed more than 50 pounds of sunflower seeds to the grosbeaks last winter and that they were at her place earlier than usual this year, clamoring for handouts.

I think it was in the winter of 1944 that I saw my first evening grosbeak. We had a window feeder, and one morning I looked out and saw this bird, olive and yellow and black and white, and I thought just for an instant that a little green and yellow parrot had been blown in. Then I saw the beak, a typical finch beak, and knew what it must be. A quick check in the bird book proved my hunch. Later that day we saw half a dozen of them in the trees near the house, and they stayed around for a couple of weeks. And, as I said, we have had a few of them around almost every winter since.

The evening grosbeaks are unusual because they migrate from west to east rather than from north to south. Their natural home is, or used to be, out in Alberta and the Canadian Rockies. The theory is that they began migrating east in search of better feeding grounds in the winter; they came farther and farther east until they reached the East Coast in their travels. Apparently they found conditions here to their liking. Their natural food includes cedar berries, ash seeds, maple seeds, ash-leaf maple seeds and locust seeds. We have, in our area, quite a supply of all of these. And we have, too, many bird feeding stations at which kindly persons offer rations, including the sunflower seeds which are like candy to the grosbeaks. They would be fools if they didn't come back.

I have heard, time after time, that the evening grosbeaks are relative newcomers to this area, that they were unknown here until fifteen years or so ago.

That isn't so at all. They have been coming here at least seventy years. *The Birds of Massachusetts,* by Griscom and Snyder, says that the first great flight into Massachusetts occurred in the winter of 1889–90, and they were seen all the way to Revere Beach. Since then, they have been regular winter visitors in increasing numbers and with a longer season in recent years.

The grosbeaks have been irregular in their coming, however. In 1944, they came in large flocks in October. In 1952 they didn't arrive until January. But they have been here in some number almost every year except the winters of 1942–43, 1944–45, and 1947–48. The biggest flights of them appeared in 1943–44, 1945–46, and in 1952–53, 1953–54, and 1954–55. Then there seemed to be a slack-off one winter, with good-sized flocks ever since.

New York City's first record of evening grosbeaks apparently was in 1911. But 1916 was the date of the biggest early migration into New York, and it got the most publicity. That year they went all the way to Portland, Maine, in considerable numbers, and stayed there until May 11.

In the spring, the evening grosbeaks compete with the squirrels for the new buds on the elm and maple trees. Probably by then they have cleaned out most of the natural seeds they are particularly fond of, and maybe the people who put out the sunflower seeds all winter have begun to ease off in their charity.

One thing about the evening grosbeaks is that you will most often see them in the hours before noon. In the short days of winter they work short hours, seldom being out and around after midday. In early afternoon they go back to their roosting places, usually in a clump of pines or hemlocks, and call it a day. One reason may be that in this way they burn up less energy and need less food. All birds have very high metabolism and burn their feed-energy fast when they are in flight. Roosting, they can slow down the engines, as it were, and put that energy into keeping warm. This theory is enforced somewhat by the fact that as the days grow longer and warmer they extend their hours of activity. The scouting party that came over here arrived about 10 A.M. and left before 11, probably to pick up a meal in Canaan and call it a day.

THERE was a tree, always. I don't know where they got an evergreen that size—it towered almost to the ceiling of the church—but it was awesome in that land of few trees and most of them cottonwoods. Farther south, down where there were a good many Mexican-Americans, they decorated cottonwoods with home-made angels and birds cut out of shiny metal from tin cans and they made fake snow for the branches from cotton with flaked-up mica to give it a proper glisten. But most of the people in my small town were from the Midwest and had to have a real pine, or fir, or spruce.

There was the tree. It was set up in the church, as I say, down in front beside the pulpit, so the pews could hold everybody in town and give everybody a view. It didn't matter about sects. This wasn't a church Christmas. It was the community's Christmas.

There was the popcorn, and there were the cranberries. For a week before Christmas half the kitchens in town smelled of popcorn. It was popped by the bushel. And Bill Hall, who ran the general store, ordered a barrel of cranberries. Half of them were sold for cranberry sauce, but half were saved for the tree. Then every kid big enough to use a needle was set to work. Popcorn and cranberries were strung, yards and yards of them. And the little kids, not big enough to do the stringing, made paper chains in school, yards and yards of paper chains, smeary with paste and smudgy with fingers, but every color of the rainbow.

There was candy, hard candy, gumdrops, stick candy, red and green and frosty white. It came in wooden buckets, big buckets, and the grownups put it in paper bags. Paper bags of candy, at least two hundred of them, maybe three. And there were oranges. Oranges weren't everyday fare. You had to order them special, and Bill Hall ordered them, ten or twelve crates.

There were the gifts. Dolls for the girls, tin whistles and rubber balls for the boys. I have no idea where they came from, but there they were, bushel baskets full of them.

There were candles. Every year there was the question about the candles. There were those who said, "We won't go if there are candles on the tree," and there were those who said, "We won't go if there *aren't* candles on the tree." So there were candles, and everyone went. But Clarence Smith supervised the candles, put them on the tree, and Earl Brown and Bob Probst sat in the front row with buckets of water handy, just in case. There never was a fire.

Christmas Eve was the time. Right after supper, with just time to clear away the table and put on the Sunday clothes. By eight o'clock the church was packed.

The preacher, Adna Moore, opened the service. He went to the lectern and opened the big Bible to the book of Luke and began reading, "Now it came to pass in those days," and right on through the first twenty verses of the second chapter. He finished reading, spread his hands in quiet blessing, and nodded to Chris Straub, who took over. Chris said, "Thanks, Reverend. Now the girls will sing 'Holy Night' for us."

A group of older girls giggled and sang "Oh, Little Town of Bethlehem." Chris said, "I guess the boys are going to sing 'Holy Night,' " and the boys giggled and sang "Deck the Halls." Chris said, "Confound it, *everybody* will sing 'Holy Night'!" And that time he had his way. Everybody sang "Holy Night."

Chris kept watching the door, fidgeting. Finally there was the sound of sleigh bells outside. The doors opened and Chris said, "All right, Ed. Come on!" Ed Schlote, the fattest man in town, appeared, waddled down the aisle, red-faced, red-suited, white-whiskered and beaming. But halfway down the aisle something happened. It wasn't Ed Schlote. It was Santa Claus. You could feel the wave of belief all over the church, in grownups as well as children.

He came down the aisle, paused to look at the tree with its popcorn and cranberries and paper chains and lighted candles, and he said, "What a beautiful tree!" His voice was awed. And everybody knew it was the most beautiful Christmas tree in the world. Then he turned to the boxes and baskets and began calling out names. He knew every child in town and he called them, one by one, to come down and get a bag of candy, an orange, a toy. It took forever, maybe an hour, but not once was there a break in that web of belief. And when he left, shouting, "Merry

Christmas to all, and to all a good night!" the sound of sleigh bells hung in the cold, starlit night a long, long time. Listening now, half a century and 2,000 miles away, I can still hear those bells.

I DON'T SET much store by New Year's Day except as a date on a calendar. Winter has just begun and there won't be anything really new, except another snowstorm, until March. But we all have to live by clocks and calendars, to some degree at least, and we have a long-standing habit of taking inventory now, casting back to see what the past twelvemonth amounted to and what it means, if anything. So be it.

The totting up has been somewhat simplified for me this year by a letter from a total stranger who was curious about why I live on a farm and write about life in the country. He had no quarrel with me, but he did want to know why. His letter brought to mind a letter from another man, a few weeks ago, who said he missed "straight-from-the-shoulder belligerency" in my attitude toward life. Thinking about both these letters, I have been summing up and examining the totals. Some of the findings may have meaning beyond the personal.

Many of us who live in the country, whether it be on a farm, in a village or in the far fringes of the suburbs, live there by choice. We came and we stay because we want to live close to the land, to what we think of as natural reality. We have no quarrel with life in the cities or with city folk; but city life has artificial aspects that have little appeal for us. Rural life can be, and in the past often was, cramped and limiting, but it need not be. It really is the individual, not the place, that dominates or knuckles under, and it seems easier for some of us to be in control of our lives away from the mass pressures of the city. It is easier to maintain perspective on life and mankind somewhat apart from the crowd.

That perspective involves certain natural phenomena. Try as he may, man cannot totally divorce himself from his environment. Yet in the big city one is insulated from the earth itself by such a prosaic thing as pavement. Such fundamental matters as rain and snow are nuisances in the city, despite all man's efforts to abate them. It seems to some of us that man should know the earth of his own origins, should be able to touch the earth and know the benevolence of rain. He should be able to see grass grow, and trees, and see the crops that feed him and all his kind. If he is to know where he lives, what particular part of the universe he inhabits, he should be where he can face the sky and feel the earth and even see the stars. Otherwise he becomes so ingrown, so overwhelmed by the crowd, that he forgets who he is, or where he is.

As for "straight-from-the-shoulder belligerency," it seems to me that there are already too many belligerents. I would prefer more calm, quiet voices and more men seeking truth and understanding. More men who say, without overtones of hysteria, "Wait. Look. See where you are hurrying and what you are hurrying past before you have gone over the horizon." I say that most of man's troubles are man-made, and that belligerency does little to solve those troubles. It seems incredible that anyone should even think man's problems were created by the sun, the stars, the wind, the rain or the everlasting hills. What gain is there, what element of peace or comfort, in being belligerent about the state of the weather or the lay of the land?

I happen to believe there is a considerable degree of

freedom in human choice, but that the price of certain choices is higher than some of us are willing to pay. Those of us who have chosen to live somewhat apart from the crowd decided that the satisfactions were worth the price. Otherwise we would not be here.

Emerson once wrote, "He who knows what sweets and virtues are in the ground, the waters, the plants, the heavens, and how to come to these enchantments is the rich and royal man." The language is a bit lush. Thoreau would have said it better and with more bite. But there are those of us who still believe in the truth of it. I wouldn't call the verities and natural truths "enchantments," because some of them have their stubborn and even difficult and painful aspects. But they are truths we should all recognize. And at the very top of the list I should put the simplicity of cause and effect. Too often, man has tried to ignore or legislate out of existence this fundamental truth,—that one must plant before he reaps, that one must earn before he spends, that one must learn before he understands. Cause, and effect. And the greatest teacher in such matters is the earth, nature, life itself.

So there is some of the substance of my summarizing and appraisal. There are a few of the things that go into this particular countryman's appraisal of himself and his purposes. That is why I live where I live and write what I write. I never found better reasons to live anywhere else or spend my time and energy doing anything different.

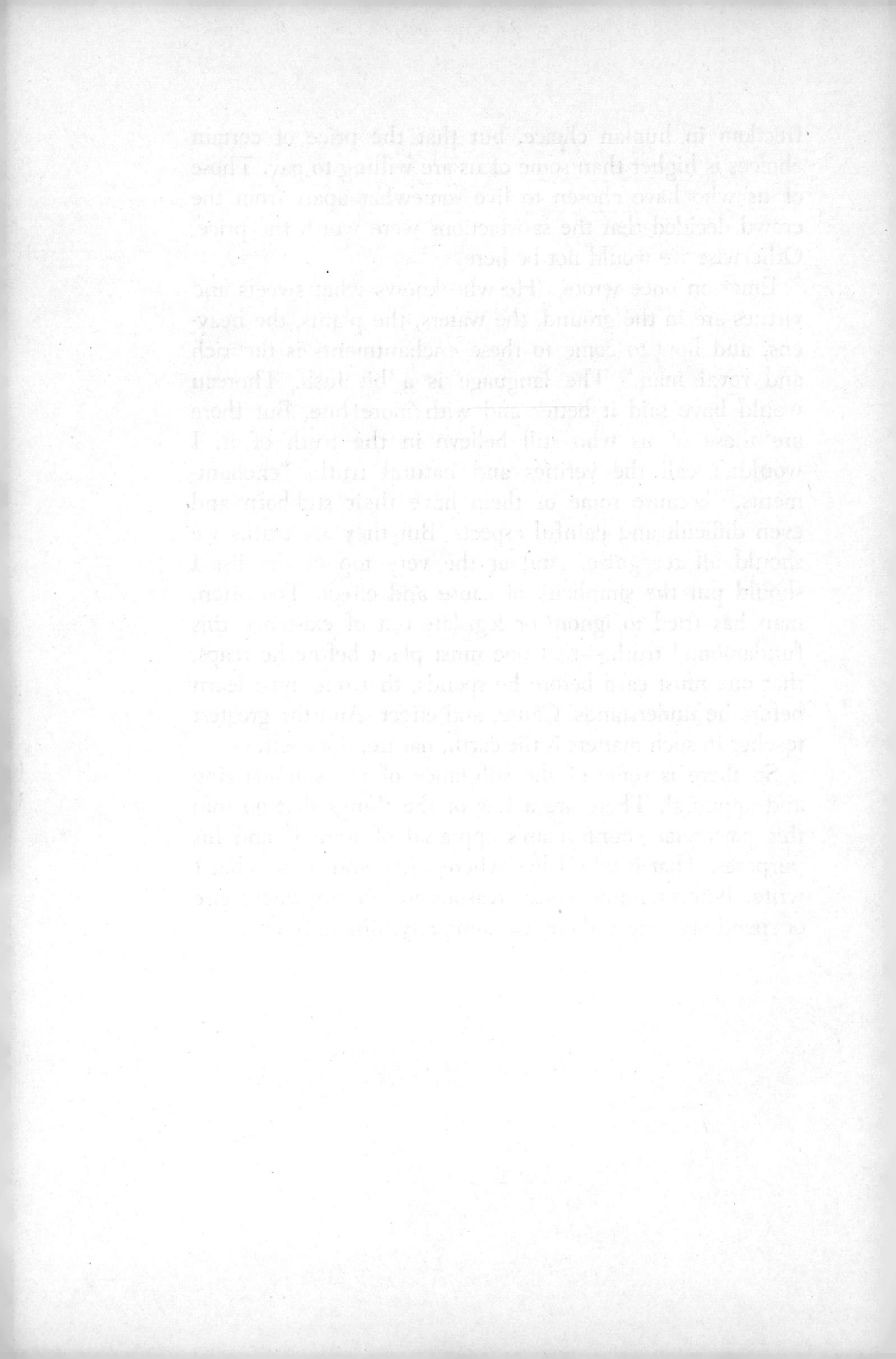